Theology against Religion

Theology against Religion

Constructive Dialogues with Bonhoeffer and Barth

by
TOM GREGGS

t&t clark

Published by T&T Clark International
A Continuum Imprint
The Tower Building, 11 York Road, London SE1 7NX
80 Maiden Lane, Suite 704, New York, NY 10038

www.continuumbooks.com

A section of Chapter 5 (pages 111–116) is a re-written version of several pages of ' "Jesus is Victor": Passing the Impasse of Barth on Universalism', © 2007 Scottish Journal of Theology. Originally published in *Scottish Journal of Theology* 60:2 (2007), 196–212. Reprinted with permission.

A section of Chapter 9 (pages 209–214) is a re-written version of several pages of 'Inter-Faith Pedagogy for Muslims and Christians: Scriptural Reasoning and Christian and Muslim Youth work', © 2010 Discourse. Originally published in *Discourse* 9:2 (2010), 201–25. Reprinted with permission.

British Library Cataloguing-in-Publication Data
A catalogue record for this book is available from the British Library

ISBN: 978-0-567-46279-4 (hardback)
978-0-567-10423-6 (paperback)

Typeset by Newgen Imaging Systems Pvt Ltd, Chennai, India
Printed and bound in India

This book is dedicated to three friends since school days
– Chris Allen, Steven Jamieson and Mark Perkins.

TABLE OF CONTENTS

ACKNOWLEDGEMENTS

The activity of writing a book is often imagined as one born of solitude and quiet hours in a study or the library. True, there are plenty of times when that is the case. But there is also a very real sense in which the writing of a book is a communal activity – an activity born of conversations, friendships and dialogues into which one is initiated and initiates others. Certainly, the writing of this book would not have been possible without a significant number of people, and it is only right that I acknowledge their contributions.

Much of this book was written during an eight-month research leave, funded by the Promising Researcher Fellowship and the Learning and Teaching Institute of the University of Chester. I am grateful to the Vice-Chancellor, to Professor Neville Ford and to Professor Jethro Newton for enabling the financial support for this leave. I am particularly grateful, from the period of my application for leave, to my then Head of Department, the Revd Professor Ruth Ackroyd, for her guidance: she never failed to support, encourage and facilitate, and since her well deserved retirement, she is sorely missed. Of course, my being absent from the university for two terms determined a heavier load had to be carried by my colleagues, and I am grateful to the theology team at Chester for their efforts, especially to Dr Hannah Bacon, Professor Celia Deane-Drummond, Dr Wayne Morris and Dr Steve Knowles. My research student, Nathan Paylor, proved a wonderful substitute teacher for my classes during my leave, and I am indebted to him for taking such care of my courses; I am also in his debt for checking all of the references and citations in this book. Professor David Clough and Revd Robert Evans not only helped alongside the other members of the department in covering my absence, but have been constant sources of wisdom, support, guidance and trips to the pub; they are a blessing to me. The final stages of this book were completed during my transition to a new post at the University of Aberdeen, and I look forward with anticipation to working alongside my colleagues there.

Much of the writing of the book was made more bearable by the hospitality of different institutions and individuals. St John's College, Durham, hosted me as a visiting research fellow at the start of my leave, and I am grateful to all of the staff there for their support, and especially to Dr Richard Briggs and his family for their hospitality and friendship. The principal, Revd Dr David Wilkinson, was my minister as a teenager in Liverpool, and his continued prayer and support, along with that of Revd Alison Wilkinson, are unendingly appreciated. The Department of Theology and Religion at Durham was equally welcoming, and I am most grateful especially to Professor John Barclay, Professor Paul Murray and Dr Robert Song for their time, hospitality and conversations.

Further time was passed at La Salle University, Philadelphia, with the Kelly family. Geffrey Kelly not only spent long hours discussing Bonhoeffer and Barth with me, but also welcomed me into his home; in fact, I felt like an adopted member of the family, and I am so grateful for the hospitality that he, Joan, Brendan, Mike and Susan (and their extended family) showed to me. I do not know where to begin in thanking Geff and Joan for the time I spent with them.

My longest sojourn during research leave was spent at the University of Virginia, where I was College of Arts and Sciences International Visiting Scholar and Visiting Professor in Religion. During my time there, the doctoral students not only bore my teaching with good grace, but a number were also willing to read and discuss early drafts of the chapters of this book. I learned so much from them, and I am grateful for their time and thoughts. The faculty also welcomed me warmly, and I learned much of 'southern hospitality'. It is wrong for me to name individuals, but several people overwhelmed me with hospitality. It was heartening to be reminded of England during conversations and meals with the Head of Department, Professor Kevin Hart, who was generous with his time. Professor Chuck Mathewes was a constant lunch and coffee (and the occasional scotch) partner. Matt Puffer, along with Becca and the newly born Will, could not have been any more friendly, hospitable or generous; Matt is a doctoral student who shows great promise, and whose work on Bonhoeffer and Barth is certain to prove important. Professor Valerie Cooper embodied southern hospitality; ever-ready for lunch, a trip to the cinema, or a church visit, she also made me feel at home by poking friendly fun at my eccentric English ways, and my time at UVa would have been much the poorer without her presence. The two people to whom I owe the most, however, are Professors Peter and Vanessa Ochs. They welcomed me into their home; saved me from snow storms; let me teach some of their classes; talked faith, theology and philosophy with me; shared *Shabbat* with me; included me in birthdays and celebrations; introduced me to their friends; and most importantly, laughed and laughed with me. Of God's many blessings, they are certainly two of the most precious in my life – people to learn from, alongside and with, about the glory of God.

Beyond my time in different communities, there are numerous other people who must be thanked for their support, friendship and guidance. From the theological community, I am particularly grateful to Dr Nick Adams, Dr Mark Edwards, Revd Dr Jason Fout, Professor Ivor Davidson, Dr David Grumett, Dr Douglas Headley, Dr Mike Higton, Revd Dr Steve Holmes, Dr Rachel Muers, Revd Professor George Newlands, Revd Dr Stephen Plant, Professor Jeffrey Pugh, Revd Professor Ben Quash, Professor Janet Martin Soskice, Dr Susannah Ticcitiati, Revd Professor John Webster, Revd Professor Ralf Wüstenberg, Dr Simeon Zahl and Professor Laurie Zoloth. Many of these people have not only shaped and formed this book through conversation, but have read and commented on sections or chapters; the book would be much the poorer without their contributions. Professor David Ford has remained a constant dialogue partner, supporter and friend through the period of writing this book. He has helped to shape not only my thoughts on several of the topics herein, but also the way in which I think and do theology. Dr Paul Nimmo has been my most constant source of theological friendship. A confidant, counsel, encourager, critic and adviser, he is a wise and true friend.

Friends who do not share my love of theology have remained loyal, and have given me welcome breaks from the intensities of research, thinking and writing. Through the period of writing this particular book, I am especially grateful to Chris and Nancy Allen, Annemarie and Lynton Bell, Andrea Chan, Bryony Creswell, Sarah and Jonathan Davidson, Dan and Becks Farr, Neil and Esther Flynn, Rick Gayton, Edward and Kirsty Gayton, Catherine and Narada Haralambous, Andy and Fleur Heyworth, Jack Hodd, Faryal Iqbal, Susan and Andy James, Steven Jamieson, Anthony Partington, Mark Perkins, Alex Skinner, Daniel and Karen Richards, Alastair and Helen Shepherd, Meriel Tolhurst-Clever, Dominic Traynor, and Karen and Alison Williamson. My church community has continued to support me, and Elm Hall Drive Methodist Church in Liverpool has had to endure far too many sermons on idolatry or inter-faith issues while these areas have occupied my thinking.

The constant in all things in my life has been my family. My dad's faith and ministry has always been one which has been all too aware of the dangers of religion and religiosity, and my mum's common-sense approach to the Christian life has embodied the sort of ethic that I hope this book might engender. My parents have never failed me throughout my whole life, and knowing their love for me has been the foundation for everything else. My sisters, Ann and Colette, are my closest friends, and they now have a new addition, my nephew Billy, to bolster their numbers in poking fun at me. My nan, Patricia, is an ever-present joy in my life, a great source of fun and a wonderful friend in times of need. My Auntie Ann and Joan have been unfailing in their support and love. I owe my family so much, and I thank them for all they do for me.

I have sought in this book in some ways to engage in theology proper. God is wonderfully and gloriously complex, magnificent beyond all imagination, worthy of all praise and adoration. For all of my concerns about religion, I remain a (hopefully self-critical) pietist. As such, I will never cease to be amazed by God's abundant plenitude of grace for the world, and even for me. The book is offered in thanksgiving and to His praise and glory.

ABBREVIATIONS

A&B   *Act and Being: Transcendental Philosophy and Ontology in Systematic Theology*. Dietrich Bonhoeffer. Translated by H. Martin Rumscheidt. Edited by Wayne Whitson Floyd, Jr. DBWE vol. 2. Minneapolis: Fortress Press, 1996.

BBNY   *Barcelona, Berlin, New York 1928–1931*. Dietrich Bonhoeffer. Translated by Douglas W. Stott. Edited by Clifford J. Green. DBWE vol. 10. Minneapolis: Fortress Press, 2008.

CCCC   'The Christian Community and the Civil Community'. In Karl Barth, *Community, State and Church: Three Essays by Karl Barth*. Garden City: Doubleday, 1960.

CD   *Church Dogmatics*. Karl Barth. Edited by G. W. Bromiley and T. F. Torrance. 4 vols. Edinburgh: T&T Clark, 1936–77.

C&F   *Creation and Fall: A Theological Exposition of Genesis 1–3*. Dietrich Bonhoeffer. Translated by Douglas S. Bax. Edited by John W. de Gruchy. DBWE vol. 3. Minneapolis: Fortress Press, 1998.

Christology   'Lectures on Christology'. In Dietrich Bonhoeffer, *Berlin: 1932–1933*. Translated by Isabel Best and David Higgins. Edited by Larry L. Rasmussen. DBWE vol. 12. Minneapolis: Fortress Press, 2009.

ChrL   *The Christian Life: Church Dogmatics Volume IV, Part 4 Lecture Fragments*. Karl Barth. Translated by Geoffrey W. Bromiley. Edinburgh: T&T Clark, 1981.

CS   'Church and State'. In Karl Barth, *Community, State and Church: Three Essays by Karl Barth*. Garden City: Doubleday, 1960.

Discipleship   *Discipleship*. Dietrich Bonhoeffer. Translated by Barbara Green and Reinhard Krauss. Edited by Wayne Whitson Floyd, Jr. DBWE vol. 4. Mineappolis: Fortress Press, 2001.

Ethics   *Ethics*. Dietrich Bonhoeffer. Translated by Reinhard Krauss, Charles C. West and Douglas W. Stott. Edited by Clifford J. Green. DBWE vol. 6. Minneapolis: Fortress Press, 2005.

EvTheol   *Evangelical Theology*. Karl Barth. Translated by Grover Foley. London: Weidenfeld & Nicolson, 1963.

FGG   *Fragments Grave and Gay*. Karl Barth. Translated by Eric Mosbacher. Edited by Martin Rumschiedt. London: Collins, 1971.

GD   *The Göttingen Dogmatics: Instruction in the Christian Religion*. Vol. 1. Karl Barth. Translated by Geoffrey W. Bromiley. Edited by Hannelotte Reiffen. Grand Rapids: Wm. B. Eerdmans, 1990.

HoG   'Humanity of God'. In Karl Barth, *God, Grace and Gospel*. Trans-
           lated by James S. McNab. SJT Occasional Papers 10. Edinburgh:
           Oliver & Boyd, 1959.
LJCHC   *Learning Jesus Christ through the Heidelberg Catechism*. Karl
           Barth. Grand Rapids: Wm. B. Eerdmans, 1964.
LPP   *Letters and Papers from Prison*. Dietrich Bonhoeffer. Translated
           by Isabel Best, Lisa E. Dahill, Reinhard Krauss and Nancy Lukens.
           Edited by John W. De Gruchy. DBWE vol. 8. Minneapolis: Fortress
           Press, 2009.
LT   'Life Together'. In Dietrich Bonohoffer, *Life Together and the
           Prayerbook of the Bible*. Translated by Daniel W. Bloesch and
           James H. Burtness. Edited by Wayne Whitson Floyd, Jr. DBWE
           vol. 5. Minneapolis: Fortress Press, 2005.
Rom(II)   *The Epistle to the Romans*. Karl Barth. Translated by Edwyn C.
           Hoskyns. Oxford: OUP, 1968.
SC   *Sanctorum Communio: A Theological Study of the Sociology of the
           Church*. Dietrich Bonhoeffer. Translated by Reinhard Krauss and
           Nancy Lukens. Edited by Clifford J. Green. DBWE vol. 1. Min-
           neapolis: Fortress Press, 1998.
ToC   *The Theology of Calvin*. Karl Barth. Translated by Geoffrey W.
           Bromiley. Grand Rapids: Wm. B. Eerdmans, 1955.
ToS   *The Theology of Schleiermacher: Lectures at Göttingen, Winter
           Semester of 1923/24*. Karl Barth. Translated by Geoffrey W. Bromiley.
           Edited by Dietrich Ritschl. Edinburgh: T&T Clark, 1982.
WGWM   *The Word of God and the Word of Man*. Karl Barth. Translated by
           Douglas Horton. London: Harper, 1957.

Chapter 1

INTRODUCTION

We live in an age in which there has been a clear resurgence of religion. Secularism has not, as it had anticipated, moved fully in a singular and unitary direction, usurped religion, and sounded the final note.[1] To write a book, therefore, entitled *Theology against Religion* may not seem the most appropriate or wise theological enterprise in the contemporary setting. At a time when fundamentalisms of theistic and atheistic varieties have gained power and coverage in politics and the media, there seems, rather, to be a need for theology to engage with the dual movements of secularism and pluralism, and to deal with religion and the religions in relation to these.[2] Emphasizing the connectedness of different religions, and expressing any exclusivism with a significant degree of caution might seem a more beneficial work for theology today than advocating theology's opposition to religion.[3] Furthermore, in an intellectual culture of post- (or hyper-) modernity, the very suggestion of an overarching concept such as 'religion' can itself be seen to offer a dangerous undermining of particularity. It places together various different and distinct movements into a singular (and potentially western, imperialist and Christian) universal of 'religion'. This seems to presuppose that each individual religion

---

1   On this theme, see, for example, Peter L. Berger, 'The Desecularization of the World: A Global Overview', in *The Desecularization of the West*, ed. Peter L. Berger (Grand Rapids: Wm. B. Eerdmans, 1999); Grace Davie, *Europe: The Exceptional Case. Parameters of Faith and the Modern World.* (London: Darton, Longmann & Todd, 2000); Timothy Jenkins, *Religion in English Everyday Life: An Ethnographic Approach* (New York & Oxford: Berghahn Books, 1999); Philip Jenkins, *God's Continent: Christianity, Islam, and Europe's Religious Crisis* (New York: OUP, 2007); and Timothy Jenkins and Ben Quash, 'The Cambridge Inter-Faith Programme: Academic Profile' (http://www.interfaith. cam.ac.uk/en/resources/papers/cip-academic-profile).
2   On fundamentalism, see Martyn Percy, *Words, Wonders and Power: Understanding Contemporary Fundamentalism and Revivalism* (London: SPCK, 1996); Youssef M. Choueiri, *Islamic Fundamentalism. Revised Edition* (London: Cassell, 1997); Youssef Choueiri, 'The Political Discourse of Contemporary Islamicist Movements', in *Islamic Fundamentalism*, ed. Abdel Salam Sidahmed and Anoushiravan Ehteshami (Boulder: Westview, 1996); and (in terms of approaches to scripture in Christian fundamentalism) James Barr, *Fundamentalism* (London: SCM, 1977).
3   One might see this kind of approach in the work of the likes of John Hick. See John Hick, *God and the Universe of Faiths : Essays in the Philosophy of Religion* (London: Macmillan, 1973); John Hick, *God Has Many Names: Britain's New Religious Pluralism* (London: Macmillan, 1980); John Hick, *Problems of Religious Pluralism* (London: Macmillan, 1985); John Hick, *An Interpretation of Religion: Human Responses to the Transcendent* (London: Macmillan, 1989).

is to some degree equivalent, with variance coming only in terms of individual instantiations of universally normative religious concepts such as 'God', 'ritual', 'symbol', 'holy text' and so on: difference, distinction and particularity are removed by religion's meta-narrative. There are, therefore, potential pitfalls both in seeking to articulate a theology against religion and even in speaking of religion as a concept in and of itself in the current cultural, political and intellectual climate.

Furthermore, were this not problematic enough, to engage in this task in constructive dialogue with Bonhoeffer and Barth might also not seem to be a wise enterprise to undertake. In the first instance, there is significant discussion about whether these two thinkers should be seen as working on a singular project with regard to the critique of religion or the positive proposal of a religionless Christianity – differences of terminology which might belie profound differences of approach. Bonhoeffer certainly critiques Barth on the grounds of the latter's failure to follow through the promise that his theology offers with regard to secular expressions of Christianity; and while Barth offers a critique of religion, Bonhoeffer suggests that it might be possible to articulate a completely religionless Christianity.[4] The question of whether Barth and Bonhoeffer's work on religion is one project or two has determined that, in the opinion of the present author, an over-emphasized chasm has been formed between their theologies, despite the obvious similarities that exist. And this has, in turn, determined that systematic theology has responded by discussing the relationship between the two historical figures, rather than forming their theologies on this theme for contemporary engagements in dogmatics. The distrust that some constituents of the Bonhoeffer and Barth communities have at times had for each other has exacerbated this issue, and has determined that – rather than fulfilling the promise that Barth's and Bonhoeffer's theologies offer for contemporary constructive theology – there has been a predominantly historical engagement with their work on these themes. This has come at the expense of allowing their work to inform theology today – a task surely more true to the method of both theologians.[5]

Despite these significant issues, this book advocates that the engagement in describing and advocating a theology against religion is not only possible but useful for the contemporary theological context. A theology against religion may not only allow for a clearer sense of the nature of theological discourse, but may also provide important dogmatic content for the doctrines of God (a theme which pervades this book), salvation and the church. Furthermore, in a setting in which religion is a much discussed topic in politics, world-affairs and the media, thinking theologically about religion may help Christians to form a clearer sense of

---

4   On these themes, see Chapters 2–4 of this book for a detailed discussion.
5   The exception to this is the recent book on worship by Matthew Myer Boulton, *God against Religion: Rethinking Christian Theology through Worship* (Grand Rapids: Wm. B. Eerdmans, 2008). However, this book is directed singularly at liturgy and worship in Christian theology. This comment is not to undermine the extremely good exegetical and constructive nature of the work (and its wise instincts), but to note the different focus of attention in the present work.

what they mean by the term. This in turn may aid sensitive engagements with the symbiotic sphere of the secular, and with those others from the plurality of other faith traditions that are referred to as 'religious'.

A THEOLOGICAL NOT A SOCIOLOGICAL DISCUSSION

This book seeks to offer a theological, rather than a sociological or anthropological, engagement with the concept of religion.[6] It seeks to speak from the perspective of Christian theology about what might be meant by religion as a category for, in the first instance, Christianity: what does it mean to speak of Christianity as the Christian *religion*? In this way, this book does not seek to engage in any universalizing discourse around a reductionist approach to religion which sees each individual religion as one instantiation of a universal essence.[7] Its primary concern and focus is Christianity and what the term 'religion' means for Christian *theology*. Thus, no universalized categorization of religion is desired, but what is desired is simply a discussion of the nature of religion from the perspective of Christian theology. Even though what is meant by a religion is a question which is shared across other academic disciplines and perhaps even other religious traditions, the words of MacIntyre should not be forgotten: these shared concerns do not provide individual traditions with

> a neutral standard in terms of which their respective achievements can be measured. Some problems are indeed shared. But what importance each particular problem has varies from tradition to tradition, and so do the effects of failing to arrive at a solution.[8]

---

6 I have tackled the theme of the need for a *theological* engagement with the category of religion, in relation to both Barth and Bonhoeffer, elsewhere. See Tom Greggs, 'Bringing Barth's Critique of Religion to the Inter-Faith Table', *Journal of Religion* 88, no. 1 (2008); and Tom Greggs, 'Religionless Christianity in a Complexly Religious and Secular World: Thinking through and Beyond Bonhoeffer', in *Religion, Religionlessness and Contemporary Western Culture*, ed. Stephen Plant and Ralf K. Wüstenberg, *International Bonhoeffer Interpretations* (Frankfurt am Main: Peter Lang, 2008).

7 As one sees in the likes of Freud, Nietzsche, Feuerbach, Marx et al., and also in the likes of any approach which focuses upon the phenomenological and the universal in terms of religion, as is the case with Tillich, who sees religion as 'the self-transcendence of life under the dimension of spirit', and even in recognizing the ambiguity of religion, connects it with culture, morality and nature, as three other universals which interpenetrate each other and religion: see Paul Tillich, *Systematic Theology: Combined Volume* (Welwyn: James Nisbet & Co., 1968), vol. 3, pp. 100–13; for an introduction to Tillich on religion, see Mary Ann Stenger, 'Faith (and Religion)', in *The Cambridge Companion to Paul Tillich*, ed. Russell Re Manning (Cambridge: CUP, 2009). An excellent critique of phenomenologically driven approaches to theological accounts of religion can be found in Wolfhart Pannenberg, *Basic Questions in Theology: Collected Essays Volume 2* (Minneapolis: Fortress, 2007), pp. 65–118; Pannenberg argues for a deeply particularist approach to the history of religions.

8 Alasdair MacIntyre, *Whose Justice? Which Rationality?* (London: Duckworth, 1988), p. 348. The thinking contained in the present book is 'traditioned' thinking. In seeking to discuss religion, it

In this way, the present book seeks to engage in elemental thinking for Christian theology about the theological interpretation of religion, in a primary discourse which is believed to be necessary prior to an engagement in discussions about the relation between the religious and the secular, or about a theology of the religions (plural). There will clearly be a degree of overlap between the task of elemental thinking about the nature of religion from a theological perspective and discussion of the religious and the secular and of theologies of the religions.[9] However, before theology engages in these two enterprises, it would seem wise to consider what religion is from a theological perspective. In seeking to do this, this book draws on two major Protestant theologians of the twentieth century who discuss what religion is from a theological perspective, and seeks to offer some constructive suggestions for Protestant theology today.[10]

The need for the Christian theologian to engage with the concept of religion arises, moreover, out of scripture. Throughout scripture, there is an ambivalent relationship expressed with regard to religion and religious observance. Pure religion is defined not in terms of correct ritualistic engagement, but instead in terms of caring for widows and orphans in distress, and keeping oneself undefiled by the world.[11] Even sacrifice seems at times to be redefined in a manner which transcends religious observance.[12] The Psalmist, for example, writes: 'The sacrifice acceptable to God is a broken spirit; a broken and contrite heart, O God, you will not despise.'[13] Proverbs in a similar vein states: 'To do righteousness and justice is more acceptable to the LORD than sacrifice.'[14] In Hosea, it is put thus: 'For I desire steadfast love and not sacrifice, the knowledge of God rather than burnt offerings.'[15] Indeed, to some degree, one might say that there is a development within scripture from a religious to a non-religious or anti-religious expression of God. The development from polytheism, to henotheism, to proto-monotheism, to anidolatrous (but still localized) monotheism, to exclusive but universalized

---

recognizes (again in the words of MacIntyre): 'There are no preconceptual or even pretheoretical data, and this entails that no set of action, no matter how comprehensive, can provide a neutral court of appeal for decision between rivals' (p. 333).

9   The book discusses these themes in relation to theologies of the religion and inter-faith dialogue in Chapters 8 and 9.

10   Clearly, other theological approaches will not follow the same theological trajectory as is offered here. In drawing on Bonhoeffer and Barth, this book also draws on the theological heritage in which they themselves stood, and in which this book itself stands. Indeed, the critique of religion in both Barth and Bonhnoeffer may well rely for its cogency upon its Protestant milieu.

11   James 1.27; cf. 1 Tim. 5.4. There is, indeed, a comparable shift even in the Old Testament with regard to this and the category of the holy; see R. W. L. Moberly, *The Old Testament of the Old Testament: Patriarchal Narratives and Mosaic Yahwism* (Minneapolis: Fortress, 1992), esp. pp. 99–104.

12   It is clear in scripture (and in the ancient world) that sacrifice is somehow elementally connected with religion.

13   Ps. 51.17. All quotations from the Bible are taken from the *New Revised Standard Version*.

14   Prov. 21.3.

15   Hos. 6.6; cf. Mt. 12.7.

monotheism, to the incarnation suggests a trajectory away from religion to a non-religious conception of the nature of God:[16] the divide between the secular and the sacred is broken down once and for all in Christ in whom there is no longer any distance between God and humanity.[17] Throughout the forthcoming chapters (and particularly in Parts II and III of this book) recourse will be made to scripture in connection with some of these themes.

However, the very engagement in the task of speaking about religion theologically inevitably has implications for thinking about religion in relation to other faith traditions practised by living communities of people. While there is a tremendous danger in universalizing religion, and any discussion which seeks to offer paralleling or corresponding presentations of different and particular faiths should and will be avoided, within a discussion of Christianity as a religion there will be a need to discuss religion as a human phenomenon more broadly than simply within the confines of the Christian faith. While this may seem to fall victim to the same flaws discussed above in terms of essentialist and reductionist approaches to religion, the limitations and limited intentions of this discussion should also be noted. Even this aspect of the present work arises, too, *from the perspective of Christian theology*: if Christianity is a religion, how does it relate to other similar (but particular and distinct) human phenomena with which it might loosely be grouped? How should these others be understood in relation to Christianity from the perspective of a Christian theology of religion (as a prior engagement to a theology of the religions)? What makes, for example, Hinduism, Judaism and Islam *theologically* distinctive as entities from other communities or organizations such as trade unions, political parties or large non-governmental organizations? How should theology engage with this distinction between religions and other communities or

---

16 Space does not allow a thorough engagement in these themes here. However, one might note the progression from the idea of ancestral deities (see Albrecht Alt, *Essays in Old Testament History and Religion* (Sheffield: JSOT, 1989), pp. 1–77), to the early Yahwist cult localized to Sinai/Horeb with some form of henotheism suggested in the texts, to a proto-monotheism found in the one God who dwells within the temple, to a more universalized form of monotheism brought about by the exile. One may see this development in theology proper as completed within scripture in Mark 15.38–9, in which the veil is rent and God is seen most clearly in the dead Jesus. On early Yahwism and Israelite Religion, see, for example, John Day, *Yahweh and the Gods and Goddesses of Canaan* (Sheffield: Sheffield Academic Press, 2000); R. Albertz, *A History of Israelite Religion in the Old Testament Period, Vol. 1* (London: SCM, 1994); H. H. Rowley, *Worship in Ancient Israel: Its Forms and Meaning* (London: SPCK, 1967); and Moberly, *The Old Testament of the Old Testament*.

17 In contrast to religious conceptions which are attuned to the presence of God in, for example, the material or culture, which might on one level be seen to be a breaking down of the secular–sacred divide, the conception that this book works with is nervous of drawing lines from culture to God, and is nervous of generalized christological (or so-called incarnational) patterning. It is also conscious of the fact that such culture based or material conceptions often locate God in only certain cultural referents and not others, emphasizing the (albeit now different) distinction between that which is sacred and that which is not.

groups, prior to articulating the relationship between the religions? It is this discourse which, to some degree, the present work seeks to address in the service of broader theological concerns.

Once again, there is a scriptural imperative for engaging with such themes. Not only is religion spoken of as a category in a specifically Judaeo-Christian way in the Bible, but other religions are also discussed from that perspective. While this is often in a confrontational way in terms of pollution of the Yahwist cult, the very engagement in these issues demonstrates a degree of connectivity between the cult of Yahweh and that of other 'gods': there is clear condemnation of God's worship being related in someway to Baal, Molech and the gods of the Canaanites, but this very concern recognizes a degree of continuity (or relationality in terms of discontinuity) between the actions of Israelite religionists and other surrounding religionists.[18] Furthermore, in the New Testament, there is engagement with themes surrounding the interrelation of those of different religions, whether they be Samaritans or pagans.[19] Jesus asserts in relation to a Roman centurion who believes in Jesus' ability to cure his servant: 'Truly I tell you, in no one in Israel have I found such faith. I tell you, many will come from east and west and will eat with Abraham and Isaac and Jacob in the kingdom of heaven' (Mt. 8.10–11). Furthermore, Jesus enters into discussion with a Samaritan woman about where the appropriate place to worship God is. Regarding the issue of whether the correct cultic practice should be undertaken at Gerezim or Jerusalem, Jesus states:

> the hour is coming when you will worship the Father neither on this mountain nor in Jerusalem. You worship what you do not know; we worship what we know, for salvation is from the Jews. But the hour is coming, and is now here, when the true worshipers will worship the Father in spirit and truth, for the Father seeks such as these to worship him.[20]

Given Jesus' engagement in the relationship between different religious expressions of the nature of God, and scripture's record of this, it is surely imperative for the contemporary theologian to reflect upon such themes today.

---

18   And, indeed, to a degree, the assimilation with surrounding cultic practices: one can note Canaanite influences on Psalms 29 and 74, for example. For further on this, see, for example, Day, *Yahweh and the Gods and Goddesses of Canaan*.

19   For further and more focused discussion of biblical texts on religious others, see Gerald O'Collins, *Salvation for All: God's Other Peoples* (Oxford: OUP, 2008), chapters 1–11; Tom Greggs, 'Preaching Inter-Faith: Finding Hints about the Religious Other from the Good Samaritan', *Epworth Review* 36, no. 3 (2009); and Tom Greggs, 'Legitimizing and Necessitating Inter-Faith Dialogue: The Dynamics of Inter-Faith for Individual Faith Communities', *International Journal of Public Theology* 4, no. 2 (2010), 202–10.

20   Jn 4.21–3.

THE NEED TO SPEAK SIMULTANEOUSLY OF SECULARITY, RELIGION, PLURALISM AND GOD

Related to the preceding discussion of the need to engage theologically with the concept of religion is the issue of the symbiotic relationship between the religious and the secular. As David Martin puts it:

> The religions and the secular are in one sense opposites but in another way intertwined. There is almost nothing regarded as religious which cannot also be secular, and almost no characteristic appearing in secular contexts which do not also appear in religious ones.[21]

The concept of the religious presupposes that of the secular, just as the concept of the secular presupposes that of religion:[22] each defines an area or space in which the other somehow is not present. This very distinction arose in light of minimal secular settlements following the religious wars of the sixteenth and seventeenth centuries,[23] with the creation of shared (political) space exempt of religious commitment for those of different faiths in order to settle disputes. Indeed, this creation of 'neutral space' is itself indicative of a further concept which relates symbiotically to those of religion and secularity – pluralism. Secular settlement arose out of a clash of religious commitments, itself a manifestation of a pluralistic religious situation.[24]

In recent years, one has been able to see the extreme effects of these symbiotic relationships unhelpfully aggravating a world situation in which fundamentalisms have burgeoned like weeds in a garden. In the words of David Ford,

> The pathologies of the religions are of course made worse by their mirror opposites in the secular sphere, as the extremes reinforce each other. Unwise,

---

21 David Martin, *The Religious and the Secular: Studies in Secularization* (London: Routledge & Kegan Paul, 1969), p. 3; cf. chapter 4.

22 On the symbiotic nature of concepts surrounding the terms 'religious' and 'secular', see Talal Asad, *Formations of the Secular: Christianity, Islam, Modernity* (Stanford: Stanford University Press, 2003), pp. 2–8. On the evolution of the concept of 'religion', see Jenkins, *Religion in English Everyday Life*, p. 9.

23 See Jenkins and Quash, 'The Cambridge Inter-Faith Programme: Academic Profile', pp. 2–3.

24 Even today, aggressive secularists often advocate religious plurality as the base reason for a secular society, citing religious plurality as being responsible for wars, conflicts and social unrest. See, for example, Richard Dawkins, *The God Delusion* (London: Black Swan, 2007). For a history and a typology of atheisms, the reader is directed to Pannenberg, *Basic Questions in Theology: Collected Essays Volume 2*, pp. 184–200; and David Fergusson, *Faith and Its Critics: A Conversation* (Oxford: OUP, 2009), chapter 1. Fergusson also offers a sensitive engagement with Dawkins' thought in chapters 2 and 3 of his book.

fundamentalist religious dogmatisms feed off unwise, fundamentalist secular ideologies, and vice versa.[25]

This is undoubtedly true, and further complexified by the pluralist setting of contemporary society. Whereas throughout the nineteenth century religious pluralism in most settings implied variations of one religious tradition (for example, in England, a fear by the Church of England of religious pluralism found in the form of Roman Catholics and the increasingly large number of Nonconformists),[26] migration throughout the latter half of the twentieth century has determined that, especially in Europe, there is now a variance in terms of the presence of different world religions, with significant religious minorities present in many political states. Even in largely homogenous religious societies, mass media, films and the internet (as well as foreign travel) provide almost instant access to other religions and cultures throughout the world. To employ a popular cliché, the world is now a very small place. Furthermore, the so-called 'clash of civilizations' has intensified and destabilized this already existing pluralism. Pluralism has been a determining factor in the rise of secular and religious fundamentalisms, both of which are united in desiring to restore a situation of religious homogeneity to nations, and each of which is exacerbated by the other as it responds to the situation of pluralism and to the other opposing fundamentalism.

The danger for theology in responding to this situation of a complexly secular and religiously pluralist society is that it can become a two-faced Janus, engaging in two distinctive conversations (one with secularists and the other with religionists) without recognizing the complex interplay and exchange of issues that exists between these seeming polarities. Theology all too often can engage in dialogue with secularists by emphasizing how sophisticated and 'adult' its thinking is in contradistinction to more juvenile co-religionists, simultaneous to dialoguing with members of other religions by pointing to commonalities and continuities between one religion and another. Furthermore, in engaging in these two conversations, theology runs the danger of construing the symbiotic relationship between the secular and the religious in unhelpful asymmetrical ways. Engagement with other religions can actually become an exercise determined by secular or political agendas, aimed at modifying or de-intensifying particularist religious commitment. The need for co-engagement of religious traditions is often seen not as being internal to the religious traditions themselves, but as external to them as a result of concerns over community cohesion and geo-political conflict: inter-faith can often be politically or secularly motivated, rather than theologically grounded. Without careful theological thought about what 'religion' as a category might

25   David F. Ford, 'God and Our Public Life: A Scriptural Wisdom', *International Journal of Public Theology* 1 (2007), 76.
26   Clearly, in the instance of Roman Catholicism, the fear was also in part concerned with British subjects being beholden to a foreign head of state.

mean, there is the danger that inter-religious engagement (even, and perhaps most especially, in its homogenized liberal form) marches to the beat of an externally authoritative secular drum which sounds a resolutely non-theological religious tone. Indeed, the two faces of Janus may be connected in this way: an acceptance of non-theological definitions of religion in dialogue with secular intellectual authorities leads to a bland and simplistic lowest common denominator form of religiosity in engagement with those of other religious traditions. In this, the bass drum of the Enlightenment clearly sounds loudest. The bringing of religion into the secular, political sphere arises out of a desire to reduce the intensity of religious commitment (out of a fear of extremism) rather than to seek the wisdom that faith traditions might in themselves offer to the *polis*.

Recognizing this unhelpful symbiosis does not determine, however, that the symbiosis is not able to be re-engaged in a constructive and helpful manner for theology, and that secular engagements in the definition of religion offer no positive constructive elements: to fail to attend to these critiques could determine that decisive theological material is lost. However, to understand this symbiosis and secular engagement with religion in a theologically appropriate manner involves the recognition of a further asymmetrical relationship of terms. These terms, for Christian theologians, are 'God' and 'religion'. Here, the secular critique of religion is decidedly helpful. It aids the theologian in realizing that the divine projection that stems from human religiosity cannot stand in continuity with the ontological nature of God. When one is able to recognize that God is not merely the product of human religiosity, which like all created things belongs to this world (as does the so-called 'god' it creates), one is able to note that all religious speech about God (even if raised by God's grace to correspond to some degree to God's nature) is only ever the speech of religionists about God, rather than definitional and limiting of God's nature. From a theological perspective, secular critiques of religion help theologians to realize that their speech about God is religious, and that however good and appropriate that speech may be, it must always guard itself from confusing its own speech with God *in se*. By reminding the theologian of the need to be self-critical in her religious speech about God, secular critiques of religion may come to help the theologian to focus on the true subject of theological enquiry – God in all of God's otherness to creation – rather than to confuse God with an idol of human religious imagining. Secular critiques of religion may help, therefore, to identify religion and the religious nature of speech about God, and thereby to make theology alert to the danger of confusing so-called 'god' with God. By reminding us of the propensity to engage in acts of idolatry and religion, secular critiques point theologians towards the very Godness of God, which cannot simply be captured in human language, ritual or conceptualization. It is clearly not the case that one can speak of God in a fully religionless manner; but theology can and should be prepared to turn scepticism about religious speech back on itself and the fellow religionists with whom it engages, in order to remember the absolute otherness of God at moments when they are tempted to speak *vox dei*.

When these relationships of terms are recognized, the person of faith is enabled to realize that, even in her best moments, she speaks as a religionist, and that she should not confuse the God of her imagining (even if that imagining by grace has correspondence to God) with God in Godself, in God's self-sufficient life. The symbiotic relationship of the terms 'secular' and 'religious' with the term 'God' provides useful dogmatic material for theology proper. When thinking about God is brought back to the symbiotic relationship between the secular and the religious, theology can be rearticulated in a manner which is helpful both to religionists and to secular authorities. When secular critiques of religion are theologized, theologians are able to articulate a more intense and more particular version of faith, which recognizes the nature of God's otherness. These intensive articulations of faith do not undermine particularity or lead to a lowest common denominator religiosity, but are able nevertheless to offer the possibilities of a simultaneously more faithful and more positive engagement with a post-Christendom world, marked by secular and pluralist forces. It is this reconstrual of the relationship between secularism, pluralism, religion and God that this book wishes to explore in its constructive sections, in order to replace a dangerous vicious cycle of mutually reinforcing fundamentalisms with a virtuous cycle of more particularist but open expressions of faith: the integrity of the particular religionist is maintained, but there are new potentials for openness to the world.

DIALOGUING WITH BONHOEFFER AND BARTH

In order to explore the issues outlined, this book will engage in constructive dialogue with Karl Barth (1886–1968) and Dietrich Bonhoeffer (1906–45). The book seeks to build upon the dialogue that occurred between Barth and Bonhoeffer around the Christianization of the critique of religion.[27] In seeking to engage with both of these theologians simultaneously, this book advocates that both Barth and Bonhoeffer are travelling along the same trajectory with regard to the theological critique of religion. To put forward this perspective, it is necessary to enter into an historical discussion of their theologies so as to lay foundations in order to think with and from them constructively.[28] This book is, therefore, in part historical (in examination of Bonhoeffer and Barth) and in part constructive

---

27   Bonhoeffer and Barth both accepted the critiques of religion offered by the sceptics of the nineteenth century, but interpreted and understood these from a theological perspective in such a way as to allow the critiques to fulfil a theological purpose and re-orientate the focus of theological discourse away from religion and back to God.

28   On the activity of thinking with Bonhoeffer, see John W. de Gruchy, 'With Bonhoeffer, Beyond Bonhoeffer: Transmitting Bonhoeffer's Legacy', in *Dietrich Bonheoffer's Theology Today: A Way between Fundamentalism and Secularism?*, ed. John W. de Gruchy, Stephen Plant and Christiane Tietz (Gütersloh: Gütersloh Verlaghaus, 2009).

(in Parts II and III).[29] In that way, the theology contained herein might best be described as *formative*, as it seeks to form the work of others for the theological setting of today. For those readers who are more interested in the constructive proposals that this book offers than in the historical exegesis of Bonhoeffer and Barth, reading the concluding sections of Chapters 2, 3 and 4 should suffice in laying the foundations for the theology which follows. In doing this, however, something will be lost in terms of the exciting work of Bonhoeffer and Barth which is discussed in greater detail in the bodies of those chapters. Nevertheless, this book intends ultimately to offer some new and creative thinking that engages *with and from* Bonhoeffer and Barth, rather than simply seeking to think *towards* their thought. The book seeks, therefore, to engage Barth and Bonhoeffer in dialogue with each other, and then to enter into that dialogue with contemporary concerns and discussions. Since Bonhoeffer's later writings are so telegrammatic and suggestive, the book will seek to think from these aphorisms and exciting suggestions of theological promise in new and creative ways.

One of the difficulties in engaging in a dialogue with Barth and Bonhoeffer surrounds the appropriate use of language for the constructive engagement with them. While Bonhoeffer speaks arrestingly of 'religionless Christianity', for Barth there seems to be (at least in the early work) no suggestion of any possibility of a Christianity without religion. However, if both theologians are taken as being engaged in the prophetic admonition of religion one might see a greater level of connectedness in their thoughts: Bonhoeffer is offering his prophetic admonition from the perspective of the possibilities of what Christianity might be (and indeed might need to be), and Barth from the perspective of what Christianity is. If we take this as our basis, then the different terminological turns of phrase can be seen as being ones which (while not quite synonymous) point theology along the same trajectory. This theme will be explored in detail in Chapters 2 to 4. Ultimately, the uniting concept of the two thinkers might be thought to be the Christianization of the critique of religion in the service of an anti-religious theology. For two theologians who worked in different ages to the present one, it is this direction for theology which is taken to be the basis of the constructive engagement for our own world situation.

SYNOPSIS OF PARTS

The first part of this book seeks to establish motifs in Barth and Bonhoeffer's theology around the theme of religion. Establishing that the two theologians are moving along the same trajectory of thinking, the book will advocate that there are certain markers that are present for a theology against religion. These markers,

---

29   This in itself parallels Bonhoeffer's own work in SC; see SC, p. 291.

arising from historical, exegetical and hermeneutical consideration of Barth and Bonhoeffer, will be the basis for the constructive theology that follows. In this way, the theology contained herein seeks to shape the theology of the past for the concerns and questions of the present.

The formative engagements that follow the historical discussion seek to articulate a theology after Christendom which is concerned to engage with a society marked by a complex relationship between pluralistic religious expressions and secularism. While these twin concerns of secularism and pluralism cannot be artificially separated (and certainly will not be within this volume), the second part of the book addresses what might be thought to be the articulation of a theology against religion in a secular setting. It asks questions of what a doctrine of salvation might look like in such an age, and offers a constructive engagement in ecclesiology at a time when there are falling numbers in congregations. Given the comparative weakness of the church at this time, a third chapter of this part seeks to navigate the relationship between the church and the *polis* in a way which takes a theological interpretation of the critique of religion seriously.

Clearly, the discussions in Part II of this book have implications for a pluralist setting as well (after all, making sense of salvation for those of other faiths as well as none and interpreting the church beside the synagogue, mosque or temple will be necessary aspects of these discussions), and the third chapter of Part II (on the *polis*) acts a bridge to Part III. However, the focus of the third part is more directly concerned with religious pluralism. The three chapters in this part seek to engage theologically with the concept of religion which operates as a precursor to articulating a Christian theology of religions (Chapter 8), prior to engaging in a discussion of inter-faith dialogue (Chapter 9). The book is brought to a conclusion with a chapter which addresses the theological motifs of mystery and hope.

The degree to which this book keeps in operation the concepts of religion, secularism and pluralism in seeking to articulate a theology against religion will determine whether it has fulfilled its desire to express a theologically sensitive account of religion for the church, academy and world in a post-Christendom setting.[30]

---

30 While dominantly systematic in approach, this book does overlap into the field of public theology. In the words of Storrar and Morton, 'Public theology has to do with the public relevance of a theology which has at the core of its Christian identity a concern for the coming of God's Kingdom in the public world of human history.' (William F. Storrar and Andrew R. Morton, 'Introduction', in *Public Theology for the 21st Century: Essays in Honour of Duncan B. Forrester*, ed. William F. Storrar and Andrew R. Morton (London: T&T Clark, 2004), p. 1). The concern of the present book is to address theologically themes relevant to the life of the church and society, offering articulations of theology in the contemporary conditions of post-Christendom.

PART I

CHRISTIANIZING THE CRITIQUE OF RELIGION: BARTH AND BONHOEFFER

Chapter 2

BARTH'S EARLY DISCUSSIONS OF RELIGION

INTRODUCTION

Karl Barth's engagement with the category of religion is one of the most significant, yet understudied, aspects of his theological thought.[1] In distinction to Schleiermacher and in continuity with Feuerbach,[2] Barth offers a fierce critique of religion in order to cut out at root any talk of 'God in man'.[3] Indeed, the influence of Feuerbach on Barth is profound. In his introductory essay to the English translation of Feuerbach's *The Essence of Christianity*, Barth states that 'the attitude of the anti-theologian Feuerbach was more theological than that of many theologians',[4] and that 'the content of his anti-theology may have such a significant bearing on the

---

1   The only major works on Barth's engagement with religion are Garrett Green, 'Challenging the Religious Studies Canon: Karl Barth's Theory of Religion', *Journal of Religion* 75 (1995); and Garrett Green, *Barth on Religion: The Revelation of God as the Sublimation of Religion* (London: T&T Clark, 2007). Green offers a new translation of §17 of CD. While his work offers much to the understanding of this paragraph, and issues of translation will be discussed in this book, the translation offered in CD is the one which will be quoted in this book, unless otherwise indicated. Other discussions of Barth on religion can be found in: J. A. Di Noia, 'Religion and the Religions', in *Cambridge Companion to Karl Barth*, ed. John Webster (Cambridge: CUP, 2000); Greggs, 'Bringing Barth's Critique of Religion to the Inter-Faith Table'; and Boulton, *God against Religion,* chapter 1. Addressing religion in §69, and the relationship of religion to the religions, see Geoff Thompson, 'Religious Diversity, Christian Doctrine and Karl Barth', *International Journal of Systematic Theology* 8, no. 1 (2006); and George Hunsinger, *How to Read Karl Barth. The Shape of His Theology* (New York & Oxford: OUP, 1991), pp. 234–80.
2   For Schleiermacher on religion, see Freidrich Schleiermacher, *The Christian Faith*, ed. H. R. Mackintosh and J. S. Stewart, trans. H. R. Mackintosh and J. S. Stewart, English translation of the second German edition (Edinburgh: T&T Clark, 1968), §§6–10. For Feuerbach on religion, see Ludwig Feuerbach, *The Essence of Christianity*, trans. George Eliot (New York: Harper & Row, 1957). On Barth's engagement with Feuerbach, see John Glasse, 'Barth on Feuerbach', *The Harvard Theological Review* 57, no. 2 (1964). For an introduction to the influence of Marx, Luther and Calvin (as well as Feuerbach) on Barth's understanding of religion, see Boulton, *God against Religion*, pp. 30–5.
3   Feuerbach, *The Essence of Christianity*, p. xxx.
4   Ibid., p. x.

problematic features of modern theology . . . that decisive theological material might escape us if we refused to hear him.'⁵ If Schleiermacher and Calvin are dominant voices from the tradition with whom Barth discusses the dogmatic enterprise, it is Feuerbach who leads him to the very need for discussion. For Barth, Feuerbach was concerned more than any other philosopher with the problem of theology; was more theologically skilled than most modern theologians; and penetrated the contemporary theological situation more effectively than any thinker of his time.⁶

This chapter seeks to outline the way in which Barth engaged in *theologizing* and *Christianizing* the *critique* of religion in opposition to the inheritance of the liberal theology he had received from his mentors. This turn to the critique of religion has far-reaching implications, not least in terms of Barth's doctrine of revelation. In order to lay the foundations for further constructive work on the theologizing of the critique of religion, this chapter will examine Barth's early material on religion, and will focus on Barth's work on this theme up to *Church Dogmatics* I/2. The reason for focusing on this section of Barth's work in the current chapter is that, while Bonhoeffer had read *Church Dogmatics* up to II/2,⁷ he only really engages with Barth's thought on religion up to I/2. There is, thus, in this chapter a discussion of various of Barth's early works which touch on religion and an exegesis of *Church Dogmatics* paragraph 17. Discussion of Barth's work on this topic in his writings from II/1 onwards is reserved for Chapter 4. With a mind to the next chapter (on Bonhoeffer), and recognizing the relationship between the two concepts of religion and revelation, this chapter also contains a discussion of Barth on revelation, and seeks to offer some guidance in order to avoid certain common pitfalls in approaching Barth's theology. It is hoped in all of the discussion that follows that an exegesis of Barth is offered which makes it possible for one to see his work as moving along the same path as that of Bonhoeffer.

EARLY DISCUSSIONS OF RELIGION

Even in Barth's very early academic work, the theme of the relationship between Christianity and the concept of religion is present.⁸ In his 1916 essay, 'The Strange

5   Ibid., p. xi.

6   Ibid., p. x.

7   Andreas Pangritz, *Karl Barth in the Theology of Dietrich Bonhoeffer*, trans. Barbara Rumscheidt and Martin Rumscheidt (Grand Rapids: Wm. B. Eerdmans, 2000), pp. 61–2. While Barth's CD vol. II seems to have influenced Ethics (as Pangritz observes, p. 62), Bethge is correct about Bonhoeffer's lack of reaction to the dogmatic content of CD II/2: 'there is no record of Bonhoeffer's reaction to Barth's doctrine of predestination' (Eberhard Bethge, *Dietrich Bonhoeffer*, ed. Edwin Robertson, trans. Eric Mosbacher, et al. (London: Collins, 1970), p. 746). The lack of a record of a direct reaction by Bonhoeffer to aspects of Barth's theology could equally well be made for CD II/1 as well, as the work of Marsh makes clear. See Charles Marsh, *Reclaiming Dietrich Bonhoeffer: The Promise of His Theology* (Oxford: OUP, 1994).

8   Indeed, even prior to his academic career, Barth's sermons demonstrate that he sees religion as a more and more ambiguous affair: 'Barth spoke of religion as being like the colour that is painted

New World within the Bible',[9] the theme of religion is already present, and religion is one of the three motifs around which Barth responds to the liberal inheritance of theology.[10] Barth's use of 'religion' as a category at this early stage is not systematic, and he criticizes religion as well as stating that there is more than simply religion in the text of scripture, finally differentiating the religion of God from any historical instantiation of religion, including Christianity: 'in the Bible . . . the theme is, so to speak, the religion of God and never once the religion of the Jews, or Christians, or heathen'.[11] Although not fully worked through, one can already see the concerns that Barth is beginning to express with regard to the way in which Christianity might function as a religion and how it might relate to theoretical approaches to religion.[12]

One sees a similar lack of systematic engagement with the concept of religion in the first edition of *Römerbrief*. In this volume, religion is used in a generally negative manner, and is often linked with the concept of morality and pitted against the gospel. However, it is only in the second and revised edition of Barth's *The Epistle to the Romans* that one begins to see the organization of Barth's thought on religion in a more directly conceptual way.[13] It is to this volume that one should turn first in attending to Barth's theologizing of the critique of religion.

The Epistle to the Romans

In editing and revising *Romans*, Barth engaged in making the concept of religion a major aspect of his thought.[14] His reflections on chapter seven of Paul's epistle, under the title of 'Freedom', come to be focused on religion – 'The Frontier of Religion',

---

over wood or stone. Outwardly, the wood or stone is pretty but underneath everything remains the same. In the same way, religion is very often simply a façade or belief which conceals the greatest unbelief. . . . There can be little doubt that Barth saw himself in the role of the modern-day Amos.' Bruce L. McCormack, *Karl Barth's Critically Realistic Dialectical Theology* (Oxford: Clarendon Press, 1995), p. 99.

9   This is published in WGWM, pp. 28–50.

10   WGWM, pp. 41–5.

11   WGWM, p. 45.

12   The same is true of Barth's engagement with von Harnack and the thought of Overbeck. On this, see Eberhard Jüngel, *Karl Barth: A Theological Legacy*, trans. Garrett E. Paul (Philadelphia: Westminster, 1986), pp. 59–60.

13   For a more detailed engagement of the way in which the first edition of *Römerbrief* relates to the second, see Green, *Barth on Religion*, pp. 6–8; and McCormack, *Karl Barth's Critically Realistic Dialectical Theology*, pp. 282–8. The second, revised edition was published in 1922. The Hoskyns translation is of the sixth edition, which – with the exception of the preface – is unaltered from the second.

14   Indeed, McCormack asserts that the 'most immediate consequence of [the critically realistic] starting-point was the fact that criticism of religion moved to the centre of Barth's concerns.' McCormack, *Karl Barth's Critically Realistic Dialectical Theology*, pp. 130–1.

'The Meaning of Religion' and 'The Reality of Religion'.[15] However, even at earlier points in the book, one can already see in *Romans* Barth's contrasting of Christ to religion. Rather than being the founder of a religious tradition, or indeed a religious figure, for Barth, Christ's unique status cannot be undermined by connecting Him simply with other comparable figures who founded religious movements in a history-of-religions approach to theology.[16] This is not to say that Christianity is not a religion. While Barth is able to state that '[t]he Gospel of Christ was not concerned with inventing new rites and dogmas and institutions', he also asserts (in the very next sentence) that '[e]verywhere it [Christianity] can be seen quite naively borrowing religious material already in existence.'[17] Thus from its very foundation, Christianity has engaged in becoming a religion – the very thing that it was not destined to be. Barth sees a purpose in this, however, as it leads the Christian back to grace and faith: 'by grace alone do we become aware of the sense that is non-sense . . . and therefore the appropriation of the sense in the non-sense of the world of religion can only be by faith.'[18] The purpose of Christianity *qua* religion, therefore, is to lead people to its own non-sense which directs people back to grace. Thus, the critique of religion should not stand alone, without being thought of from a christological perspective as directing the Christian towards Christ from the 'non-sense' of religion. Barth's negativity about religion is always checked by its capacity to function in leading people to Christ. Thus, Barth's approach to religion is never *fully* negative.[19] He writes: 'If religion is nebulous and lacking in security, so also is everything which is exalted to oppose religion. Anti-religious negation has no advantage over the affirmations of religion. To destroy temples is not better than to build them.'[20] The critique of religion is – in *Romans* – firmly theologized in a christological way, reflecting on the function of religion in leading people back to the need for grace in Christ.

This dialectic of religion leading people to the need for grace is developed throughout chapter seven of *Romans*. While the first part of the seventh chapter is directly negative, Barth offers the potential of a positive purpose for religion as well: 'We have been concerned with the negative truth. But religion has also a positive truth'.[21] This is best summarized in the following passage:

> Religion compels us to the perception that God is not to be found in religion. Religion makes us to know that we are competent to advance no single step.

---

15 Cf. J. A. Veitch, 'Revelation and Religion in the Theology of Karl Barth', *Scottish Journal of Theology* 24, no. 1 (1971), 7.

16 Rom(II), p. 117.

17 Rom(II), p. 192.

18 Rom(II), p. 193.

19 Cf. McCormack, *Karl Barth's Critically Realistic Dialectical Theology*, p. 282, regarding Rom(II): 'Barth made it quite clear that there is no grace without the experience of grace. His critique of religion was not directed against religion as such but against *Religion an sich* – religion for its own sake.'

20 Rom(II), p. 136.

21 Rom(II), p. 240.

Religion, as the final human possibility, commands us to halt. Religion brings us to a place where we must wait, in order that God may confront us – on the other side of the frontier of religion. The transformation of the 'No' of religion into the divine 'Yes' occurs in the dissolution of this last observable human thing.[22]

The inability of humans to reach God through religion makes them rely on God's initiative through His grace. Thus, religion serves as a step on the path (although the path is a dead end until God acts) to recognizing the graciousness of God.

However, there are more radically negative moments that stand in contrast to this (almost) positive purpose for religion. Religion is seen as the product of 'the serpent's sermon on the theme of a direct relation between man and God', and thereby becomes 'the occasion of sin' and sin's 'working capital' by which people are removed from direct relation to God and are 'thrust into disunion'.[23] Even when Barth speaks of the 'No' of religion in which the 'Yes' of God is hidden, this does not necessarily mean that religion itself is a positive thing, any more than sin can be seen as such in relation to grace. Barth, having hinted at a positive purpose for religion, often goes on to guard against any confusion of religion's positive purpose with the idea of religion being a positive thing. For example:

Death is the meaning of religion; for when we are pressed to the boundary of religion, death pronounces the inner calm of simple and harmless relativity to be at an end. Religion is not at all to be 'in tune with the infinite' or to be at 'peace with oneself' . . . But religion is an abyss; it is terror.[24]

Or again: 'Religion is the KRISIS of culture and of barbarism. Apart from God, it is the most dangerous enemy a man has on this side of the grave. For religion is the human possibility of remembering that we must die'.[25] Barth is also concerned to point out that religion leads to a lack of wholeness in humans, splitting them in two, in a way which makes it impossible to know which person one truly is – the inward or the natural.

The Theology of Schleiermacher

The theme of religion is also discussed in Barth's lectures on the theology of Schleiermacher.[26] In these lectures, significant time is spent exegeting the opening

---

22 Rom(II), p. 242.
23 Rom(II), p. 248.
24 Rom(II), p. 253.
25 Rom(II), p. 268.
26 Clearly, in the context of this book, the key question is not whether Barth has interpreted Schleiermacher correctly, but what resonances his interpretation had for his developing theologizing of

paragraphs of Schleiermacher's *The Christian Faith*.[27] Schleiermacher's use of the concept of religion and his category of *Gefühl* gave religious experience a positive role within theology and the Christian faith more broadly. However, the effect of this was to make Christianity just one species of a broader genus of piety. In order to differentiate between Christianity and other religions, Schleiermacher postulated a hierarchy of pieties, with an evolutionary progression through fetishism to polytheism to monotheism.[28] At the height of this hierarchy lies Christianity. In Barth's words:

> in the light of the demonstration of the facticity and universality of the sense of absolute dependence in §§ 3–6 he [Schleiermacher] wants to prove that in the historical world of this mysterious basic factor Christianity takes one of the highest places, indeed, the very highest place. He does this by postulating a series in which monotheism as its climax is secretly declared to be Christian monotheism and is shown to be the irresistible result of a consistent natural development of the religious spirit or feeling that has already been proved to be present and universal.[29]

Barth questions Schleiermacher's approach of basing Christian theology on the overarching category of religion.

> Cannot this simple thing be summed up in the thesis that Christianity is a *historically conditioned religion*? A *religion:* it thus participates in the established fundamental fact of religion in general; it has an inner aspect, the feeling of absolute dependence, which has here a special form on the highest monotheistic stage as the consciousness of redemption; but thus far it is not a specific entity manifested and operative in history. A *historically conditioned religion:* thus far it takes on shape and extension among historical things; it has an outer side, the person of its founder, which gives it tone and color and with which its specific expression is indissolubly connected; but thus far it is also a relative entity, and with its special crystallization of everywhere identical elements it stands alongside others of the same kind.[30]

Barth's concern here is the relativizing of the unique nature of Christian faith. Schleiermacher's work on revelation does little to assuage Barth's concerns:

---

religion. The issue of Barth's interpretation of Schleiermacher is, therefore, sidestepped in this work. For an excellent recent discussion of Barth's engagement with Schleiermacher (principally around the doctrine of election), the reader is directed to Matthias Gockel, *Barth and Schleiermacher on the Doctrine of Election: A Systematic-Theological Comparison* (New York: OUP, 2006).

27   ToS, pp. 211–43.
28   Cf. Schleiermacher, *The Christian Faith*, §§3–4 and 7–10.
29   ToS, p. 226.
30   ToS, p. 232.

Purely wraithlike is the possibility that *true revelation* might mean that God communicates himself as he is in and for himself; we do not have the organs that are necessary to receive such a communication. All revelation is simply 'God in relation to us,' that is, a modification of our self-consciousness.[31]

Even where Schleiermacher does establish the distinctiveness of Christianity, Barth is concerned that this is done from the perspective of 'the watchtower of philosophy of religion'.[32] Thus, one can see that for Barth in his discussion of Schleiermacher's *Christian Faith*, religion stands in contrast to the category of revelation, and thereby undermines the unique claims of Christian revelation and the person of Jesus Christ.

The Göttingen Dogmatics

One finds a further discussion of religion as a category in Barth's earliest lectures on dogmatics in Göttingen. Barth differentiates his own approach to theology from that of those who are 'investigators of religion in general and of Christianity in particular'.[33] Barth is not as negative as one might imagine he would be with regard to this approach to the discipline:

There is nothing dangerous or suspect about this if we at least know how to walk warily around the burning bush [Exod. 3.2ff.]. This is just one aspect of scholarship like any other, and on these academic pastures, and in good company, one can spend one's life most honorably.[34]

However, Barth by contrast is unwilling in his own method, and thereby in the method he implies that his students should follow, merely to end there. Instead, he writes:

What are *you* going to say? Not as one who knows the Bible or Thomas or the Reformers or the older Blumhardt, but responsibly and seriously as one who stands by the words that are said: *you?* And *what* are you going to say? Not how impressively or how clearly or how well adapted to your hearers and to the present age – these are all secondary concerns – but *what?*[35]

Rather than targeting what has come to be termed an 'outsider approach' to religion, Barth's concern with religion as a category is aimed far more at those who

---

31 ToS, p. 235.
32 ToS, p. 236.
33 GD, p. 5.
34 GD, p. 5.
35 GD, p. 6.

begin their theologies with discussion of religious consciousness as a direct and natural human knowledge of God. Thus, Barth addresses older instances of the use of the word 'religion'. In this, he is clear that the target he has in sight is not the way in which the word functions for the likes of Zwingli or Calvin, even though a cursory glance at their works might create the opinion that they are engaging with religion in a way that Barth would wish to reject. He states:

> We have only to read the first pages of these books to be convinced that we do not have here a theology of religious consciousness. What God is, we of ourselves know as little as a scarab knows what a man is, Zwingli tells us. It would be Luciferian and Promethean arrogance to want to know what God is in any other way than through God himself. Calvin, too, will link the knowledge of God directly to self-knowledge only insofar as insight into our poverty, nakedness, and ruin through the fall compel us to ask after God.[36]

Barth's concern here with religion as a category of theological speech is related directly to his view that revelation is the only way in which humans may know God. For Barth, therefore, any notion of natural religion, even one which sees Christianity as its supreme form, must be removed from theology. In discussing revelation and critiquing any view of the historical progression of religions, he asserts forcefully: 'A ramp is built so that one may easily ("casually"!) climb up from the general history of the spirit and religion to Jesus at the top, that is, to revelation. We must smash this ramp, or at least see that revelation is not there at the top.'[37] Religion and revelation can never, for Barth, be seen as continuous: God does not make Himself known in religion, and those who seek to know something of God should not look there, other than for detail of what humans have believed about God.

It is not difficult to identify the target that Barth has in his eye in these discussions, and this target comes further into focus in *Göttingen Dogmatics* in Barth's discussion of 'The Concept of Religion'. In his opening to this section, Barth makes clear (if in a somewhat overstated way)[38] his own allergy to religion as a theological concept:

> You have probably never heard me use the words 'religion,' 'religiosity,' and 'religious' except when quoting the thoughts of others; then they are apposite.

---

36   GD, p. 9. Cf. Barth's 1922 lectures on Calvin: 'We have here a criticism of religion that we might well feel reminds us of Feuerbach. True piety shows itself in the genuine zeal that never tries to conceive of God as our own presumption dictates but seeks the knowledge of the true God in God himself, conceives of him only as he himself reveals himself and declares himself, namely, as Father and Lord, reaches out after his righteousness, and has more fear of offending him than of death itself' (ToC, p. 273).

37   GD, p. 61.

38   As well as what has already been cited, Barth also discusses Israel's religion in relation to the Christian religion in GD, p. 145; and there is a discussion of religion under his section 'Jesus the Kyrios' on p. 125.

Similarly, in my vocabulary the words 'religious knowledge,' 'religious history,' 'religious philosophy,' and 'religious psychology' denote something which, if it is not entirely mistaken, still has no place in theology as I see it. . . . I do not propose to advance my own view of religion. I have no interest in this concept . . . [39]

Instead, the dominant aspect of Barth's engagement with religion is once more to distance himself from the theology of Schleiermacher. Within the ten pages on the theme of the concept of religion, Barth spends nine of them discussing the church father of the nineteenth century. The fierceness of Barth's critique is almost beyond measure:

I can no longer hear or pronounce the word 'religion' without the adverse recollection that in modern intellectual history it has in fact been a flag denoting the place of refuge to which Protestant and a good deal of Roman Catholic theology began a more or less headlong retreat when it no longer had the courage to think in terms of its object, that is, the Word of God, but was glad to find at the place where the little banner of religion waved a small field of historical and psychological reality to which, renouncing all else, it could devote itself as a true 'as though' theology, at peace with the modern understanding of science. Behind the alien word 'religion' and all that it entails, and also behind the word 'piety,' which some prefer, there lies concealed either shamefully or shamelessly a confession that as moderns we no longer dare in principle, primarily, and with uplifted voice to speak about God. Even with the best dialectical accommodation, I cannot today detach this historical background from even the better sense of the word *religio*.[40]

One can begin to note here a questioning of Barth's previous *potentially* positive purpose for religion, which had stood in tension with the negative use of the term. This is only gestured at and hinted at, but there is an indication that for Barth it is difficult to have anything positive to say about the theme, and what little there is that does appear positive (the 'better sense of the word' in the passage quoted above) points only to the very different way in which Calvin and Zwingli used the term. The reason Barth gives for this move is that he is concerned that Schleiermacher has made Jesus Christ 'simply one specimen of the genus' of religious leaders;[41] and that Schleiermacher has described a God who is 'a something, a neuter, not a He.'[42] Barth is also critical of Schleiermacher's theology in relation to other religions, and

39   GD, p. 181.
40   GD, p. 182.
41   GD, p. 184.
42   GD, p. 187.

not – perhaps – quite in the way one might be first led to believe. Instead, Barth is critical of the all-encompassing and dominant universal in Schleiermacher's thought which merges all religions together: 'As regards the different religions, the insight is simply that they are all one, that the whole religious world is an indivisible totality into which they all merge. In every way the universum is contemplated and worshiped.'[43] To some degree, therefore, the critique of religion in the Göttingen lectures is essentially a critique of Schliermacher's thought on the subject.

RELIGION IN *CHURCH DOGMATICS* I/2, §17

Barth's most sustained and detailed engagement with the concept of religion comes in the second part volume of his *Church Dogmatics* §17 'The Revelation of God as the Abolition [*Aufhebung*] of Religion'.[44] Under the overarching discussion of 'The Doctrine of the Word of God', Barth discusses religion in Part III of *Church Dogmatics* I/2 – 'The Outpouring of the Holy Spirit'. That Barth places the discussion of religion under a pneumatological heading is significant. Barth's discussion of religion here falls within the section where he treats the way in which revelation reaches humanity – the subjective appropriation of revelation through the third mode of God's triune being. Barth's concern here is the *reception* of revelation, and it is under that topic that he feels it necessary to discuss within this theme the concept of religion. His question runs, therefore, along the following lines: is revelation received in religion? To this question, Barth offers a dialectical response with a very resounding and loud 'no', and a much more tentative and quiet 'yes'. This 'yes' is not that of his *Romans* (in which religion led to the inability to know God and therefore the need for revelation and grace), but is connected far more to the subjective reception of the objective revelation of God in Jesus Christ. Given the historical existence of Christianity, Barth finds it necessary to discuss the purpose and role of religion in relation to Jesus Christ and to the Holy Spirit. In this, Barth is not using religion as a concept by means of which to distance his theology from that of Schleiermacher, as had previously been the case: indeed, Schleiermacher is mentioned only three times in the 81-page paragraph. Instead, Barth is offering a constructive engagement with the concept of religion, as a concept related to his true interest of theology and as religion pertains to that primary academic discipline. As Green asserts:

> Barth thus belongs among those theorists of religion who approach the subject indirectly, out of a primary interest in some other issue. A parallel might

---

43   GD, p. 189.
44   On issues relating to the translation of *Aufhebung* in Barth, see Green, *Barth on Religion*, pp. 5–6. Although the original translation will be used, the reader is reminded of the Hegelian concept that this word implies, and the German term will be placed in parentheses as appropriate.

be found in a thinker like Freud, who likewise comes to religion out of a prior interest in something else: he finds that he must deal with religion because of the psychological power of human wishes. Thus just as Barth, guided by his theological interest, defines religion in terms of divine revelation, so Freud, guided by his psychoanalytic interest, defines religion in terms of human desires.[45]

Paragraph 17 is a much understudied and often poorly presented aspect of Barth's thought, and it is thus necessary to discuss each of its three sections, seeking to extract the conceptual and analytical points.[46] Key to my analysis is the suggestion that Barth's application of the term 'true religion' (the positive aspect of the dialectic) requires very careful recognition of the limitations of its terms. Far from serving to give Barth's work on religion a more positive spin than his preceding work on the subject, this paragraph offers an even more critical engagement with the topic than is found in *Romans*. As Boulton puts it:

> If religion is primarily the human attempt to offer works in order to stand aright before God in *The Epistle to the Romans*, in *Church Dogmatics*, it is also the rejection of God's 'self-offering and self-manifestation.' . . . Not only does human offering make actual the separation of sin, it also forestalls the divine self-offering, setting up a religious 'human manufacture' in its stead.[47]

The Problem of Religion in Theology

Because the Holy Spirit is the foundation of the possibility and reality of the event of God's revelation to human beings, revelation as a determination of human existence has 'at least the aspect and character of a human phenomenon.'[48] As a result of this, Barth finds it appropriate to enter into a discussion of religion. Here, Barth affirms the universal nature of religion as a human phenomenon:

> 'Christianity' or the 'Christian religion' is one predicate for a subject which may have other predicates. It is a species within a genus in which there may be other species. Apart from and alongside Christianity there is Judaism, Islam, Buddhism, Shintoism and every kind of animistic, totemistic, ascetic, mystical and prophetic religion. And again, we would have to deny revelation

---

45 Ibid., p. 13.
46 For a more descriptive engagement in exegesis of this text, see ibid., pp. 12–22.
47 Boulton, *God against Religion*, p. 58.
48 CD I/2, p. 281.

as such if we tried to deny that it is also Christianity, that it has this human aspect, that from this standpoint it can be compared with other human things, that from this standpoint it is singular but certainly not unique. We have to recognise the fact calmly, and calmly think it through.[49]

Christianity clearly, for Barth, exists alongside all other human expressions of religion. Its unique claims differentiate Christianity from other religions, but not to the degree that Christianity ceases to belong to the same genus as these other religions. Even in its best form, for Barth, Christian piety belongs on the same scale as all other pieties.[50] However, that this is the case does not determine that the subject of theological speech should be religion; this was the mistake of Protestant theology in the nineteenth century: 'The real catastrophe was that theology lost its object, revelation in all its uniqueness. And losing that, it lost the seed of faith with which it could remove mountains, even the mountain of modern humanistic culture.'[51] While Barth seems to concede to Schleiermacher the universal nature of religion, and Christianity's belonging to that genus, Barth's primary concern is to continue to discuss how to articulate the true subject of theology – revelation in all its uniqueness – in relation to the concrete and historical phenomenon of religion. Barth accepts, with the likes of Freud and Feuerbach, the inevitability of religion, but – unlike these secular critics – he seeks to think about the category of religion from a theological perspective. No simple answers are allowed here: no longer can religion be contrasted to Christianity as a 'faith'; Barth's critique is deeper and much more searching than that. The problem of the 'problem of religion' is, instead, as follows: 'where we think that revelation can be compared or equated with religion, we have not understood it as revelation.'[52] The issue is, therefore, whether or not there are any lines of continuity between the revelation of God and religion. The basis for the reception of revelation is not and cannot be religion; and religion is not and should never be confused with revelation. Contrary to certain presentations of Barth which seem to suggest a lack of interest in the human subject,[53] the historical or the particular,[54] Barth's concern

---

49   CD I/2, p. 281.

50   CD I/2, p. 282.

51   CD I/2, p. 294.

52   CD I/2, p. 295.

53   For example, Barth's theology is sometimes presented as if it falls under the critique of Tillich regarding a theological propensity towards a 'demonic absolutism which throws the truth like at the heads of people not caring whether they can accept it or not' (Paul Tillich, *Systematic Theology Vol. 3: Life in the Spirit; History and the Kingdom of God* (Welwyn: James Nisbet & Co., 1964), p. 199; cf. John Webster "Introducing Barth", in *The Cambridge Companion to Karl Barth* (Cambridge: CUP, 2000), p. 9). See also Clifford J. Green, *Bonhoeffer: A Theology of Sociality. Revised Edition* (Grand Rapids: Wm. B. Eerdmans, 1999), p. 262; cf. pp. 258–68.

54   Although this is a common critique of Barth's theology (and especially his doctrine of election), the most thorough-going version of it can be found in Richard H. Roberts, *A Theology on Its Way? Essays on Karl Barth* (Edinburgh: T&T Clark, 1991), chapter 1. Roberts argues that there is an overly

here is to address the appropriate way in which to speak of humanity in relation to the reception of God's revelation:

> Revelation is God's sovereign action upon man or it is not revelation. But the concept 'sovereign' – and in the context of the doctrine of the Holy Spirit we can presuppose this as 'self-evident' (although not at all self-evidently) – indicates that God is not at all alone, that therefore, if revelation is to be understood, man must not be overlooked or eliminated. And the same is true of religion, whether by that we mean the Christian religion in particular or human religion in general, to which the Christian religion belongs.[55]

Barth recognizes the place of humans in the reception of revelation, and – as a collective and historical entity – the place of religion. Barth does not feel that the category of religion can be ignored in discussing revelation. However, far from offering a positive discussion of religion, Barth's engagement with how humans receive revelation has its context in the powerful statement: 'because we remember and apply the christological doctrine of *assumptio carnis* . . . we speak of revelation as the abolition [*Aufhebung*] of religion.'[56]

Religion as Unbelief

Having established the universal nature of religion and recognized Christianity's religious nature as an instantiation of religion, Barth goes on to define religion from the standpoint of revelation. It is difficult to overestimate the negativity with which Barth does this. His definition of religion as *Unglaube* (unbelief, or – better – faithlessness) forms part of his polemic against the replacing of revelation with religion. Religion is 'the attempted replacement of the divine work by a human manufacture', in which humans venture to grasp at God.[57] For Barth, there can be emphatically no continuity between religion and revelation: 'Revelation does not link up with a human religion which is already present and practised. It contradicts it, just as religion previously contradicted revelation. It displaces it, just as religion previously displaced revelation'.[58] Indeed, the knowledge of God that humans claim to have through religion is not knowledge of God at all, but knowledge of the anti-God. Barth writes of this knowledge in the harshest of terms: 'It is never the

strong influence of Hegel and Kant on Barth that leads him along the path of idealism to the resulting destruction of real human time. Similar versions of this critique can be found in G. C. Berkouwer, *The Triumph of Grace in the Theology of Karl Barth*, trans. Harry R. Boer (London: Paternoster, 1956); and Ben Quash, *Theology and the Drama of History* (Cambridge: CUP, 2005), pp. 122ff.
55   CD I/2, pp. 295–6.
56   CD I/2, p. 297.
57   CD I/2, p. 302.
58   CD I/2, p. 303.

truth. It is a complete fiction, which has not only little but *no* relation to God.'[59] In asserting this, Barth differentiates between the so-called 'God' of religion and the true God who makes Himself known in the revelation of Jesus Christ by the power of the Holy Spirit. It is this christocentric turn which is key to Barth's mature work on religion. Revelation is not simply an abstract concept, but is concretely and objectively the person of Jesus Christ, and it is this *person* who is the contradiction of religion:

> Jesus Christ does not fill out and improve all the different attempts of man to think of God and to represent Him according to his own standard. But as the self-offering and self-manifestation of God He replaces and completely out-bids those attempts, putting them in the shadows to which they belong. . . . He replaces all the different attempts of man to reconcile God to the world, all our human efforts at justification and sanctification, at conversion and salvation.[60]

For Barth, it is Jesus Christ who is the only basis on which one can identify religion as idolatrous and self-righteous: He is the one who exposes religion as unbelief.[61] Because Barth's critique of religion is pursued from a christological perspective, it is clear that for him the only real critique of religion can come from Christ, and all other versions of this critique (even theological ones) fail: neither mysticism nor atheism can deal appropriately with religion precisely because of this.[62] It is Jesus who reveals religion to be idolatrous, self-righteous and self-centred. Having laid these foundations, Barth goes on to discuss the way in which one might nevertheless speak of a true religion.

True Religion

The sub-paragraph on true religion might suggest at first glance that Barth overcomes his negativity about religions in general by a positive engagement with Christianity as a unique revelation of God. Here, the Hegelian dialectic can be seen to come to the fore.[63] Certainly, there is much to this: Barth does not want to follow the paths of atheism or of mysticism that he has just rejected. However, if Barth is critical in his first two sub-paragraphs, it is the third which is in some ways the most critical of all in terms of the Christian religion.[64] One does well to note that Barth does not simply assert in this paragraph that Christianity is the true

---

59 CD I/2, p. 303, emphasis added.
60 CD I/2, p. 308.
61 CD I/2, p. 315; cf. pp. 315–22.
62 CD I/2, pp. 314–15.
63 This, I think, is the essence of Garrett Green's presentation.
64 In this way, I suspect my reading varies slightly from that of Green, 'Challenging the Religious Studies Canon', and that of Thompson, 'Religious Diversity, Christian Doctrine and Karl Barth', 6–9.

religion, but explains in what *ways* one can speak of Christianity as the true religion and, by implication, in what ways one cannot. Because Christianity is a religion in response to God's revelation in Jesus Christ who *is* the abolition [*Aufhebung*] of religion, the manner in which Barth can speak of Christianity as the true religion requires careful consideration. Indeed, Barth begins not by stating that in this section he *will* assert that Christianity is the true religion, but that in the preceding paragraphs he has done this already: 'The *preceding* expositions have established the fact that we can speak of "true" religion only in the sense in which we speak of a "justified sinner."'[65] Rather than offering a justification of the truth of the Christian religion in and of itself, Barth rejects the possibility that one can ever claim the truth of religion. He starts his very next paragraph: 'Religion is never true in itself and as such. The revelation of God denies that any religion is true'.[66] It is only after having forcefully asserted this that Barth goes on to speak about the way in which to differentiate between the Christian religion and other religions, something he has not done until this point.

In examining the way in which Barth differentiates between the Christian religion and other religions, it is necessary always to hold in mind that the analogy which Barth uses to speak of the true religion in relation to Christianity is *strictly* that of the justified sinner. That is to say: any speech about the essential truth or goodness of religion cannot be maintained, just as one cannot speak of the truth or goodness of sin. It is not *because* of its religion that Christian claims are true, but *despite* its religion, just as it is not because of sin that a human is justified, but despite her sin. In God's grace, Christianity is enabled to become true, but this does not offer any positive message to religion *per se*: 'grace is the revelation of God. No religion can stand before it as true religion. No man is righteous in its presence. It subjects us all to the judgment of death. But it can also call dead men to life and sinners to repentance.'[67] Barth's engagement with the category of religion (even theologically) is not, therefore, a way of differentiating Christianity from other religions: for Barth, that would involve proving that Christianity is not guilty of idolatry and self-righteousness.[68] Instead, Barth's account of the category of religion is a theological (or perhaps more accurately christological) appropriation of the critique of religion as applied to Christianity, and not to the other religions:

> it is our business as Christians to apply this judgment first and most acutely to ourselves: and to others, the non-Christians, only in so far as we recognise ourselves in them, i.e., only as we see in them the truth of this judgment of

---

These both see the final section of the paragraph as a more positive engagement with religion – the reconstitution of religion, as the synthesis moment of the Hegelian dialectic.

65   CD I/2, p. 325, emphasis added.
66   CD I/2, p. 325.
67   CD I/2, p. 326.
68   CD I/2, p. 326.

revelation which concerns us, in the solidarity, therefore, in which, anticipating them in both repentance and hope, we accept this judgment to participate in the promise of revelation.[69]

Christianity's truth in part lies in God's judgement of it. This again relates to the subjective appropriation of revelation: what Christians accept is the revelation of Jesus Christ who exposes religion as unbelief. Barth writes in a sermonic tone:

> this judgment affects the whole practice of our faith: our Christian conceptions of God and the things of God, our Christian theology, our Christian worship, our forms of Christian fellowship and order, our Christian morals, poetry and art, our attempts to give individual and social form to the Christian life, our Christian strategy and tactics in the interest of our Christian cause, in short our Christianity, to the extent that it is *our* Christianity . . . [70]

In receiving revelation, revelation should not be thought of as becoming 'Christian' or 'ours'. Barth continues in this section of the paragraph to speak out against religion, while still recognizing the inevitability of its continuing forms. This attempt at a religious reception of revelation involves a contradiction:

> we can and must perceive that for our part we and our contradiction against grace stand under the even more powerful contradiction of grace itself. We can and must – in faith. To believe means, in the knowledge of our own sin to rely upon the righteousness of God which makes an infinite satisfaction for our sin. Concretely, it means, in the knowledge of our own contradiction against grace to cleave to the grace of God which infinitely contradicts this contradiction.[71]

The revelation of God does not replace religion, but identifies religion as a contradiction to grace. However, grace is grace, and able thereby even to be the ultimate contradiction of that contradiction. Importantly, it is not as a religion of grace that Christianity is true: Barth points to versions of Buddhism which he terms 'Japanese Protestantism' to indicate that; only the name of Jesus Christ is Christianity's truth.[72] That Christianity is able to recognize this is an act of God's grace in the event of the outpouring of the Holy Spirit. This gracious work of the Spirit determines that there can be real subjective appropriation of revelation, despite the religious nature of Christian activity:

> there is a knowledge and worship of God and a corresponding human activity. We can only say of them that they are corrupt. They are an attempt born of

---

69   CD I/2, p. 327.
70   CD I/2, p. 327, emphasis original.
71   CD I/2, p. 338.
72   See the excursus, CD I/2, pp. 340–4.

lying and wrong and committed to futile means. And yet we have also to say of them that (in their corruption) they do reach their goal. In spite of the lying and wrong committed, in spite of the futility of the means applied, God is really known and worshipped, there is a genuine activity of man as reconciled to God.[73]

This is not because of the religion of these people (even though it is a religion of grace), but in contradiction to the wrongful engagement in religion in which they have partaken. Concretely, what this all means for Barth is this: 'through the name of Jesus Christ there are men who believe in this name.'[74] Here, we return effectively to Barth's starting point with the problem of religion: religion is contradicted by Jesus Christ but there are people who confess the name of Jesus Christ. In relation to this name, Barth is able to state that in the Christian religion there is a divine act of creation;[75] a divine act of election;[76] a divine act of justification and the forgiveness of sins;[77] and a divine act of sanctification.[78] Even in these affirmatory ways, however, Christianity *qua religion* is never affirmed – only its relation to the name of Jesus.[79] There are numerous examples of this rejection of Christianity *qua* human religion throughout this discussion, such as: 'For the sum total of the qualities of even the Christian religion is simply this, that it is idolatry and self-righteousness, unbelief, and therefore sin.'[80] Barth never moves beyond critiquing religion because revelation contradicts religion, even the religion which pays testimony to God's grace in revelation. Barth's paragraph in *Church Dogmatics* on religion offers throughout, therefore, a christological critique of religion with regard to the way in which revelation is known through the work of the Holy Spirit in relating objective revelation to humanity subjectively.

IN THE CONTEXT OF REVELATION: OVERCOMING SOME COMMON MISUNDERSTANDINGS

Thus far this chapter has discussed Barth's work on religion. There has been throughout, however, a passing engagement with the recurring and symbiotic theme of the doctrine of revelation which has made the discussion necessary.

---

73 CD I/2, p. 344.
74 CD I/2, p. 346.
75 CD I/2, pp. 346–8.
76 CD I/2, pp. 348–52.
77 CD I/2, pp. 352–7.
78 CD I/2, pp. 357–61.
79 Cf. Veitch, 'Revelation and Religion', 13–14.
80 CD I/2, p. 354.

Given the unbreakable bond that exists between revelation and religion as topics in Barth's work, and the fact that his work on religion was critiqued by Bonhoeffer who advocated that Barth replaced religion with a 'positivism of revelation',[81] it is necessary to turn to a brief discussion of revelation in order to set aside some misunderstandings of Barth's work.

Barth's theological method and starting point is dominantly christological. This could hardly be denied, and his christocentrism is a point noted even by those who know his work simply by reputation. Because of this, there is sometimes a lack of sensitivity with regard to presentations his work on revelation. His work on this topic does not only involve God's objective revelation to humanity (in the second mode of God's triune being), but also God's subjective revelation to humanity (in the third mode of God's triune being).[82] Given that Barth's §17 falls under a pneumatological section of his work, it is important – for all of the dominance of christology in Barth's discussion – to pay due attention to the work of the Spirit in revelation.[83] This may, indeed, prevent misunderstandings regarding Barth's doctrine of revelation.

The role of the Spirit in revelation is a theme which Barth discussed even in his early lectures and writings. In his *Göttingen Dogmatics*, Barth is already confronted with the problem of the possibility of confessing Christ as Lord in spite of the idolatry of religion. Barth's solution as to how this might be possible is articulated in terms of the work of the Holy Spirit:

> But if the claim of what is called religion to be a relationship with God is true, then the riddle confronts us once more – how can there be such a thing as religion? We agreed, however, to concede to the first Christians that they *did* believe in God and confess him with their Iēsous Kyrios. Let us allow these Christians themselves to tell us how they regarded this fact, the decisive fact in their lives. It really was for them an inexplicable fact. We are forcefully pointed to this by their answer: *oudeis dynatai eipein; Kyrios Iēsous, ei mē en pneumati hagiō* (1 Cor. 12.3). Note the *oudeis* and the *ei mē [!] en pneumati*

---

81   See the section on 'Positivism of Revelation' in Chapter 3 of this book.

82   The lack of engagement with Barth's doctrine of the Spirit is something I have discussed before: for further detail, see Tom Greggs, *Barth, Origen, and Universal Salvation: Restoring Particularity* (Oxford: OUP, 2009), esp. chapter 5. On Barth's pneumatology, see Philip J. Rosato, *The Spirit as Lord. The Pneumatology of Karl Barth* (Edinburgh: T&T Clark, 1981); James J. Buckley, 'A Field of Living Fire: Karl Barth on the Spirit and the Church', *Modern Theology* 10, no. 1 (1994); Eugene F. Rogers, Jr, 'Supplementing Barth on Jews and Gender: Identifying God by Analogy and Spirit', *Modern Theology* 14, no. 1 (1998); Eugene F. Rogers, Jr, 'The Eclipse of the Spirit in Karl Barth', in *Conversing with Barth*, ed. John C. McDowell and Mike Higton (Aldershot: Ashgate, 2004); and George Hunsinger, 'The Mediator of Communion: Karl Barth's Doctrine of the Holy Spirit', in *The Cambridge Companion to Karl Barth*, ed. John Webster (Cambridge: CUP, 2000).

83   See Trevor A. Hart, *Regarding Barth: Essays toward a Reading of His Theology* (Carlisle: Paternoster, 1999), pp. 7–11.

hagiō. A new element comes in here which is not identical with their faith and confession but is obviously an a priori of their faith and confession.[84]

The *sine qua non* of faith and confession is the event of God the Holy Spirit.

This point is developed in *Church Dogmatics* in which Barth spends considerable time discussing the work of the Holy Spirit in revelation. According to Barth, the Holy Spirit is God Himself, who can be present with the creature without in any way reducing His divinity. It is as Holy Spirit that God effects a relation with the creature,[85] and indeed grants the creature life. He is the freedom of God to be with the creature.[86] For Barth, it is as the Holy Spirit that God opens humans up to the possibility of revelation, determining that the revelation of God comes not only from above but also terminates within the human.[87] The Holy Spirit, therefore, guarantees what humans (in religion) cannot – a personal, human participation in revelation; true instruction and guidance; and the possibility of speaking of Christ in such a way as to witness to Him.[88] It is the Spirit of God who frees humans to be children of God and it is by the Spirit that sinful humans become capable of receiving the divine speaking.[89] Humans remain human in this relation, and God remains God. This issue determines that, unlike religion in which humans ultimately can only find confidence in themselves, '[t]o have the Holy Spirit is to let God rather than our having God be our confidence.'[90] The assurance of faith must come from without, not from within ourselves – only from God, as an event of His Spirit.[91]

This is a theme Barth expounds further in *Church Dogmatics* I/2, §16 (the paragraph which immediately precedes that on religion), in which he addresses 'The Freedom of Man for God'. In this paragraph, Barth asserts:

According to Holy Scripture God's revelation occurs in our enlightenment by the Holy Spirit of God to a knowledge of His Word. The outpouring of the Holy Spirit is God's revelation. In the reality of this event consists our freedom to be the children of God and to know and love and praise Him in His revelation.[92]

The crucial issue that Barth addresses here is that of the revealedness of God – that God's self-revelation does not take place in a vacuum. While from the side of

---

84   GD, p. 125.
85   On revelation as relation rather than a 'thing', see Hart, *Regarding Barth*, pp. 26–7.
86   CD I/1, p. 450.
87   CD I/1, p. 451.
88   CD I/1, pp. 453–4.
89   CD I/1, p. 456.
90   CD I/1, p. 462.
91   CD I/1, p. 466.
92   CD I/2, p. 203.

God, the reality of revelation is answered in the act of the revelation of the person of Jesus Christ, from the side of humanity, revealedness is achieved for us by the Holy Spirit, who is the foundation for the subjective reality of revelation.[93] It is this which Barth expounds in this paragraph. Significantly, for Barth, it is not God alone, but God and humanity together, who 'constitute the content of the Word of God attested in Scripture.'[94] The place in which this reality takes place and is identified is the church. However, it is crucial that, for Barth, God is not bound by the church, but the recipients of His revelation are.[95] Pneumatology takes priority over ecclesiology: the latter is a doctrinal subset of the former.[96] This is a theme that Barth addresses throughout his work, a point often missed by those who critique him. Even in his earliest dogmatic lectures, Barth can state:

> I hope I am ready at any time to be open to God's Word as in fact it may be spoken to me also in nature, history, art, and, who knows, even my own heart and conscience. All this is true (we have, of course, still to speak about it in principle). Nevertheless – we have to add, and again in the words of the Second Helvetic – we leave all that to God's omnipotence.[97]

The point is not that God is unable to reveal Himself outside of the normal patterns, but simply that the church is the normal place in which God's revelation will take place. Indeed, Barth is even able to state that God is able to reveal Himself in a dead dog.[98] However, the key issue is that subjective reality can never be an independent theme: all that is said about us can only be said because of our existence in Christ.[99] It is the Spirit who brings the words of Christ into hearing, freeing humans to be met by God: it is the event of the Spirit which is the subjective possibility of the revelation of Christ.[100]

It is also worthy of note that Barth does not simply offer a doctrine of revelation as a thing in itself.[101] His doctrine of revelation is the self-revelation of the

---

93   CD I/2, p. 204.
94   CD I/2, p. 207.
95   CD I/2, p. 211. Cf. Colin E. Gunton, 'The Triune God and the Freedom of the Creature', in *Karl Barth: Centenary Essays*, ed. S. W. Sykes (Cambridge: CUP, 1989), p. 65.
96   For the theological significance of this, see Chapter 6 of this book.
97   GD, p. 34.
98   CD I/1, p. 55.
99   CD I/2, p. 240.
100   CD I/2, pp. 242ff.
101   Quash cites the danger of a certain form of Barthianism which confuses theology (or the doctrine of revelation) with the revelation itself, something of which one can never accuse Barth: 'Where this position is vulnerable to critique . . . is in the fact that it is the *theology* that can sometimes be seen as doing the positing.' Ben Quash, 'Revelation', in *The Oxford Handbook of Systematic Theology*, ed. John Webster, Kathryn Tanner and Iain Torrance (Oxford: OUP, 2007), p. 334. As is seen in this chapter (and throughout this book), this cannot be levelled as a charge against Barth.

self-revealing God. Rather than a set of principles or dogmas being revealed, for Barth revelation is always the revelation of the Word of God who is Jesus Christ. This Word of God is known in three forms, which are not three different words but one Word in three ways[102] – the Word revealed, in scripture and preached.[103] But there is a clear asymmetrical relationship of dependence in this:

> The presupposition which makes proclamation proclamation and therewith makes the Church the Church is the Word of God. This attests itself in Holy Scripture in the word of the prophets and apostles to whom it was originally and once and for all spoken by God's revelation.[104]

The preached word has its dependence on scripture; and scripture has its dependence on Jesus Christ, to whom it pays testimony in anticipation (in the Old Testament) and in recollection (in the New Testament). It is the Word of God made flesh that is the basis of both of the other forms of the three-fold form. As Barth arrestingly puts it: 'Revelation in fact does not differ from the person of Jesus Christ nor from the reconciliation accomplished in Him. To say revelation is to say "The Word became flesh." '[105] The other two forms of revelation have their dependence entirely on this Word made flesh, this person of Jesus Christ – the same Jesus Christ whom Barth later describes as the *Aufhebung* of religion. In Barth's words, 'The Bible and proclamation both appeal to this fact [Jesus Christ] that has been given here and now. They cannot reproduce it as a given fact. They cannot bring it on the scene themselves. They can only attest and proclaim it.'[106] The hierarchy of order that exists in Barth's three-fold form of the Word of God should not be ignored, and neither should the effect of this on Barth's own dogmatic method.

The engagement in dogmatics is for Barth an exercise which must take place in humility. This is a point many of his opponents fail to recognize. Theology is a reflection on the proclaimed word, which is itself dependent on scripture, which is dependent on the Word made flesh of Jesus Christ. The proper attitude of theology which Barth advocates is thus one of faithfulness and prayer, both of which are necessary and essential for theological enquiry.[107] The recognition of the necessary humility with which doctrine should engage with revelation is seen in Barth's description of the task of dogmatics as a 'laborious movement from one partial

---

102 CD I/1, §4.4. On the three-fold form (and indeed its relation to Feuerbach), see Trevor Hart, 'The Word, the Words and the Witness: Proclamation as Divine and Human Reality in the Theology of Karl Barth', *Tyndale Bulletin* 46, no. 1 (1995). In relation to hermeneutics, see Werner G. Jearnold, 'Karl Barth's Hermeneutics', in *Reckoning with Barth: Essays in Commemoration of the Centenary of Karl Barth's Birth*, ed. Nigel Biggar (Oxford & London: Mowbray, 1988), pp. 86–9.

103 CD I/1, §4.1–3.

104 CD I/1, p. 88.

105 CD I/1, p. 119.

106 CD I/1, p. 120.

107 CD I/1, p. 23.

human insight to another'.[108] For Barth, the engagement in dogmatics is not an engagement in creating a system of Christian truth.[109] Instead, church proclamation is the raw material of dogmatics – and never vice versa.[110] One should never think, therefore, that dogmatics is some kind of secretive and salvific higher knowledge of God and the world; its focus is plainly the Sunday sermon.[111] Barth is clear, furthermore, of the relationship that exists between proclamation (as a third form of revelation) and dogmatics: dogmatics is required because, although proclamation is the command of God to the church, the human execution of that command is fallible.[112] Dogmatics thus serves church proclamation as *gnosis* or *intelligere* to the church's *pistis* or *credere*.[113] However, and this is key, dogmatics is neither a higher stage of faith or knowledge of faith than preaching, nor a higher or a better source of knowledge than preaching, nor an end in itself – unlike preaching.[114] Dogmatics as an exercise, therefore, is to be desired by the church to ensure that proclamation is an act engaged in responsibly, and it is the task of dogmatics to try to meet this desire. The task of dogmatics for Barth relates, therefore, to the investigation of how, at each given point, it is best to speak of God, revelation and faith, while all the time remembering that God is in heaven and dogmatics firmly belongs to the earth.[115] As a result, dogmatics can counsel but not give orders to the church.[116] Proclamation is essential; and dogmatics exists only because of it. Any suggestion that Barth engages in an exercise of presenting revelation in his work, or that his dogmatics is somehow 'revealed' (which certain critiques seem to suggest) is clearly disallowed by Barth right from the early stages of his theology. Were this distancing of theology from revelation not enough, Barth also raises repeatedly the theme of mystery as a means of theologically 'de-assuring' theology as discipline.[117]

Certainly, one cannot simply say that Barth replaces religion with his own dogmatic system, as if that system were itself revealed. For all that Barth is a theologian of revelation, dogmatics is obviously never revealed: theology does not take the place that religion might have once enjoyed, but is instead a humble discipline, which seeks to serve the Word of God in the proclamation of the church, which is dependent on the Word of God in scripture, which in turn is testimony to the Word of God made flesh (revelation). Theology is, therefore, perhaps best described as a fourth order (rather than a second order) discipline, which takes its subject as the proclamation of the church.

---

108   CD I/1, p. 14.
109   As Hauerwas puts it regarding Barth: 'Who and what Jesus is, is something which can only be told, not a system which can be considered and described.' Stanley Hauerwas, *With the Grain of the Universe: The Church's Witness and Natural Theology* (London: SCM, 2002), p. 180.
110   CD I/1, p. 79.
111   CD I/1, p. 81.
112   CD I/1, p. 82.
113   CD I/1, p. 83.
114   CD I/1, pp. 83–4.
115   CD I/1, p. 85.
116   CD I/1, p. 87.
117   CD I/1, pp. 154–5; see also Chapter 10 of this book on mystery.

What is meant by church proclamation is also something that Barth discussed. There is the danger in advocating that proclamation is the basis for theological reflection that the theological enterprise itself becomes overly narrowly focused on the proclamation of certain fields of preaching which are themselves defined in narrow confessional ways. Barth was, however, from earliest times deeply ecumenical in his approach to what counted as church proclamation. Even in his Göttingen days, in response to the issue of whether God spoke only through the preaching of his own Reformed tradition, Barth was clear that this was not the case:

> I accept the preaching of the Reformed church first, but also that of the Lutheran, United, and Methodist churches, and I expect to hear God's Word as well from the Irvingites, the Christian Catholics, and the Salvation Army. I am also glad to have heard God's Word in Roman Catholic preaching.[118]

Furthermore, while theology's normal engagement is with revelation in this third form of the Word of God as preaching, this does not determine for Barth that God is not free to speak in other ways. In Barth's words,

> I will open my ears wide to be convinced that God's Word might even come through voices that belong to no church, that are perhaps directed against every church, that have nothing to do with what we call religion, and yet that I have to listen to if I am not to be disobedient to the heavenly voice [cf. Acts 26.19].[119]

Thus Barth engages in what might be termed a 'centred' as opposed to a 'bounded' approach to preaching. He writes: 'In my view the important point is not whether we draw the circle of what we call Christian preaching more broadly or more narrowly. What counts is (a) that it really is a circle with a center, and (b) that we take seriously what takes place within this circle.'[120] Within these parameters, the freedom of God to reveal Himself knows almost no bounds. This is a theme which continues in the early volumes of *Church Dogmatics*, in which Barth is happy to affirm God's ability to speak in unexpected ways – through political philosophy, music, nature or even the grotesque.[121] The distinctive issue is not that God does not speak to individuals through these irregular means, but simply that these things (for the collective) cannot become the basis for the proclamation of the church:

> God may speak to us through a pagan or an atheist, and thus give us to understand that the boundary between the Church and the secular world can still take at any time a different course from that which we think we discern.

---

118 GD, p. 34.
119 GD, p. 34.
120 GD, p. 34. On centred and bounded groups in relation to theology, see Richard B. Hays, 'Postscript: Seeking a Centred, Generous Orthodoxy', in *New Perspectives for Evangelical Theology: Engaging with God, Scripture and the World*, ed. Tom Greggs (Abingdon: Routledge, 2010).
121 CD I/1, p. 55.

Yet this does not mean, unless we are prophets, that we ourselves have to proclaim the pagan or atheistic thing which we have heard.[122]

Barth does not doubt that God communicates Himself in these many different ways; his concern regards whether these things should become the authoritative or normative basis for congregational proclamation.[123]

CONCLUSION

The above discussion demonstrates that religion is a theological concept for Barth which is evident from his early writings onwards. His engagement with religion marks a Christianization of the nineteenth-century critique of religion, principally arising from Feuerbach. The theme around which the discussion of religion revolves is the right way in which to speak of human knowledge of God. In this, Barth seeks to set himself in contradistinction to Schleiermacher, for whom religion is a positive concept. For Barth, religion is an inevitability of human life, but is a phenomenon which is born of the human willingness to engage in idolatry.[124] Barth is concerned, in speaking about the manner in which humans know God, that it is *God* that they know. This knowledge of God, for Barth, from a Christian perspective, can only come through God Himself, in the person of the Holy Spirit, who ensures that the revelation of God that takes place outside of the human being finds a terminus inside of the human being. For Barth, therefore, revelation and religion are symbiotic theological motifs. However, one cannot simply confuse Barth's own theological enterprise with revelation itself, as if Barth believed his work in some ways to be determinative of the bounds and definitions of that revelation. For him, theology is a humble discipline, which engages in fourth order statements, in reflection upon revelation in church proclamation, which is derived from revelation in scripture, which is derived from the true Word of God, Jesus Christ. Having traced Barth's theological discussions of religion, it is necessary in the next chapter to turn to the use and appropriation of those ideas by one of Barth's students and theological interlocutors, Dietrich Bonhoeffer.

---

122   CD I/1, p. 55.

123   This is a theme that is very much related to Barth's discussion of the lights and the Light, and secular parables of the kingdom, discussed in Chapter 4 of this book.

124   For a discussion of Barth on idolatry, see David Clough, 'Karl Barth on Religious and Irreligious Idolatry', in *Idolatry: False Worship in the Bible, Early Judaism and Christianity*, ed. Stephen C. Barton (London: T&T Clark, 2007).

Chapter 3

BONHOEFFER'S RELIGIONLESS CHRISTIANITY

INTRODUCTION: THEOLOGIZING THE CRITIQUE OF RELIGION

Like Barth's engagement with religion, Bonhoeffer's 'religionless Christianity' and 'non-religious interpretation' belong to a line of thought begun in the nineteenth century with certain critics of religion, including Feuerbach, Freud, Nietzsche and Marx. Rather than defending Christianity against such critiques, Bonhoeffer seeks to think with them in order to engage in a truer articulation of theology proper. As with Barth, for Bonhoeffer the critiques levelled at Christianity help the self-articulation of Christian theology to correspond more genuinely to the subject it seeks to describe: while the critiques are enemies of religion, they are unexpected friends of theology. His most significant interlocutors are Nietzsche and Freud, in comparison to Barth for whom the dominant interlocutors were Feuerbach, Marx and (to a lesser degree) Freud.[1] However, Bonhoeffer's purpose and method is entirely congruous with Barth on this point: he seeks to think theologically around such themes.

This primarily theological purpose of religionless Christianity is what provides his concept with its worth in an age which is not simply marked by the unidirectional aggressive form of secularization that Bonhoeffer's sociological presentation

---

[1] On this, see Dumas (albeit, he overstates the distinction between Barth and Bonhoeffer): André Dumas, *Dietrich Bonhoeffer: Theologian of Reality*, trans. Robert McAffee Brown (London: SCM, 1971), p. 183, cf. p. 294. On Nietzsche and Bonhoeffer, see Peter Frick, 'Friedrich Nietzsche's Aphorisms and Dietrich Bonhoeffer's Theology', in *Bonhoeffer's Intellectual Formation*, ed. Peter Frick (Tübingen: Mohr Siebeck, 2008); Stephen Plant, *Bonhoeffer* (London: Continuum, 2004), pp. 49–52; and Bethge, *Dietrich Bonhoeffer*, pp. 84–5. On Bonhoeffer and Freud, see Green, *Bonhoeffer: A Theology of Sociality*, p. 17. On Bonhoeffer and Feuerbach, see Ralf K. Wüstenberg, *Bonhoeffer and Beyond: Promoting a Dialogue between Religion and Politics*, International Bonhoeffer Interpretations (Frankfurt am Main: Peter Lang, 2008), pp. 29–30; and Sabine Dramm, *Dietrich Bonhoeffer: An Introduction to His Thought*, trans. Thomas Rice (Peabody: Hendrickson, 2007), p. 217.

seems to offer.[2] Importantly, human autonomy and secularization are not, for Bonhoeffer, primarily sociological categories but theological ones for a world which has not simply come of age by itself, but which has come of age *by Jesus Christ*.[3] Nor can one think simply of religionless Christianity as in some ways a concept which allows for a translation of terms from religious to equivalent secular ones:[4] despite some suggestions that tend in this direction, there is no evidence of this remotely being present in Bonhoeffer, who continues to use terminology (in both German and Greek) such as church, baptism, sacrament and repentance. Bonhoeffer's work is far more profound than a simple translation into the language of 'modern man and woman'. Rather, Bonhoeffer transforms the critique of religion into the tantalizing suggestion that there is now a need to think in a religionless way[5] – not simply because this critique determines the need to do so, but, according to him, also because it accords with the very message of God in scripture. In this way, the critique of religion moves from being an indicative description of human sinfulness (as one sees in Barth) to becoming a subjunctive or an optative theological possibility of or desire for religionlessness.[6]

Many helpful historical summaries of Bonhoeffer's work on religionless Christianity exist. While these will be referenced throughout, it is not the purpose of this chapter simply to rehearse summaries already made with scholarly precision elsewhere, and their sensitive identification of the careful turns of phrase in the letters relating to religionlessness and the secular interpretation of scripture.[7] Instead, the overarching nature of this book is to engage formatively

---

2 For Bonhoeffer's sociological reading of a unified secularization thesis, see LPP, pp. 362–4, 425–8, 450, 475–81 and 499–504. On the problematic nature of a unified secularization thesis, see, for example, Martin, *The Religious and the Secular*; David Martin, *Reflections on Sociology and Theology* (Oxford: Clarendon Press, 1997); Berger, 'The Desecularization of the World: A Global Overview'; and Asad, *Formations of the Secular*. On Bonhoeffer's limited engagement with sociology, see Peter Selby, 'Christianity in a World Come of Age', in *The Cambridge Companion to Dietrich Bonhoeffer*, ed. John W. de Gruchy (Cambridge: CUP, 1999), pp. 237–8.

3 LPP, p. 451 (the translation of the SCM 1971 edition of LPP is preferred here: see p. 342). I have tackled this theme in more detail elsewhere, and the reader is directed there for a more nuanced justification of this point: Greggs, 'Religionless Christianity in a Complexly Religious and Secular World: Thinking through and Beyond Bonhoeffer'.

4 Heinrich Ott, *Reality and Faith: The Theological Legacy of Dietrich Bonhoeffer*, trans. Alex A. Morrison (London: Lutterworth Press, 1971), pp. 60–1; Dumas, *Dietrich Bonhoeffer: Theologian of Reality*, p. 183.

5 On the critique of religion and non-religious Christianity, see Pangritz, *Karl Barth in the Theology of Dietrich Bonhoeffer*, pp. 87–94.

6 On indicative, subjunctive and optative moods in theology, see David F. Ford, *Self and Salvation: Being Transformed* (Cambridge: CUP, 1999), pp. 257–62; and David F. Ford, *Christian Wisdom: Desiring God and Learning in Love* (Cambridge: CUP, 2007), pp. 45–51. The desire for a religionless Christianity is something Barth believed one could not hope for this side of the fall; see Boulton, *God against Religion*, p. xvii.

7 For an introduction to the issues surrounding Bonhoeffer's religionless Christianity, see Selby, 'Christianity in a World Come of Age'. A more fulsome and detailed account is provided in

and constructively with theological approaches to the critique of religion. Thus, this chapter seeks to see Bonhoeffer's work on religionless Christianity not as an historical puzzle to be solved, but as a theological resource for contemporary articulations of the faith. To resource theology in this way, there is a clear need to engage in historical reflection around those who first thought in this way: building from Bonhoeffer involves understanding what Bonhoeffer himself might have meant; exegesis will be important; and helpfully the scholarship in this field has made considerable progress in its historical work. However, the chapter does not proceed, as much of the work on religionless Christianity and secular interpretation has done, in offering a single, packaged definition of Bonhoeffer's terms. Instead, it sees Bonhoeffer's discussion of religionless Christianity as a *partially formed but programmatic* call to theology. His thinking, therefore, is not an end point to his theology, but a midpoint in his theology – a suggestion of the *trajectory* he is on. That religionlessness has been seen as an end point has arisen by virtue of the tragic circumstances of Bonhoeffer's untimely death. But the very genre of this theology (the letter and outline of the book), and the interrogative mood of much of his writing determines that these are ideas *in via* rather than being mature and final assertions. In the first section of this chapter, it is argued that standing as ideas in the midpoint of a theological trajectory, religionlessness arises *from* somewhere, and can be seen more in continuity with Bonhoeffer's earlier works than is sometimes supposed: it marks in some ways an analytical reflection on the mood and nature of his theology up to this point, identifying the key contribution that his thinking has made and seeking to think about how this can be pursued programmatically (or perhaps subjunctively or optatively). Bonhoeffer has clearly journeyed to a point, and is thinking at this stage about where to take his theology further; however, he is not on a different path or journey to the one he has thus far taken.

Thinking in terms of trajectories also helps in considering the relationship of Bonhoeffer's thought to that of Barth.[8] It is this which forms the substantive engagement of the second section of this chapter. The chapter argues that the charge of 'positivism of revelation' should be unpacked in relation to Schleiermacher and Bultmann; places Bonhoeffer entirely on the same road on which Barth is also treading; and suggests indeed that they may also stand closer than Bonhoeffer imagines. Bonhoeffer's religionless Christianity does not mark a fork in the road in which he might walk with Barth or leave that direction altogether, but is a continuing along the same path on which Barth has set him. Thus, these theologians should be engaged together, and not separated off into different theological discussions.

Ralf K. Wüstenberg, *A Theology of Life: Dietrich Bonhoeffer's Religionless Christianity*, trans. Doug Stott (Grand Rapids: Wm. B. Eerdmanns Publishing Co., 1998).

8   Bonhoeffer himself understood the issue of trajectories, identifying a line for 'all genuine Christian thinking from Paul, Augustine, Luther, to Kierkegaard and Barth' (BBNY, p. 460).

The final substantive section of this chapter seeks to identify some directive instructions to aid in the journey along the path of theologizing with the critique of religion. These are not complete, fully expounded articulations of what Bonhoeffer definitively meant (such a task is considered as futile for the telegrammatic nature of Bonhoeffer's writing on these themes), but are suggestions of where Bonhoeffer might wish to lead us. In that way, they seek to follow the trajectory that Bonhoeffer is on, rather than seeing religionless Christianity as simply an end point in his thought.

CONTINUITY WITH THE EARLIER BONHOEFFER

For as radical and prophetic as Bonhoeffer's reflections on 'religionless Christianity' are, and for all that his thought could not help but be influenced by his setting and by the events taking place around him, there is nevertheless a significant level of continuity between these later thoughts and concerns that Bonhoeffer had from his earliest days as a theologian. Even a brief examination of the corpus preceding the prison letters demonstrates this.[9] To understand what is meant by 'religionless Christianity', it is therefore necessary to reflect on Bonhoeffer's related concerns and considerations of religion from earlier works which highlight these themes. It is hoped that this work will help to unpack and exegete Bonhoeffer's later dense and telegrammatic turn of phrase.[10]

Sanctorum Communio

Themes relating to religion are more than evident in Bonhoeffer's first doctoral thesis, *Sanctorum Communio*. Given that the topic of the book is relationship between the church and the world, it is hardly surprising that these themes arise. Clearly, one cannot see the mature reflections of Bonhoeffer on religion as present within the book, and there is a relatively clear separation between church and world in Bonhoeffer's thinking at this time. Indeed, there are several instances in the thesis in which religion is discussed positively.[11] Although clearly particularist in stance, such passages as the following demonstrate that for Bonhoeffer, in his earliest writing, religion is not simply a negative category:

> The general concept of religion has no intrinsic social implications. The idea of
> the holy in its general sense as a religious category is actualized not in social

---

9   I have attended here primarily to Bonhoeffer's major writings. Because of the ultimate constructive purposes of this book, space does not allow as thorough an exploration of these themes as found in more dominantly historical reflections. For more detailed studies, see Wüstenberg, *A Theology of Life*; and Pangritz, *Karl Barth in the Theology of Dietrich Bonhoeffer*.

10   Although at certain points my own analysis disagrees with it, the most useful and scholarly exposition of the reason why it is not necessary to choose between a 'systematic' and an 'historical' reading of Bonhoeffer on religion is without doubt articulated in Wüstenberg, *A Theology of Life*, pp. 90–7.

11   Even Schleiermacher on religion is discussed relatively positively in SC, p. 64.

interaction, but in the solitude of the soul with God. The mystic, too, is religious.
If it is nevertheless a fact that religion is for the most part social in character,
primarily due to psychological causes that are more or less accidental (the need
to communicate, as in Schleiermacher, the receptive-active human nature, as in
Seeberg). These causes demonstrate the possibility, but not the necessity, of religious community. This directs us back from the general concept of religion to the
concrete form of religion, which for us means the concept of the church.[12]

While different categorizations or interpretations of what is meant by religion are
critiqued, Bonhoeffer is happy to speak of the church as a 'concrete form of
religion'.[13] Bonhoeffer's discussions of Schleiermacher, Scheler, Scholz et al.
determine that reflection on what is meant by religion must form some part of the
theological sociology in which he is engaging.

However, for Bonhoeffer even at this stage, there is already a reflection (unsys-
tematized albeit) on the separation of the church, Christ or the Christian faith from
religion. One sees this clearly in such assertions as:

Now the relationship of Christ to the church can be stated by saying that in
essence Jesus Christ was no more the founder of the Christian religious community than the founder of a religion. The credit for both of these belongs to
the earliest church, i.e., to the apostles. This is why the question whether Jesus
founded a church is so ambiguous. He brought, established, and proclaimed
the reality of the new humanity. The circle of disciples around him was not the
church; its history prefigured the inner dialectic of the church. It was not a
new religion recruiting followers – this is the picture of a later time. Rather,
God established the reality of the church, of humanity pardoned in Jesus
Christ – not religion, but revelation, *not religious community, but church.* This
is what the reality of Jesus Christ means.[14]

However, Bonhoeffer seems unwilling to follow through this line of thinking to its
logical end point, and in the next sentence retreats into a more acceptable and cautious orthodoxy: 'And yet there is a necessary connection between revelation and
religion as well as between religious community and the church.'[15] This is not to
say, however, that the connections that Bonhoeffer posits are always positive, and
at moments we are able to glance at the mature man sitting and writing in his cell:

There are basically *two ways to misunderstand the church, one historicizing
and the other religious; the former confuses the church with the religious*

---

12   SC, p. 133.
13   Indeed, in preparation for publication, he deleted a section of the original thesis following this
discussion which was more critical of Schleiermacher.
14   SC, pp. 152–3.
15   SC, p. 153.

community, the latter with the Realm of God. . . . The second misunderstanding does not take seriously the fact that human beings are bound by history; this means that historicity either is objectified and deified, as in Catholicism, or simply is regarded as accidental, as subject to the law of death and sin.[16]

The capacity to separate the church from a religious community determines that there can be no simple equation of the church and the religious community.

The lack of this simple equation arises, furthermore, from an unwillingness even in this most ecclesial of Bonhoeffer's works to separate the church and the world into binary categories. Clifford Green's words are appropriate:

> In *Sanctorum Communio* Bonhoeffer is not yet asking about the relation of Christ to 'secular' people who may be outside the church institution. But he does explicitly say that it would be wrong to regard the empirical church and the world as ultimate antagonists; the line of encounter and decision is found *within* the church itself . . . [17]

Indeed, the words of Green are borne out very clearly by Bonhoeffer himself: 'it would not be correct to define the empirical church and the world as ultimate opposites.'[18]

Act and Being

Themes relating to religion are also discussed in Bonhoeffer's second doctoral thesis, *Act and Being*.[19] In this thesis, one sees a definitive (but not uncritical) Barthian turn in Bonhoeffer's thought:[20] 'faith is something essentially different

---

16   SC, pp. 125–6. One can also see here the beginnings of parallels to Bonhoeffer's later concerns over radicalism and compromise: Ethics, pp. 153–7.

17   Green, *Bonhoeffer: A Theology of Sociality*, p. 61.

18   SC, pp. 282–3.

19   Indeed, although this is not discussed in Wüstenberg's work on A&B, there is even discussion of Dilthey (in an albeit limited manner). See A&B, pp. 29 & 127–8; cf. Wüstenberg, *A Theology of Life*, pp. 41–6.

20   Pangritz articulates the appropriate way in which to speak of Bonhoeffer's engagement with Barth in A&B: 'The acuity of critique of Barth . . . should not deceive one into ranking Bonhoeffer with the colleagues at the Berlin faculty in their opposition to Barth. The converse is more likely: precisely because he feels close to him . . . Bonhoeffer endeavors to work out as clearly as possible the differences which nevertheless exist between them.' Pangritz, *Karl Barth in the Theology of Dietrich Bonhoeffer*, p. 29.

from religion.'[21] Bonhoeffer also realizes some of the issues associated with theological reflection on the religious a priori:

The difficulty lies in the concept of the religious a priori, in spite of the latitude Seeberg accords it. If we are to assume that the compelling ability to receive revelation and, by implication, to believe, is given with this a priori, we have already said too much. The natural human being has a *cor corvum in se*. Natural religion, too, remains flesh and seeks after flesh. If revelation is to come to human beings, they need to be changed entirely. Faith itself must be created in them. In this matter, there is no ability to hear before the hearing. . . . Having been wrought by God, faith runs counter to natural religiosity, for which the religious a priori noted by Seeberg certainly holds good. According to Luther, revelation and faith are bound to the concrete, preached word, and the word is the mediator of contact between God and human beings, allowing no other 'immediateness'. But then the concept of the religious a priori can be understood only to imply that certain mental or spiritual forms are presupposed for the formal understanding of the word, in which case a specifically religious a priori makes no more sense. All that pertains to personal appropriation of the fact of Christ is not a priori, but God's contingent action on human beings.[22]

Thus, for Bonhoeffer, the question is not so much whether human beings possess a religious a priori (as seems to be a later concern),[23] but what this religious a priori means for theology – a natural religion which is itself born of sin, only overcome by the act of God on humanity.

However, Bonhoeffer raises the issue of continuity in this work. He diagnoses problems with Barth's theology with regard to this:

it remains unclear (even in Barth) how the religious act of human beings and God's action in faith are to be thought, without dividing them into two – by nature different – spheres, or without suspending either the subjectivity of God or the fact that human beings were encountered in their existence. People can inspire religious acts of every kind, but God alone can give faith as utter readiness to hear; only God indeed can hear. The act of faith upon which we reflect cannot be distinguished from the religious act, whereas faith, being effected by God, is only in the act and never something one just comes across. But from that it follows that the I of faith, which is to be God's as well as

---

21 A&B, p. 93; this is a position that Bonhoeffer suggests Barth exemplifies entirely.
22 A&B, p. 58.
23 Cf. LPP, p. 363.

mine, also can never be something one just comes across but is something that
acts only in each act of faith.[24]

For Bonhoeffer, the concern of *Act and Being* is that of divine and human continuities – how the acts of humans and the act of God relate.[25] In this, Bonhoeffer is
determined that the whole of a person is recognized. In relation to the act of faith
brought about by God, Bonhoeffer asks: 'Is the new I to be thought of in unity with
the empirical total-I, or does it remain its "heavenly double"? This is where Barth's
concept of act becomes an issue.'[26] For Bonhoeffer, it is not simply the case that
there is a need to speculate on the relationship between divine and human acts, but
it is also necessary to discuss the way in which human particularity and identity can
be preserved. One can see here the beginnings of Bonhoeffer's later need to emphasize the Bible's concern with the *whole* human person, the *anthropos teleios*.[27]

   Act and Being also contains significant other areas of thought which might be
seen as setting Bonhoeffer on his track to his mature speculations. One can detect
elements of his admiration for Rudolf Bultmann, especially in relation to
Bultmann's capacity, in Bonhoeffer's mind, to be able to deal with the whole of a
person.[28] Bonhoeffer also criticizes sharply the tendency to make God into a mere
'religious object', enabling humans to become their own 'creator and bearer of a
world'.[29] Barth's reproach of Schleiermacher's method is praised by Bonhoeffer,
and there is the beginning of his reflections on the 'spatializing' of God: 'There is
no God who "is there" [*Einen Gott, den "es gibt", gibt es nicht*]; God "is" in the
relation of persons, and the being is God's being person [*das Sein ist sein
Peronsein*].'[30] Indeed, perhaps in keeping with the latter quotation, Bonhoeffer
posits an ontology without metaphysics,[31] a point which Bruce McCormack sees
as being not only central to the meaning of 'religionless Christianity' but also to
the continuity between Barth and Bonhoeffer's thought.[32]

Creation and Fall

Several themes and turns of phrase that appear in Bonhoeffer's 1932 lectures on
creation and sin are reminiscent of later ideas formed in Tegel prison. To a degree,

---

24   A&B, p. 93.
25   Cf. Marsh, *Reclaiming Dietrich Bonhoeffer*, p. vii.
26   A&B, p. 99.
27   LPP, p. 456.
28   A&B, p. 100.
29   A&B, p. 138.
30   A&B, p. 115.
31   Cf. Dumas, *Dietrich Bonhoeffer: Theologian of Reality*, pp. 112–17; and Bethge, *Dietrich Bonhoeffer*, pp. 776–7.
32   Bruce L. McCormack, *Orthodox and Modern: Studies in the Theology of Karl Barth* (Grand
Rapids: Baker Academic, 2008), p. 133.

the very activity of engaging at an early stage in one's career in considering the doctrine of creation to some extent moves beyond concerns with what might be commonly thought of as religion: the doctrine of creation is an attending to the *saeculum*, to this world. Bonhoeffer's focus in these lectures on the Hebrew Bible (in all of its earthiness) is also significant for his later suggestions that the Old Testament should be read in light of the New.[33] Furthermore, in his reading of the early chapters of Genesis, Bonhoeffer at one point asserts: 'Even Darwin and Feuerbach could not use stronger language than is used here. Humankind is derived from a piece of earth.'[34] Bonhoeffer's reading of these creation narratives is not, therefore, a movement to the borders of secular thought in order to posit of a god of the gaps,[35] and he emphasizes the earthiness (the this worldliness) of the human being.[36] In this work, it is also possible to see several notable turns of phrase and concepts which are developed later. For example, Bonhoeffer considers the place of God at the boundary and centre of human lives. He writes: '*God is at once the boundary and the center of our existence.*'[37] Bonhoeffer also considers what it means no longer to be able to live before God, and yet needing to do so.[38] While the concepts that underlie these phrases certainly develop, the early seeds of later ideas, and the questions which provoke Bonhoeffer's thought, are beginning to be present.

With regard to religionless Christianity, significantly in these early lectures Bonhoeffer considers the temptation of the serpent to be a temptation to replace simple obedience with 'the pious question': the fall is, therefore, a fall into piety, redolent of idolatrous and metaphysical approaches to God:

> [T]he serpent purports somehow to know about the depths of true God beyond this given word of God – about the true God who is so badly misrepresented in this human world. The serpent claims to know more about God than the human being who depends on God's word alone. The serpent knows of a more exalted God, a nobler God, who has no need to make such a prohibition. . . . Only as the pious serpent is it evil.[39]

In seeking to know more about God in this way, humans, according to Bonhoeffer, try to master God, and leave the path of obedience,[40] engaging instead (negatively) in 'the first religious, theological conversation'.[41] Bonhoeffer makes it

---

33 See the introduction to C&F by de Gruchy (p. 10); cf. LPP, pp. 213–14, 394 and 447–8.
34 C&F, p. 76.
35 Cf. LPP, pp. 405–7, 475–80 and 450.
36 C&F, p. 77.
37 C&F, p. 86; cf., for example, LPP, pp. 366–7 and 405–7.
38 C&F, p. 90.
39 C&F, p. 106.
40 C&F, p. 108.
41 C&F, p. 111; cf. Rom(II), p. 247, in which Barth makes a similar point regarding religion.

clear in his discussion of the fall that the choice for humanity was between God and a false god [*Götze*], with the false god portraying itself as true.[42] His later concern about false presentations of God brought about by religion are, therefore, present in some form at this very early stage of his theology. The attempt to be as God (*sicut deus*) is for Bonhoeffer at the heart of the drive to be pious: 'In what does humankind's sicut deus consist? It consists in its own attempt to be for God, to have access to a new way of "being-for-God", that is, in a special way of being pious.'[43] Although religion is not a primary concern, the related concept of piety clearly is for Bonhoeffer at this stage in his theological thinking.

Christology

If concerns about piety in his 1932 lectures precede Bonhoeffer's questions about religion in his prison writings, Bonhoeffer's 1933 lectures might be thought of as preceding questions about who Jesus Christ is for us today. In these lectures, Bonhoeffer is emphatic in his presentation of the *promeity* of Jesus Christ, which is key to his later considerations.[44] He writes:

> The being of Christ's person is essentially relatedness to me. His being-Christ is his being-for-me. This *pro-me* is not to be understood as an effect that issues from Christ or as a form that he assumes incidentally, but is to be understood as the being of his very person. The very core of his person is *pro-me*. This is not a historical, factual, or ontic statement, but rather an ontological one . . . [45]

Furthermore, there are implications of this for the Christian, since Christ is formed as community, for Bonhoeffer, by virtue of His being *pro me*.[46] Not only does Bonhoeffer display, therefore, an emphasis on the dominant question throughout the lectures of who Christ is (in contrast to how we might espouse this), but in so doing and in emphasizing the *promeity* of Christ's person, he also demonstrates his scepticism regarding the capacity of metaphysics to espouse the doctrine of the person of Christ.[47]

---

42   C&F, p. 114.
43   C&F, p. 116.
44   For example, LPP, pp. 362–4 and 501. For an excellent recent discussion of *promeity*, see Philip Ziegler, 'Promeity in the Christologies of Bonhoeffer and Kierkegaard', paper presented at the American Academy of Religion (Atlanta, 2010).
45   Christology, p. 314.
46   Christology, p. 323.
47   Cf. parallels with Barth in I/2, §15.1.

Moreover, Bonhoeffer continues his discussion of christology not only by talking in terms of the centrality of Christ,[48] but also by considering this in light of piety in relation to our religious personality:

> The center of our existence is (not) the center of our personality. This is not a psychological statement, but rather an ontological(–)theological one, because it refers not to our personality but rather to the persons we are before God. Christ is not the center that we can see is here but rather the center according to our faith.[49]

The idea of Christ as the centre of our lives, not in terms of what is seen (piety) or in terms of human personalities but in terms of the theological and ontological reality of Christ, is clearly anticipatory of Bonhoeffer's later concerns. Similar anticipations to later works can also be found in Bonhoeffer's discussion of the power of Christ being found in His weakness: 'If we speak of the human being Jesus Christ as we speak of God, we should not speak of him as representing an idea of God, that is, in his attributes as all-knowing and all-powerful, but rather speak of his weakness and manger.'[50] Furthermore, while much of this sounds very Barthian, one does see in Bonhoeffer's lectures on christology a willingness on the part of Bonhoeffer to question certain dogmatic assumptions, which had been accepted by Barth, including the doctrine of the virgin birth.[51]

Discipleship

It may seem strange to see lines of continuity between Bonhoeffer's later work on religionlessness, and his most devotional work, *Discipleship*. Indeed, in his *Letters and Papers from Prison*, Bonhoeffer even questions his earlier theological commitments himself: 'I thought I myself could learn to have faith by trying to live something like a saintly life. I suppose I wrote *Discipleship* at the end of this path. Today I clearly see the dangers of that book'.[52] However, Bonhoeffer continues the last (oft-quoted) sentence as follows: 'though I still stand by it.'[53] Indeed, a letter which contains reflection on the unutterability of the name of God,

---

48 Christology, pp. 324–7.
49 Christology, p. 324; cf. the 1966 translation: 'The fact that Christ is the centre of our existence does not mean that he is the centre of our personality, our thought and our feeling . . . he is our centre even when Christian piety is forced to the periphery of our being' (Dietrich Bonheoffer, *Christology* (London: Collins, 1966), p. 62).
50 Christology, p. 354; cf. LPP, pp. 479–80.
51 Christology, pp. 354–5 (and discussion of various other ambiguities regarding the biblical testimony, pp. 356–60); cf. LPP, p. 373.
52 LPP, p. 486.
53 LPP, p. 486.

upon the religious evolution of the Old Testament, and upon the importance of the penultimate things also contains a reflection pointing back to ideas hinted at in *Discipleship*.[54] Any assertion that *Discipleship* and *Letters and Papers from Prison* stand in diametric opposition to each other fails to reflect with sufficient subtlety on lines of continuity in thinking which, as one could hardly otherwise expect, do exist. Certainly, there are shifts in Bonhoeffer's thinking, and much that follows in *Letters and Papers* stems from struggling with his earlier ideas (see the section 'A Positive Wealth of Positivisms' in this chapter below), but one must also pay close attention to the dialectic of continuity and discontinuity present between his reflections on Christian discipleship and those on religionless Christianity. Indeed, both discussions concern how best to live in light of Jesus Christ in the present, and both abound in reflection on how best to live with an anxiety about religion – in *Discipleship*'s terms how best to live as a Christian in the world, outwith the religious walls of the monastery.

One clear place for continuity can be seen in Bonhoeffer's emphasis on the person of Jesus, rather than any system, being the key to his theological reflection: not even grace is the key, and this religious principle cannot be the basis for the life of faith; instead, Christ as the human for others is the key, in His reality and His personhood. As Bonhoeffer puts it, 'because Jesus is the Christ, it has to be made clear from the beginning that his word is not a doctrine. Instead, it creates existence anew.'[55] Similarly, Bonhoeffer asserts: 'we are called to follow Christ by the entire word of scripture, simply because we do not intend to wish to violate scripture by legalistically applying a principle to it, even that of a doctrine of faith.'[56] The later questions about how to understand scripture, and the question of who Jesus Christ really is for us today can be seen as extensions of these earlier concerns. Indeed, there are clear resonances with later thought in his question: 'What could the call to follow Jesus mean today for the worker, the businessman, the farmer, or the soldier?'[57]

The theme of the immediacy of Jesus Christ is also one which may help to interpret Bonhoeffer's later religionless turn. His reflection on Luke 9.57–62 suggests that the purpose of this teaching is to demonstrate that nothing, not even the law (can one see the beginnings of a line here to religion?) can stand between Jesus Christ and the one He calls.

The suffering of Jesus and the co-suffering of the Christian is an important note of continuity between *Discipleship* and the later *Letters and Papers from Prison*.[58] Bonhoeffer reflects on 'Christ-suffering' not simply as a singular and particular moment in the history of the life of Jesus of Nazareth, but also as a co-suffering with Christ for the Christian. This includes (in a way that comes to echo later work

---

54 LPP, p. 213.
55 Discipleship, p. 62.
56 Discipleship, p. 82.
57 Discipleship, p. 39.
58 Discipleship, pp. 87–8.

in *Ethics*)[59] a Christian bearing the burdens of others: 'As Christ bears our burdens, so we are to bear the burden of our sisters and brothers.'[60] Certainly, there are differences in Bonhoeffer's speaking of 'the power of Christ's suffering' and 'God's powerlessness and suffering',[61] but there is also a clear line of trajectory that can be drawn here between Bonhoeffer's earlier and later thought.[62]

There are also reflections on God and the space in which God is present within *Discipleship*. To some degree (albeit at this stage in very eschatological terms), there is a benefit to the shrinking space that the Christian church occupies in the world: 'when [Christians] have been deprived of their last inch of space here on earth, the end will be near.'[63] Theological reflection on the process of secularization, and a theologizing about that process, is evident in this book. Bonhoeffer's later and famous reflections on the shrinking space for religion in the world have prophetic forerunners in this work. The shift in his thought appears to be in terms of how Bonhoeffer feels Christians need to deal with this shrinking space. In *Discipleship*, Christians have 'no other choices but to escape from the world or to go to prison.'[64] In prison, it seems, Bonhoeffer seeks to set out a third choice. However, even this third choice of 'religionless Christianity' is hinted at in this earlier work of Bonhoeffer. The coming of Christ in human flesh brings genuine help to humanity: 'Neither a new religion nor a better religion would suffice to accomplish this goal.'[65] There is a clear distinction here of Jesus from the category of religion: what Jesus achieves, therefore, is to some degree non-religious. One can also see a parallel to this idea in Bonhoeffer's discussion of Paul on slavery, in which Bonhoeffer advocates that the work of Christ does not provide another 'religious anchor' in the world for the slave.[66]

Life Together

Bonhoeffer's other more popular level book, *Life Together*, provides further helpful clues with regard to what Bonhoeffer later means in speaking of religionless

---

59 Cf. Ethics, pp. 134–45. Cf. also here Bonhoeffer's poem, 'Christians and Heathens', LPP, pp. 460–1.

60 Discipleship, p. 88.

61 E.g., Discipleship, p. 88, cf. LPP, pp. 479–80.

62 There is much to be made of Green's assertion that '[i]n place of the power of Christ who requires ego suppression in *Discipleship*, . . . we have the weak Christ, "the one for others."' However, we cannot fail also to see that Bonhoeffer's prison thinking does arise *from* somewhere, and not simply the reading of Dilthey that Green suggests. Green appears to wish to stress discontinuity on this point, but there are also lines of continuity. See Green, *Bonhoeffer: A Theology of Sociality*, pp. 16–17; cf. p. 282.

63 Discipleship, p. 247.

64 Discipleship, p. 247.

65 Discipleship, p. 283.

66 Discipleship, p. 238.

Christianity. This is perhaps best traced to Bonhoeffer's discussion of the Christian community as '*not an ideal, but a divine reality; . . . a spiritual [pneumatishe] and not a psychic [psychiche] reality.*'[67] Bonhoeffer is wrestling here with the reality of the church, and (crucially) offers a theological reflection on this reality.[68] His fierce criticism of idealizing the image of the community arises from a deep sense of the church being an empirical community in which Christians are called to participate: 'Christian community is not an ideal we have to realize, but rather a reality created by God in Christ in which we may participate.'[69] This community is not, however, one which is marked by religious perfection or striving; rather, it is the community called by Christ, and not 'the community of pious [*frommen*] souls.'[70] This community of Christ, moreover, is one marked by 'service to one another [which] is simple and humble',[71] and in which there is a central role and essential need for the 'weak and insignificant', without whom there would be the exclusion of Christ.[72] In this short book, one can in some ways see the bridging of his thought in *Discipleship* and his thoughts in *Letters and Papers from Prison*. André Dumas neatly summarizes this development: '*The Cost of Discipleship* called for the creation of a church of disciples. It demanded saints. In describing the church as it is experienced by the disciples, *Life Together* put human beings back into it.'[73]

Ethics

It is hardly surprising that there are continuities between Bonhoeffer's *Letters and Papers from Prison*, and the (in part contemporaneous) writings contained in *Ethics*. However, once again, several themes in the latter prove helpful to unpacking the dense and exciting theological leads found in the prison letters.

Almost instantly within Bonhoeffer's considerations on 'Christ, Reality, and Good', there is a discussion which is deeply resonant with Bonhoeffer's letters on religionlessness. Bonhoeffer writes: 'If God is merely a religious concept, there is no reason why there should not be, behind this apparent "ultimate" reality, a still more ultimate reality: the twilight or the death of the gods.'[74] Certainly Bonhoeffer's *Ethics* is written against the backdrop of his perception of the secularization of Western Europe, a point which is made emphatically in his chapter 'Heritage and Decay'.[75] He sees this secularization as reaching its apex in contemporary

---

67 LT, p. 35, italics original.
68 For more on this theme, see Dumas, *Dietrich Bonhoeffer: Theologian of Reality*, pp. 131–8.
69 LT, p. 38.
70 LT, p. 39.
71 LT, p. 40.
72 LT, pp. 45–6.
73 Dumas, *Dietrich Bonhoeffer: Theologian of Reality*, p. 132.
74 Ethics, p. 48.
75 Ethics, pp. 103–33.

'*Western godlessness*', itself 'a religion of enmity toward God'.[76] Bonhoeffer's concern in this context is how the church is to witness to Jesus Christ 'in a world that has turned away from Christ after knowing him.'[77] However, in this bearing witness, Bonhoeffer is firm that:

> [t]he church's concern is not religion, but the form of Christ and its taking form among a band of people. If we let ourselves stray even the least bit from this perspective, we fall unavoidably into those programs of ethical or religious world formation from which we departed above.[78]

For Bonhoeffer in *Ethics*, there is a need to think about the whole of reality, understood christologically, as a reality in which it is impossible to live outwith the world. This impossibility arises because the reality of the world is grounded in the reality of Christ 'in which the reality of God and the reality of the world are united.'[79] For the Christian it is impossible to give up on the world as there is no Christ without the world, or to give up on Christ as there is no world without Christ: there is only one reality, 'that is God's reality revealed in Christ in the reality of the world.'[80] In Bonhoeffer's discussion of this theme, there are very clear echoes of the letters from his jail cell. This is not only in terms of the worldliness of the Christian, but also in terms of the movement away from spatial and boundary language with regard to God. Rather than 'battling over the borderline', all of reality is 'held together in Christ'.[81] There is no secular space in contrast to religious space, with one encroaching onto the other's territory, but only the Christ-reality.[82] This has radical implications for theological thought: 'Things work out quite differently when the reality of God and the reality of the world are recognized in Christ. In that way, the world, the natural, the profane, and reason are seen as included in God from the beginning.'[83] Clues to unpacking the meaning of Bonhoeffer's religionlessness and non-religious interpretations no doubt reside in such more sustained discussions of related themes.

Summary

In considering Bonhoeffer's earlier works in relation to his work on religionlessness and non-religious interpretation, one is able to see that the lines of thinking

---

76 Ethics, p. 122.
77 Ethics, p. 132.
78 Ethics, p. 97.
79 Ethics, p. 58.
80 Ethics, p. 58.
81 Ethics, p. 58.
82 Bonhoeffer here comes very close to the kind of theology of which Barth was accused – christomonism, a charge Barth refutes in his discussion of Berkouwer's work *The Triumph of Grace* in CD IV/3, pp. 173–81.
83 Ethics, p. 59.

which led to his more mature thoughts are present in his earlier work. The letters to some degree mark a way of summarizing and distilling concerns that Bonhoeffer had throughout his career as a theologian. One might be wise, therefore, while not downplaying significant shifts in Bonhoeffer's thinking, to see his letters as headline interpretations and analyses of concerns that he expressed throughout his earlier works – ways of summarizing and identifying his original contribution to theology, and the linked concern in all of his life's work. Another way of putting this is that the *Letters and Papers from Prison* mark dense reflections on what the kernel of Bonhoeffer's previous concerns for the church, the world and the Christian (and the interaction of the three) in his contemporary setting had been, and the discussions act, therefore, as an analytical springboard of previous thought from which to jump into further theological construction. This distilling is of that which had already marked his work as distinctive, and which might be thought of as the uniting conceptualization of his previous theological questions and investigations.[84]

POSITIVISM OF REVELATION

Related to the issue of continuity in Bonhoeffer's work is Bonhoeffer's intellectual relationship to the theology of Karl Barth.[85] Following Bonhoeffer's seeming condemnation of Barth's theology under the epithet of 'positivism of revelation' and the occasional none too kind words of Barth about Bonhoeffer,[86] there has been a wealth of mistrust and broken dialogue between certain members of the Barth and the Bonhoeffer 'camps'. In this section of the chapter, I will argue that there is far more continuity than has often been suggested between Barth and Bonhoeffer on the issue of theologizing the critique of religion. First, however, it is necessary to attend to what Bonhoeffer actually says, and to the way in which he unpacks a charge, which is often thrown at Barth's theology with little sense of

---

84   This seems true for a theologian who recognized that 'Christian life can become more worldly only when it is more spiritual, and more spiritual only when it is more worldly.' Carl Friedrich von Weizäcker, 'Gedanken Eines Nichttheologen Zur Theologischen Entwicklung Dietrich Bonhoeffer', in *Der Garten Des Menschlichen: Beiträge Zur Geschichlichen Anthropologie* (Munich: C. Hanser, 1977), p. 347. Translation can be found in Dramm, *Dietrich Bonhoeffer: An Introduction to His Thought*, p. 89.
85   See also Chapter 4 of this book in its discussion of the nature of Barth's theology as a moving target, and Chapter 2 on revelation and religion in Barth. For an introduction to what is meant more generally by 'positivist' approaches to revelation (in contrast to 'reductionist' approaches), see Quash, 'Revelation', pp. 332–40 (cf. 328–32).
86   For example, in Barth's letter to Superintendent Herrenbrück of 21 December 1952, in R. Gregor Smith, ed. *World Come of Age: A Symposium on Dietrich Bonhoeffer* (London: Collins, 1967), p. 70; Barth's letter to Bethge in FGG, p. 121; and in Barth's comments (albeit which notably do not name Bonhoeffer) in CD IV/3, p. 735.

its true meaning. As Clifford Green helpfully reminds us, 'Bonhoeffer's unguarded remark about Barth in a private letter should not be used to drive a wedge between these two theologians.'[87]

'Positivism of revelation' appears in three letters of Bonhoeffer. The first time it is used (30 April 1944),[88] the charge is directed at Barth with regard to the way in which he has failed to unpack 'religionless Christianity'. Bonhoeffer in this letter clearly affirms that Barth 'is the only one to have started along this line of thought' – a point which reflects more continuity than discontinuity with Bonhoeffer's own enterprise. Indeed, in this letter Bonhoeffer considers the need to unpack religionless Christianity by asking questions of Barth in terms of what his critique of religion means in reality for churches, sermons, liturgy, working people, doctrines and so forth. Bonhoeffer points to his own distinction between the ultimate and the penultimate as having 'new significance' here.[89] The second occurrence of the term (5 May 1944)[90] is focused more on substantive doctrinal questions, criticizing Barth's doctrine of revelation for its 'like it or lump it' nature on such themes as the virgin birth and the trinity: for Bonhoeffer the concern seems to be that there is no engagement by Barth in degrees of doctrinal significance, with all loci deserving equal affirmation. Here, Bonhoeffer advocates that the church stands for Barth in place where religion once dwelt, and the world is left to its own devices.[91] The third occurrence of the term 'positivism of revelation' (8 June 1944) is again directed at the lack of 'concrete guidance' for the 'non-religious interpretation of theological concepts'. This discussion is not in substantive disagreement with Barth, but concerns the process of unpacking the meaning of his critique of religion, or allowing that critique to be the dominant guiding point that Bonhoeffer believes it should be, since it marks Barth's greatest service to theology.[92]

Clearly, the content of the critique is not as harsh as it is sometimes presented as being. Furthermore, it may well be that 'positivism of revelation', far from distancing Bonhoeffer from the trajectory on which Barth was headed, places Bonhoeffer firmly on that trajectory also.[93] It is this which it is now necessary to explore.

---

87 Clifford Green, 'Trinity and Christology in Bonhoeffer and Barth', *Union Seminary Quarterly Review* 60, no. 1 (2006), 22.

88 LPP, p. 364.

89 LPP, p. 365.

90 LPP, p. 373.

91 Clearly, one must remember that the latter point must be understood in light of Barth's early theology only; Bonhoeffer did not have access to the four volume doctrine of creation found in CD III.

92 LPP, p. 429.

93 In Chapter 4, there will be a discussion of the way in which this is further demonstrated in Barth's more mature work, including the two volumes of the Doctrine of God, which – while Bonhoeffer had read them – do not mark major interlocutors for Bonhoeffer.

A positive wealth of positivisms

There is the scope for a monograph which attended singularly to the vast array of interpretations scholars have offered with regard to the way in which one should understand Bonhoeffer's three word (one in German) charge. Indeed, there is almost as much (if not more) reflection on this than the meaning of religionlessness and non-religious interpretation.[94] For some theologians, the charge is aimed more at Barthians and the Confessing Church than Barth himself.[95] Others see it as arising from a degree of misunderstanding on the part of Bonhoeffer of Barth's purpose.[96] For others, it revolves around a shift towards existential thinking on Bonhoeffer's part, compared to Barth's overarching systematic principle of christology which swallows up all else.[97] Still others consider the meaning to relate to the distinctive christological method of Bonhoeffer compared to the trinitarian method of Barth.[98] Some have suggested the ultimately positive role of religion in Barth in terms of leading humans to grace,[99] or the philosophical distinction between a theologian who is influenced primarily by Feuerbach, Freud and Marx (Barth), compared to one

---

94   Space cannot allow a thorough engagement into the details of these definitions of 'positivism of revelation', therefore, but certain aspects of them will be attended to in the footnotes. By far, the two most scholarly and useful engagements in English on the historical relationship between Barth and Bonhoeffer are Pangritz, *Karl Barth in the Theology of Dietrich Bonhoeffer*; and Wüstenberg, *A Theology of Life*. The reader should look to these for guidance on detailed issues.

95   See Pangritz, *Karl Barth in the Theology of Dietrich Bonhoeffer*, p. 77; cf. Green, 'Trinity and Christology in Bonhoeffer and Barth', 22. This seems to accord with Bonhoeffer's reaction to the Confessing Church's view of the theology of Rudolf Bultmann: see David Fergusson, *Rudolf Bultmann*, Outstanding Christian Thinkers (London: Continuum, 2000), p. 113. However, the charge of 'positivism' is still focused on Barth as well in this letter; for the Confessing Church is the charge of positivism as well as the related but distinct charge of 'conservative restoration' (LPP, p. 429).

96   Hence Friedrich-Wilhelm Marquardt, *Theologie Und Sozialismus. Das Beispiel Karl Barths*, 3rd enlarged edn (Munich: Chr. Kaiser Verlag, 1985); Gerhard Krause, 'Dietrich Bonhoeffer and Rudolf Bultmann', in *The Future of Our Religious Past: Essays in Honour of Rudolf Bultmann*, ed. James M. Robinson (London: SCM, 1971); and Hauerwas, *With the Grain of the Universe*, p. 190, according to which Bonhoeffer 'mistakenly assumes that Barth is trying to answer a question that he thought should not be asked.' While Pangritz gives an excellent defence of Bonhoeffer's understanding of Barth on this point (Pangritz, *Karl Barth in the Theology of Dietrich Bonhoeffer*, pp. 117–19), there may be a slight element of overstatement in his argument: certainly Bonhoeffer did have CD II/2 in sheet form, but he did not have access to all of Barth's preceding works in his prison cell, and even the greatest of memories cannot hold all of the detail of a thinker such as Barth. Certainly, there is an element of 'impressionism' about Bonhoeffer's charge, innate indeed to the manner in which it is made – in a letter.

97   Ott, *Reality and Faith: The Theological Legacy of Dietrich Bonhoeffer*, pp. 123–30.

98   Green, 'Trinity and Christology in Bonhoeffer and Barth', 3–5. This makes a number of significant assumptions about Barth's theology, and is deeply complex to judge in light of recent debates regarding the immanent trinity in Barth's theology. On Barth on the immanent trinity, see the ongoing debates between (principally) Bruce McCormack, and George Hunsinger and Paul Molnar; see Chapter 4, fn. 13 of this book.

99   Dumas, *Dietrich Bonhoeffer: Theologian of Reality*, pp. 178–84; cf. Green, *Bonhoeffer: A Theology of Sociality*, pp. 258, who makes a similar point. This rests on a misreading of Barth's §17.

influenced primarily by Nietzsche (Bonhoeffer).[100] Others point to the influence of the philosopher, Wilhelm Dilthey, on Bonhoeffer during the period of his prison writings.[101] For some, the issue is the dominant influence of Luther on Bonhoeffer compared to Calvin on Barth, particularly over the issue of the *extra Calvinisticum*.[102] Still others see the issue as resting in the positive meaning of 'religion' for the two theologians, with Bonhoeffer adopting an 'operational or behavioural' concept of religion in comparison to a 'morphological or institutional' one.[103] For others, it is Barth's 'all or nothing' approach that should be emphasized, especially around the issue of the virgin birth, as being at the heart of 'positivism of revelation'.[104] For others, the matter is Barth's inability to relate revelation to the world,[105] or his strong distinction of the church from the world.[106] At stake in some interpretations is Bonhoeffer's unpreparedness to create a theory of religion (and his critique of Barth's doing so), and the related issue of religion being a harmatological concept

Cf. Chapter 2 of this book: religion fulfils no more positive a role than sin does; and Barth does not replace religion with grace; rather, *Jesus Christ* (the person) is the *Aufhebung* of religion.

100 Dumas, *Dietrich Bonhoeffer: Theologian of Reality*, p. 183. There is worth in this point, but it should not be over-emphasized. Bonhoeffer, too, is influenced by Freud, as much of the literature on this topic demonstrates, just as Barth is also aware of the work of Nietszche. On the philosophical influences on Bonhoeffer, see further Peter Frick, ed. *Bonhoeffer's Intellectual Formation* (Tübingen: Mohr Siebeck, 2008).

101 Wüstenberg, *A Theology of Life*; Wüstenberg, *Bonhoeffer and Beyond*, pp. 41–55; cf. Green, *Bonhoeffer: A Theology of Sociality*, p. 16. Dilthey does exercise an influence on Bonhoeffer at this point, but Bonhoeffer has already engaged with him in A&B, and therefore any suggestion of a radical, new and dramatic discontinuity with Barth cannot be accounted for on this basis.

102 Discussed and rebutted by Pangritz, *Karl Barth in the Theology of Dietrich Bonhoeffer*, p. 60. This is, indeed, hardly a fair reading of Barth who is in some ways almost as strongly influenced by Luther as he is by Calvin.

103 Green, *Bonhoeffer: A Theology of Sociality*, p. 262; cf. pp. 258–68. However, this can hardly be used – as undoubtedly Green would not want it to be – as a wedge between Barth and Bonhoeffer. Indeed, Green's five point summary of the critique of religion on pp. 266–8 could equally well be applied to Barth as to Bonhoeffer, if one follows the interpretation of Barth offered in Chapter 2 of this book.

104 Pangritz, *Karl Barth in the Theology of Dietrich Bonhoeffer*, pp. 82–7 and 99–114. Cf. Geffrey B. Kelly, 'Bonhoeffer and Barth: A Study of the Interaction with Karl Barth in Bonhoeffer's Theology of Revelation' (Dissertation presented at the Université de Louvain, 1970). A focus on this single issue seems to overestimate its importance somewhat, as it is only mentioned once in the LPP.

105 Regin Prenter, 'Dietrich Bonhoeffer Und Karl Barths Offenbarungpositivismus', in *Mündige Welt*, ed. E. Bethge (Munich: Chr. Kaiser Verlag, 1960), III, p. 13. This fundamentally misunderstands Barth (see Chapter 2 of this book). The issues Prenter addresses are ones I have addressed before in terms of human, historical, worldly particularity. See Greggs, *Barth, Origen, and Universal Salvation*, especially the discussion of the Holy Spirit in Barth in chapter 5. Also of note is the response to Prenter of Robert T. Osborn, 'Positivism and Promise in the Theology of Karl Barth', *Interpretation* 25, no. 3 (1971), 289–90.

106 Brendan Leahy, '"Christ Existing as Community": Dietrich Bonhoeffer's Notion of Church', *Irish Theological Quarterly* 73, no. 1 (2008), 53.

for Barth compared to an historical concept for Bonhoeffer.[107] Still others analyse the distinction between Bonhoeffer and Barth in terms of different emphases in their theological approach – on the secondary objectivity of God in the former, and the primary objectivity of God in the latter.[108]

The problem with all of these approaches is that there is a need to define which Barth one is relating to which Bonhoeffer. No doubt that danger is also present in this work (and it is hoped that the preceding and following chapters help in some way to situate this clearly). However, it is certainly the case that the relationship between Bonhoeffer and Barth is far more *dynamic* than much of the secondary literature on the topic would suggest. Bonhoeffer may yet not have felt the revolutionary nature of Barth's doctrine of election, and we do well to remember that Barth had yet to embark fully on his four-volume doctrines of creation and of reconciliation. Certainly, the Barth that Bonhoeffer is aiming at is a moving target, and the concerns that underlie the charge of 'positivism of revelation' may not only be impressionistic at points. Aspects of the charge may, indeed, already be in the process of being answered not only by Barth's economic pneumatology which gives appropriate attention to the subjective appropriation of revelation, but also in Barth's doctrine of God in *Church Dogmatics* volume II.[109] Crucially, one should recognize, however, that Bonhoeffer's work on religionlessness and the positivism of revelation marks a thinking *with* rather than a reacting against Barth, who himself is continuing to think through these matters. As Robert Osborn reminds us, the key thing is that 'Bonhoeffer himself said that Barth had "*not yet*" thought through to a solution'.[110] Barth's own reaction (and clear hurt) at Bonhoeffer's comment certainly did not do much to alleviate the sense that there was some genuine level of difference between them. Undoubtedly, Barth does not think that it is ever possible to escape from religion (as Bonhoeffer at least seems to), and in this much he never truly moves beyond his claim in *The Epistle to the Romans*: 'As men living in the world, and being what we are, we cannot hope to escape the possibility of religion.'[111] But this issue cannot simply be used to place

---

107 Wüstenberg, *A Theology of Life*, pp. 64–5; cf. Wüstenberg, *Bonhoeffer and Beyond*, pp. 49–50.
108 See Marsh, *Reclaiming Dietrich Bonhoeffer*, albeit with the proviso noted by George Hunsinger, 'Review of Charles Marsh, *Reclaiming Dietrich Bonhoeffer: The Promise of His Theology*', *Modern Theology* 12, no. 1 (1996), and supported by Green, 'Trinity and Christology in Bonhoeffer and Barth', 13–14. It should be noted, however, that the idea that Christ's humanity 'adds' anything to God (Marsh, p. 14) is never directly found in Bonhoeffer, and that the emphasis Marsh places on CD II/1 would find greater support for continuity between Bonhoeffer and Barth were Marsh to discuss II/2 in as much detail: in II/2, the *promeity* of God is seen at its theological heights (see Chapter 4 of this book).
109 Marsh, *Reclaiming Dietrich Bonhoeffer*, chapter 1 is helpful on these matters, if limited by not addressing CD II/2 in detail.
110 Osborn, 'Positivism and Promise in the Theology of Karl Barth', 286.
111 Rom(II), p. 230.

these theologians into distinctive (even opposed) theological camps. Charles Marsh is correct in stating that Barth is 'the very condition of the possibility of Bonhoeffer's theological pilgrimage';[112] and we are wise to minimize rather than to maximize the differences between the two theological giants. Focusing on the distinctive moods of their theologies helps here. Bonhoeffer expresses his desire for a religionless version of Christianity as a hope (in the optative mood); Barth's discussion of religion is a description of the current life of the Christian and the church (in the indicative).

Indeed, to some degree, it may be worth seeing Bonhoeffer's articulated struggles with Barth as struggles with himself. The charge that Bonhoeffer offers Barth (of the church now standing in the place where religion once stood) is a charge that could equally well be cited of his own theology up to that point.[113] Within the reflections on the *homo religiousus*, Bonhoeffer turns the critique into a self-examination with regard to *Discipleship*.[114] To some degree, his own self-struggle with his earlier church-orientated theology is expressed as a struggle with Barth,[115] his major theological interlocutor. There is, indeed, a greater shift (even given what has been noted above) in many ways from *Discipleship* to religionless Christianity than there is from Barth's critique of religion to religionlessness. That Bonhoeffer articulates this self-struggle through discussion of Barth's work does not place distance between them, but already demonstrates that Bonhoeffer is seeking the assistance of his theological mentor in helping him to express his own constructive ideas: critically thinking from someone else's thoughts is, after all, the general practice of academic discourse. This does not serve to place Bonhoeffer outside the sphere of Barth's influence, but all the more firmly inside it. One can see this point borne out in terms of Bonhoeffer's relationship to two different theological voices, and it is to these we now turn.

What's wrong with Bultmann?

There is a tendency to see Bonhoeffer's articulation of non-religious approaches to the Bible and of religionless Christianity as shift from a more firmly Barthian perspective to a perspective that is more sympathetic to Bultmann.[116] However, this move may not be the correct one to identify. Bonhoeffer's theological home was Berlin, and his thinking therefore was a thinking *from* liberalism *to* Barth: Barth was the means for Bonhoeffer's own sense of what was wrong with the

---

112   Marsh, *Reclaiming Dietrich Bonhoeffer*, p. ix.
113   LPP, p. 373.
114   LPP, p. 486.
115   This is a point made by Gollwitzer in *Begegnung mit Dietrich Bonhoeffer. Ein Almanach*, ed. W.-D. Zimmermann (Munich: Kaiser, 1965), p. 112.
116   See, for example, Krause, 'Dietrich Bonhoeffer and Rudolf Bultmann'.

liberal enterprise. One might do well, therefore, to think of Bonhoeffer's engagement with Bultmann and Barth on these themes not as a utilizing of Bultmann to
identify what is wrong with Barth, but as a recourse back to Barth to note what is
wrong with Bultmann. The issue of Bonhoeffer's starting point may be of interest
here, as starting with Bultmann and ending with Barth (as is the form in the letters) certainly leads to the sense of Bonhoeffer ending in the Barth camp more
fully than were the opposite the case. This has greater implications, furthermore,
than simply his relation to Bultmann, as Bultmann also engages directly with
Dilthey in his 'New Testament and Mythology'.[117]

Even in Bonhoeffer's early letter of 5 December 1943, which begins his reflections on some of these themes, there are interesting points to note here. The concerns that underlie his reflections on the Old Testament in many ways parallel the
concerns that are expressed by Bultmann with regard to the New Testament.[118] By
the time that one gets to 30 April 1944, and the first charge against Barth, the
language is even more akin to that of Bultmann. Bonhoeffer's concerns about
religionless people today in light of nineteen hundred years of history feel redolent of Bultmann's statement that 'it is impossible to reinstate a past world
picture'.[119] Similarly, Bonhoeffer's assertions that people cannot be religious any
longer and that there is a dishonesty about being religious find a close parallel to
Bultmann's statement: 'we would affirm for our faith or religion a world picture
that our life otherwise denied.'[120] Crucially, however, it is *from* these questions
that Bonhoeffer arrives at Barth:[121] while not arriving entirely satisfied with where
Barth got to by that point, it is clear that there is a continued and sustained trajectory *not away from Barth but towards Barth*. One sees exactly the same point in
the letter of 5 May 1944, with Bonhoeffer moving from the questions that
Bultmann asks to the answers that Barth gives: it is on Barth's trajectory Bonhoeffer wishes to travel, and it is from Barth's answers that Bonhoeffer wishes to think
in response to the liberal theological context in which the questions are posed.[122]
When Bonhoeffer offers a similar analysis of intellectual history to Bultmann,[123]
one again sees the same trajectory in the letter of 8 June 1944. Here, on first reading it might seem that Bultmann is given the crowning glory at the end of the
successive responses to the issues Bonhoeffer has raised: Bultmann is used,
indeed, by Bonhoeffer in response to Barth's failings. But what is the point on
which Bonhoeffer ends? Bonhoeffer sets up a situation in which to respond to

117   Rudolf Bultmann, *New Testament and Mythology and Other Basic Writings*, ed. Schubert M.
Ogden, trans. Schubert M. Ogden (London: SCM, 1985), p. 23.
118   Cf. ibid., p. 3.
119   Ibid., p. 3.
120   Ibid., p. 4; cf. LPP, pp. 362–4.
121   LPP, p. 363.
122   LPP, pp. 372–3.
123   LPP, pp. 425–8, cf. Bultmann, *New Testament and Mythology and Other Basic Writings*, pp. 2–7.

liberal theology (with Bultmann as a prime example of this), and his final interlocutor, who is seen as correct in seeking to overcome theological liberalism with
his critique of religion, is Barth (even if Bonhoeffer does not think that he goes far
enough).[124] The path on which Bonhoeffer was treading was certainly not the path
of Bultmann, but a path away from Bultmann and from liberal theology. Bonhoeffer understood himself to be walking with Barth. This, indeed, is the path on
which Bonhoeffer had walked from his earliest theological days in response to the
liberal dominance of the Berlin faculty.[125]

'Positivism of revelation' set against the background of Schleiermacher

One possible way of understanding Bonhoeffer's charge against Barth is to see it in
relation to the theological father of liberalism, Friedrich Schleiermacher.[126] It may
well be that Bonhoeffer believed that Barth was ultimately influenced (if negatively) by liberal theology, and that Barth was still allowing his work to be defined
by the confines of liberal thought. Considering this point might help to unpack
what Bonhoeffer meant by positivism of revelation, and to demonstrate that Bonhoeffer is seeking to be even more Barthian than Barth, rather than engaging in a
different agenda.

   Bonhoeffer had clearly engaged with Schleiermacher's work from the early
stages of his theological formation. While still at school, Bonhoeffer read
Speeches,[127] and worked through them a second time in the summer of 1923.[128]
Discussion of Schleiermacher is found in both *Sanctorum Communio* and *Act and
Being*.[129] Indeed, in the second thesis, Bonhoeffer affirms the 'theological right
with which Barth reproached Schleiermacher for his "grand confusion" of religion and grace'.[130] Bonhoeffer, as Bethge recalls, had soon thought of Schleiermacher's work as an 'obscuration of the Reformation'.[131] However, it may well be in
Schleiermacher's work that the clue to Bonhoeffer's concerns with Barth lie.

---

124   LPP, pp. 428–31.
125   Cf. Dumas, *Dietrich Bonhoeffer: Theologian of Reality*, pp. 103–4. On Bonhoeffer's critique of
Bultmann's demythologizing, see ibid., p. 188; and Pangritz, *Karl Barth in the Theology of Dietrich
Bonhoeffer*, pp. 78–82.
126   On the relationship between Schleiermacher and Bonhoeffer, see Christiane Tietz, 'Friedrich
Schleiermacher and Dietrich Bonhoeffer', in *Bonhoeffer's Intellectual Formation: Theology and Philosophy in His Thought*, ed. Peter Frick (Tübingen: Mohr Siebeck, 2008).
127   Bethge, *Dietrich Bonhoeffer*, p. 27.
128   Ibid., p. 35.
129   For example, SC, pp. 64, 133 and 159; A&B, p. 154.
130   A&B, p. 154.
131   Bethge, *Dietrich Bonhoeffer*, p. 49.

For Schleiermacher, 'religion in general' or religiosity is not the primary interest.[132] His concern is not 'natural religion', but individual instantiations of religion, and he spends a good deal of time discussing the various confusions of words related to religion.[133] He is concerned, indeed, that the terms are employed in a confused manner,[134] and is himself quite specific about their meaning. By 'positive' is signified: 'the individual content of all the moments of the religious life within one religious communion, in so far as this content depends on the original fact from which the communion itself, as a coherent historical phenomenon, originated.'[135] Revelation, on the other hand, is defined by Schleiermacher as that which 'signifies the *originality* of the fact which lies at the foundation of the religious communion'.[136] This original element, for Schleiermacher, has a divine causality. Thus, the relationship of religion as a general category to positive individual instantiations of religion is brought about by the divine causality of revelation: revelation brings about the individual and distinctive historical category of *positive* religion. Barth, in his lectures on Schleiermacher, discusses the relation of these concepts to each other helpfully and clearly:

> Natural religion . . . is that which can be abstracted equally from the teachings of all pious societies of the top stage as the common element in all of them, even if in different determinations. What is differently determined, the individual element, is the positive element in a religion. . . . A revelation denotes the fact that underlies a religion and conditions the individual content of its pious emotions but cannot itself be explained in terms of an earlier historical relationship.[137]

Given Bonhoeffer's time in Berlin, it is hardly thinkable that his reflections on religion and on Barth on religion would not have Schleiermacher in the background. Furthermore, Bonhoeffer became interested in Barth's thought in 1924 through his cousin, Hans-Christoph von Hase,[138] a student in Göttingen, just months after Barth's lectures on Schleiermacher, which must no doubt have been freshly of interest in the minds of the students present in Göttingen. If this might have been a dim and distant point 20 years in the past for the middle-aged Bonhoeffer in the cell, Bonhoeffer's engagement with Dilthey surely places Schleiermacher back at the centre of Bonhoeffer's concerns. As Wüstenberg puts

---

132   Schleiermacher, *The Christian Faith*, p. 30.
133   In the postscript to §6, and the postscript to §10.
134   Schleiermacher, *The Christian Faith*, p. 47.
135   Ibid., p. 49.
136   Ibid., p. 50; italics original.
137   ToS, p. 233.
138   Bethge, *Dietrich Bonhoeffer*, p. 51.

it: 'Given their substantive, proximity, one can mention Schleiermacher's and Dilthey's concepts of religion under a common denominator.'[139]

What, then, does this mean for Bonhoeffer's charge against Barth of 'positivism of revelation'? Firstly, it relates to the accusation of the 'take it or leave it' nature of revelation which, according to Bonhoeffer, exists in Barth's work. Positivism points to the givenness of the individual instantiation of Christianity, its unique stand-aloneness which separates it not only from other religions but also from the world.[140] Secondly, and more fiercely, it seems that Bonhoeffer's term suggests a logical flaw in Barth's doctrine of revelation which separates it off from all other potential engagements external to itself, creating a self-enclosed circle, self-sufficient in its entirety.[141] The argument of this would go thus: the positive aspect of a religion is its individuality and distinctiveness from all else. The cause of this (according to Schleiermacher) is revelation. Barth seems to agree with Schleiermacher in his presentation to some degree, since revelation contradicts religion. But, for Barth, the very thing which is distinctive is not only *caused by* revelation, but *is* revelation. In other words, according to Bonhoeffer's critique of 'positivism of revelation', Barth says something akin to 'revelation makes Christianity a positive (unique) religion, and what is revealed is that Christianity is a religion which arises in some way out of revelation: the positivism of the Christianity, which is caused by revelation, is, thereby, revelation.' Thus, revelation, rather than being the means of establishing the distinctiveness of Christianity becomes the beginning and the end. However, this presentation fails to do full justice to §17 of *Church Dogmatics*. As has been seen in Chapter 2, it is not a concept of revelation or even grace which is the *Aufhebung* of religion, but Jesus Christ Himself. The trueness of Christian religion does not rest in revelation or grace, but its religion is contradicted in the same way in which sin is contradicted, not simply by the revelation of revelation, but by the revelation of God in the person of Jesus Christ. To a degree, therefore, the charge rests on an insensitive reading of Barth, but nevertheless that reading does not stop Bonhoeffer from sensing that Barth is on the path that he, too, should walk along: it means only that Bonhoeffer does not realize how closely and how much in step he and Barth are walking, and, given the ongoing and dynamic nature of both of their works (see above), this can hardly be a charge of mis-representation. Bonhoeffer builds upon Barth's indicative description of human religion and optatively hopes for a Christianity which can become religionless: for Bonhoeffer, there is the hope that religion need not be the 'given'

---

139   Wüstenberg, *A Theology of Life*, p. 186n; cf. pp. 73–6.

140   Cf. LPP, p. 373.

141   Cf. Richard H. Roberts, 'Spirit, Structure and Truth', *Modern Theology* 3, no. 1 (1986). Roberts claims that Barth massively subordinates the Spirit to the central encounter with the Word of God, simply completing the circle of revelation. The explanation of economic pneumatology in relation to Barth's doctrine of revelation in the present book hopefully suggests that there are problems with such presentations of Barth; see Chapters 2 and 4.

(positive) for theology.[142] He charges Barth with the task of moving *further away* from Schleiermacher's categories – otherwise put, with the task of becoming more intensely Barth. The critique is not a critique against Barth's constructive work, but a critique of the continued Schleiermacherian categories which Barth still works with as a background: Bonhoeffer does not want less Barth; he wants more.

THEOLOGICAL MOTIFS
FOR RELIGIONLESS CHRISTIANITY

Having cleared some historical ground, it is now necessary to turn to the concrete, constructive theological meaning of Bonhoeffer's non-religious interpretation and religionless Christianity. Since the purpose of this book is ultimately a formative theology shaped by the work on Barth and Bonhoeffer on religion, these comments will not focus on distinctive historical issues present in each individual letter or paralleled phrase,[143] but will instead seek to identify motifs that might be taken forward into the more programmatic chapters of this book which will follow.[144] This is already venturing from historical reflection into systematic theology, but it will be done with close attention to Bonhoeffer's prison writings.[145] This section answers the question: what are the salient theological points that Bonhoeffer's religionlessness offers? It does so only as motifs which will be returned to, with recourse to both Barth and Bonhoeffer, throughout the more constructive sections of this book. However, identifying these salient points may

---

142   It is because of this that it is so difficult to locate Bonhoeffer's model of understanding religion: '[Bonhoeffer] never really develops a theory of religion, nor is there a fixed place in him that one can point to and think they possess the interpretative key to Bonhoeffer's concept of religion. Some people find themselves agitated by Bonhoeffer's perspective' (Jeffrey Pugh, *Religionless Christianity: Dietrich Bonhoeffer in Troubled Times* (London: T&T Clark, 2008), p. 73). Pugh goes on to question himself whether Christianity could be separated from religion.

143   For example, the distinction between non-religious interpretation and religionless Christianity is not explored in detail.

144   Indeed, this form of engagement itself recognizes something of the amorphous and pluralistic nature of Bonhoeffer's understanding of the term 'religion'. As Schwöbel asserts: 'the term summarizes a contingent cluster of features which characterize the response of theology and the church to the situation of a world come of age. . . . This way of speaking of "religion" criticizes a phenomenon within Christian theology and the church'. Christoph Schwöbel, ' "Religion" and "Religionlessness" in *Letters and Papers from Prison*: A Perspective for Religious Pluralism?', in *Mysteries in the Theology of Dietrich Bonhoeffer: A Copenhagen Bonhoeffer Symposium*, ed. Kirsten Busch Nielsen, Ulrik Nissen and Christiane Tietz (Göttingen: Vandenhoeck & Ruprecht, 2007), p. 165; Schwöbel goes on to list these features and motifs as he sees them (pp. 165–75). Cf. Wüstenberg, *A Theology of Life*, p. 159.

145   A useful parallel to this move (with a more focused attention to individual terms) can be found in Bethge, *Dietrich Bonhoeffer*, pp. 274–92, and the reader is directed there for more detailed, but still theological, historical exegesis.

also help us to see how closely Barth and Bonhoeffer are working: the desire for religionlessness and the critique of religion may well be two sides of the same coin, with the same theological worth and value in terms of its content.

Anti-idolatry

Innately connected to Bonhoeffer's religionless concerns are those regarding the unutterability of the name of God. Although these discussions come before the turn to religionlessness, they nevertheless mark discussions on the path towards religionlessness, with Bonhoeffer assuring Bethge that he will not emerge from his confinement as a 'homo religiosus', and stating that his 'suspicion and fear of "religiosity" have become greater than ever' while in prison.[146] This context makes Bonhoeffer understand a point which he says has always made him think – '[t]he fact that the Israelites *never* say the name of God aloud'.[147] This is a theme to which Bonhoeffer returns little more than a week later: 'Only when one knows that the name of God may not be uttered may one sometimes speak the name of Jesus Christ.'[148] These thoughts seem deeply resonant with the later work on religionlessness, as Bonhoeffer continues: 'Only when one loves life and the earth so much that with it everything seems to be lost and at its end may one believe in the resurrection of the dead and the new world.'[149] Indeed, he then even goes on to discuss the evolution of religion in the same paragraph.

The unutterability of God's name is – to some degree – connected to the movement away from religion. That God's name cannot be uttered determines that God cannot be captured fully within the confines of human religious speech: God is no object of human conceptual or religious imaginings, but truly the Lord and the creator who is holy and beyond all comprehension.[150] In the words of Nicholas Lash: 'All human beings have their hearts set somewhere, hold something sacred, worship at some shrine. We are all spontaneously idolatrous.'[151] For Bonhoeffer, the refusal of the Israelites to utter God's name is a protection against religion which confuses God with the belief system or concept it imagines – confuses God with so-called 'god' or with its own theoretical idol.[152]

The issue of idolatry is related to that of the spatiality of God for Bonhoeffer. For him, '[e]pistemological transcendence has nothing to do with God's

---

146   LPP, p. 189.
147   LPP, p. 189.
148   LPP, p. 213.
149   LPP, p. 213.
150   Cf. concerns Bonhoeffer had at a much earlier stage of his career: A&B, p. 138.
151   Nicholas Lash, *The Beginning and End of 'Religon'* (Cambridge: CUP, 1996), p. 21.
152   On Bonhoeffer's use of the word 'God', see Dumas, *Dietrich Bonhoeffer: Theologian of Reality*, p. 193. Clearly, I am distancing myself here slightly from Green's suggestion that Bonhoeffer is not concerned with themes such as idolatry: see Green, *Bonhoeffer: A Theology of Sociality*, p. 259.

transcendence.'[153] The religious conceptualization of God is clearly not God Himself. However, there is a radicality to this theological move by Bonhoeffer, since
he does not allow God's beyondness and unutterability simply to be 'the beyond
of our cognitive faculties', which one may have recourse to with certain as yet
unsolved problems: that beyondness is the path to the superfluous *deus ex machina*.
God's transcendence is, instead, for Bonhoeffer a transcendence in which 'God is
the beyond in the midst of our lives.'[154] There is no assigning of space to God, even
a conceptual space which is beyond: this is only an intellectual version of the
building of an idol. Instead, there is the need to think of this matter christologically: in Christ, there cannot be static spatial boundaries between God and the
world, even in conceptualized terms of otherness.[155] Eberhard Jüngel provides a
helpful reflection on these themes in relation to Bonhoeffer's statement that God
allows Himself to be 'pushed out of the world'.[156] For Jüngel, this reflection is not
simply a soteriological and economic one, but one which 'contains a profound
insight into the ontological character of the divine being'.[157] Jüngel identifies this
insight in the following way:

> The metaphysical theory of the worldly omnipresence of a God who is above
> everything and nowhere corresponds much too much to the fixation of God as
> a supra-worldly 'above us.' The faith that the 'Father in heaven' above us was
> among us through the crucified Son of God and in the Holy Spirit is united
> with the Son not only for himself but as one absent is present with us and that
> as the one who 'lets himself be pushed out of the world' *comes to the world –*
> this faith grants to the theologoumenon of the omnipresence of God a mean-
> ing which reconstructs it entirely. This happens in that God's omnipresence is
> to be understood now on the very basis of his very presence on the cross of
> Jesus and not without a christologically established removal of God.[158]

Bonhoeffer's anidolatrous move not only prevents the crude identification of God
with a boundary, but also undermines a conceptual spatialization of God through
unhelpful theological reflection.

Evidently, Bonhoeffer's theological attack on idolatry is not that of a *via negativa*
or of a human construct of God's otherness, which is so articulated as to suggest

153   LPP, p. 367.
154   LPP, p. 367.
155   Bonhoeffer addressed variously the problematic issue of space boundaries for the church; this is
a parallel move to that involved in his work on theology proper. Cf., for example, Discipleship, chapter 11; Ethics, pp. 63–8.
156   LPP, p. 479.
157   Eberhard Jüngel, *God as the Mystery of the World: On the Foundation of the Theology of the
Crucified One in the Dispute between Theism and Atheism*, trans. Darrell L. Guder (Edinburgh: T&T
Clark, 1983), p. 62.
158   Ibid., pp. 62–3.

that nothing could genuinely be said of God. The very christological focus of the work – the fact that it is only in realizing the unutterability of the name of God that one can utter the name of Jesus Christ, and the construal of transcendence and immanence from the perspective of the cross – determines that it is deeply particularist, with no foray back into a religion marked by mysticism from the religionlessness that Bonheoffer sets up. Instead, it is the very secondary objectivity of God,[159] which marks the basis for Bonhoeffer's charge against idolatry: the world has not simply come of age, but has come of age by *Jesus Christ.*[160] Particularism is at the heart of religionlessness. And religionlessness itself is an innately christological concept. After all, according to Bonhoeffer '[a]ll concepts of reality that ignore Jesus Christ are abstractions.'[161]

Anti-fundamentalist

While there is an element of anachronism involved in using the term 'anti-fundamentalist' in relation to Bonhoeffer,[162] there is certainly an aspect of this to his thinking on religionlessness. This aspect is connected to the above consideration of the dangers of identifying God with a physical or conceptual space, and of boundary language. The idea of the church trying to preserve space for itself in the world is a theme which Bonhoeffer discusses negatively in terms of apologetics,[163] of knowledge and of human boundary issues.[164] Bonhoeffer notes '"God" is being pushed further and further out of life, losing ground.'[165] However, the response to this is not, for Bonhoeffer, the response of a reactive and aggressive attempt to reclaim territory which was lost. As with Barth so with Bonhoeffer, the response to this was not the attempt to 'save some room for religion in the world or over against the world.'[166] To do so would again only offer the so-called 'god' of religion, who dwells in idolatrous boundary spaces. This path ends with God being 'smuggled in somewhere, in the very last, secret place that is left',[167] into the gaps.

---

159 For an unpacking of this term, see Marsh, *Reclaiming Dietrich Bonhoeffer.*
160 LPP, p. 451 (cf. the SCM 1971 edition of LPP, p. 342).
161 Ethics, p. 54.
162 On Bonhoeffer's own context in relation to fundamentalism, see Geffrey B. Kelly, 'Bonhoeffer's Christ-Centred, Religionless Christianity and His Critique of Religio-Political Fundamentalism' paper presented at the *Tenth International Bonhoeffer Congress* (Prague, Czech Republic 2008). More generally, the reader is directed to de Gruchy, Plant and Tietz (eds), *Dietrich Bonheoffer's Theology Today: A Way between Fundamentalism and Secularism?*.
163 LPP, pp. 425–7.
164 LPP, pp. 366–7.
165 LPP, p. 426.
166 LPP, p. 429.
167 LPP, p. 457.

Fundamentalism attempts to reassert the God of power and seeks to win back space into which the world has encroached.[168] Against this 'god', Bonhoeffer argues that the God of the Bible 'who gains ground and power in the world by being powerless' must be advocated.[169] This means that the church cannot exist in crusade mode. As Bonhoeffer puts it in his *Ethics*: 'The space of the church is not there in order to fight with the world for a piece of its territory, but precisely to testify to the world that it is still the world, namely, the world that is loved and reconciled by God.'[170] This point for Bonhoeffer is deeply connected to the issue of religionlessness:

> The church can only defend its own space by fighting, not for space, but for
> the salvation of the world. Otherwise the church becomes a 'religious society'
> that fights in its own interest and thus has ceased to be the church of God in
> the world. So the first task given to those who belong to the church of God is
> not to be something for themselves, for example, by creating a religious
> organization or leading a pious life, but to be witnesses of Jesus Christ to the
> world.[171]

Religionless Christianity's refusal to identify a space in which God dwells compared to a worldly space, and its refusal thereby to engage in idolatry, determines that the very quest in which fundamentalism struggles against the world is overcome.

This does not mean, however, that Christianity should deal only with that which is weak and marginal. The very opposite is the case. Bonhoeffer asserts the genuine power and sovereignty of the Lord in the place of a falsely understood power of God, redefining what is meant by power for Christianity. Indeed, Bonhoeffer's diagnosis of the essence of religion rests in human weakness and dependency on the power of God.[172] It is precisely against this human weakness that Bonhoeffer asserts his religionlessness. For Bonhoeffer, true God (and not the so-called 'god' of religion) belongs 'not at the boundaries but in the centre, not in weakness but in strength, thus not in death and guilt but in human life and human goodness.'[173] Indeed, true God could be no other, as God is already present fully in the world, and not a concept to be exploited when people in their

---

168   For reflection on the relationship between power and fundamentalism, see Percy, *Words, Wonders and Power*. For more on the weakness of Christ in Bonhoeffer, see Green, *Bonhoeffer: A Theology of Sociality*, pp. 269–73.

169   LPP, p. 480. This clearly does not determine that one must give up on God's impassibility, as it could mark a willed self-limitation of sovereignty by God as the mode in which in the person of Jesus Christ He helps His creatures.

170   *Ethics*, p. 63.

171   *Ethics*, p. 64.

172   Green, *Bonhoeffer: A Theology of Sociality*, p. 16.

173   LPP, pp. 366–7.

weakness require 'God' to deal with the peripheral points of their lives. There is, therefore, no need to seek to push space in which God occupies forward into the world, since God already is there at the centre, not religiously but fully and genuinely in the world.

Holistic and continuous

A notable feature of Bonhoeffer's religionless Christianity is its emphasis on holistic and continuous approaches to human beings. This is a concern that Bonhoeffer expressed from *Act and Being* onwards,[174] and it has full force in the prison writings. Bonhoeffer is concerned that theology deals with the *whole* human, and not simply the inner person, since the Bible offers no such distinction between inward and outward living: 'Since human beings live as much from their "outer" to their "inner" selves as from their "inner" to their "outer" selves, the assumption that one can only understand the essence of a human being by knowing his most intimate psychological depths and backgrounds is completely erroneous.'[175] The concern of scripture is always the whole person in his or her worldliness in relation to God. A religious act for Bonhoeffer is always something which is partial and lacks wholeness, in comparison to true faith.[176] A Christian, therefore, is called to be whole:

> To be a Christian does not mean to be religious in a particular way, to make something of oneself (a sinner, a penitent, or a saint) on the basis of some method or other, but to be a man – not a type of man, but the man that Christ creates in us.[177]

After all, Jesus does not call human beings to a new religion, says Bonhoeffer, but to life – life in all of its fullness. Thus the Christian is not a '*homo religiosus*, but simply a human being, in the same way that Jesus was a human being'.[178] To have faith can never involve for Bonhoeffer an escape from the world, since 'one only learns to have faith by living in the full this-worldliness of life.'[179] It is recognizing the true worldliness of the world, and the need for the Christian to live within that worldliness in which and through which God reveals Godself, that is at the heart of Bonhoeffer's concern with wholeness.

---

174   See above.
175   LPP, p. 457.
176   LPP, p. 482; cf. Marsh, *Reclaiming Dietrich Bonhoeffer*, p. 260.
177   LPP, p. 480.
178   LPP, p. 486. While it might seem that there is a significant difference here between Bonhoeffer and Barth's theological anthropologies, the point that Bonheoffer is making is about the *style* of living that Jesus engaged in, in contrast, as he explains to, for example, John the Baptist.
179   LPP, p. 486.

This issue is not just expressed theoretically, however, for Bonhoeffer; it is also expressed personally. In his poem 'Who am I?',[180] Bonhoeffer addresses himself to the issue of the way in which he is perceived (as a religious man, perhaps) by others in comparison to the person he knows himself to be. The penultimate stanza of the poem addresses directly the issue of a divided or non-continuous identity:

Am I this [person] and tomorrow another?

Am I both at once? Before others a hypocrite

and in my own eyes a pitiful, whimpering weakling?[181]

However, the answer for Bonhoeffer lies in the wholeness of his humanity, which is grounded in the identity God has given him: 'Whoever I am, thou knowest, O God, I am thine.'

Removal of secular–sacred divide

The religionless God, who is 'the beyond in the midst of our lives' and who cannot be defined by a space which is ever being reduced in the contemporary world,[182] is a God who does not allow a neat division of secular and sacred concerns. Clearly, this point follows from those which have preceded it in this section, but these very points determine that one cannot simply identify a realm or space which is secular and one which is sacred. As Leahy puts it, 'A theological view that splits the world into two separated realms risks reducing Christianity to an individualistic project of saving one's soul.'[183] For Bonhoeffer, this conception of God is simply not possible from a christological perspective. To his mind, dividing reality into sacred and profane, or church and world, suggests the possibility of existence in only one of these two sectors, a problem both for the secular age and for the pious. Moreover, the effect of this is a giving up on reality as a whole: 'either we place ourselves in one of the two realms, wanting Christ without the world or the world without Christ – and in both cases we deceive ourselves . . . There are not two realities, but *only one reality*, and that is God's reality revealed in Christ in the reality of the world.'[184] The implications are profound:

---

180   LPP, pp. 458–60. For a commentary and some reflection on this poem, see Rowan Williams, 'The Suspicion of Suspicion: Wittgenstein and Bonhoeffer', in *The Grammar of the Heart: New Essays in Moral Philosophy and Theology*, ed. Richard H. Bell (San Francisco: Harper & Row, 1988), pp. 42–3; and Michael Northcott, ' "Who Am I?": Human Identity and the Spiritual Disciplines in the Witness of Dietrich Bonhoeffer', in *Who Am I? Bonhoeffer's Theology through His Poetry*, ed. Bernd Wannenswetsch (London: T&T Clark, 2009).

181   LPP, p. 460.

182   LPP, p. 367.

183   Leahy, ' "Christ Existing as Community": Dietrich Bonhoeffer's Notion of Church', p. 50.

184   Ethics, p. 58.

> Our categories need to change. All dualistic categories of private-public, inter-
> ior life-exterior life, God-world, ethics-piety, and active-passive have to be
> interpreted through the Christological (Chalcedonian) prism, because reality
> is 'in him' and all Christian ecclesial life is carried within this reality.[185]

Indeed, it is this unwillingness to separate the secular and the sacred realms that is
the basis of Bonhoeffer's distrust of classical metaphysics, which he associates
with religion.[186] Bonhoeffer also carries these observations through into the issue
of soteriology, using Irenaeus's *recapitulatio* as a basis for positing a universal
salvation,[187] a theme found earlier in Bonhoeffer's thought, which seems also to be
at work in his poem 'Christians and Heathens'.[188]

Part of the concern that Bonhoeffer has in removing the secular–sacred divide
in his theology is that of how to express the world's secularity (or worldliness)
theologically. It is this which leads him to consider the 'profound this-worldliness of Christianity',[189] and this which leads him to assert that '[b]efore God, and
with God, we live without God.'[190] Bonhoeffer is seeking in these discussions to
make sense of how to speak of the world in its own particularity and seeming
self-sufficiency. The worldliness of the world is a key theological concern for
him. There is, in Jüngel's words, for Bonhoeffer, a 'theological necessity to think
God in this way . . . given both by the world which factually exists "even if there
were no God" and by the nature of the God who reveals himself in the crucified
Christ.'[191] Jüngel identifies both of the concerns that Bonhoeffer seeks to face
here: first, the empirical reality of a world getting along just fine as if God did not
exist; second, the theological implications of a God who 'consents to be pushed
out of the world and onto the cross'.[192] Bonhoeffer identifies the need to think
theologically about the empirical reality of a world which has done away with
the concept of God, and he responds to that need by reflecting christologically on
the death of Christ.[193] The removal of the secular–sacred divide is also related to

---

185   Leahy, ' "Christ Existing as Community": Dietrich Bonhoeffer's Notion of Church', 51.

186   LPP, p. 364. Cf. McCormack, *Orthodox and Modern*, p. 133; Dramm, *Dietrich Bonhoeffer: An Introduction to His Thought*, pp. 200–1. This is an issue that will be discussed further in relation to Karl Barth, and in Chapter 5 of this book.

187   LPP, p. 230.

188   LPP, pp. 460–1. For further discussion of Bonhoeffer on universal salvation, see Tom Greggs, 'Pessimistic Universalism: Rethinking the Wider Hope with Bonhoeffer and Barth', *Modern Theology* 26, no. 4 (2010); and Chapter 5 below.

189   LPP, p. 485.

190   LPP, p. 479.

191   Jüngel, *God as the Mystery of the World*, p. 61.

192   LPP, p. 479.

193   There is, therefore, a degree to which the analysis of Green regarding *Mündigkeit* needs to be modified: it is not simply first an anthropological, then a theological one; certainly this order exists, but there is also a simultaneity to it. See Green, *Bonhoeffer: A Theology of Sociality*, pp. 248–57.

the issue of the distinction but interconnectedness of religious and secular concerns.[194] It is questions about secular society that lead Bonhoeffer to questions about the continuation of religion, and questions about the type of religion being espoused that lead him to question the nature of God: Bonhoeffer refuses to think religiously because of secularity, and refuses to give up on Christianity (even if it must be in a religionless form) precisely because of God. His theological reflection will not separate religious concerns from secular ones, but nor will they allow secular concerns to be considered without recourse to scripture and to God: all of these concerns have to be thought, for Bonhoeffer, from a christological perspective. As a christological concept, religionless Christianity provides, therefore, a prophetic admonition to the continued religious attitudes and behaviour of Christians. It recognizes the religious garments Christianity has worn over the ages, but is determined that the Christian faith should not be confused with a particular (and, for Bonhoeffer, passing) stage of human religious evolution. In this way, this work stands very closely to that of Barth.

CONCLUSION

Bonhoeffer sets for us a programmatic directive for theology. There is an urgency to his theology which, while his self-confessed clumsiness determines his thinking cannot be neatly packaged or reduced to a system,[195] engages the present day theologian in the task of articulating theology in a world which has come of age by Jesus Christ. In seeking to learn from Bonhoeffer what that might mean, it is helpful to see his thinking as a directive culmination of concerns he has expressed throughout his theological career: after all, even the most seemingly different of his works, *Discipleship*, he far from rejects *in toto*.[196] Religionless Christianity marks a midpoint of his theology, which sadly became an end point. It was not intended as an end point at which he had arrived, but was the suggestive path on which he was travelling. This path is one on which Karl Barth, too, was walking, and – while the very fact that they were not static but living human beings determines that they might not always have walked in synch – it is the same journey in which they are actively engaging. Clearly, Barth does not think it is possible to have Christianity without religion, but emphasizing religionlessness as an optative theological category determines that one can also see how Bonhoeffer, too, recognizes that the church can never remove religion (whatever that might be in sociological terms) from itself, but must constantly be vigilant of confusing God with religion, or separating the church from the world. Barth describes this as the case;

---

194   This, for Bonhoeffer, is a theological position comparable to the sociological position of David Martin. See Martin, *The Religious and the Secular*, chapter 4, esp. p. 3.

195   Cf. LPP, pp. 480–2.

196   LPP, p. 486.

Bonhoeffer hopes that we might endeavour for it not to be so. Seeking to identify from Bonhoeffer, therefore, motifs that might help in the articulation of a theology which is suspicious of religion for theological reasons is the best way, in the contemporary age, that one can seek to identify the direction in which Bonhoeffer was pointing, and join him in the journey that seeks to answer the question of what Christianity is, and who Jesus Christ is, for us today.

Chapter 4

AFTER RELIGIONLESSNESS: BACK TO BARTH AND FORMATIVE MOTIFS

INTRODUCTION

One of the most significant difficulties in relating the theologies of Bonhoeffer and Barth is that of interrupted generationalism. While to some degree Bonhoeffer belonged to a slightly different generation to Barth (or at least a half-generation), Bonhoeffer's untimely death determined that Barth's theological writing continued for over 20 years beyond Bonhoeffer's final letters and papers. The result of this is that, although there is a clear influence of Barth on Bonhoeffer, the Barth who influenced Bonhoeffer was a theologian who continued his own theological development for many more years. In Bonhoeffer's personal and academic writings, it is clear that he is a student of Barth,[1] but the Barth of whom he was a student was not the Barth known fully to present-day scholars. Following Bonhoeffer's untimely death, among a significant number of other publications, Barth wrote a further eight part volumes of his *Church Dogmatics*. To hold Barth to the standard of his pre-1945 work is to cut short the tremendous theological work in which he engaged after the war.

While I have already argued that Barth and Bonhoeffer are both walking along the same path with regard to the theologizing of the critique of religion, attention to Barth's mature theology allows one to see how very closely they are walking. Bonhoeffer's primary engagement with Barth seems to be with Barth's first volume of *Church Dogmatics* and the work preceding it. Although there is clear evidence that Bonhoeffer had read volumes II/1 and II/2, with the exception of Barth's ethical work in chapter VIII of the *Dogmatics* there does not appear to be sustained engagement with the work of Barth in the second volume of *Church Dogmatics*.[2]

---

1 One can see this in various of Bonhoeffer's enthusiastic and respectful letters to or about Barth: see, for example, BBNY, pp. 77 and 460; C&I, pp. 190–1 and 276–9.

2 The excellent study by Marsh demonstrates this with regard to CD II/1. See Marsh, *Reclaiming Dietrich Bonhoeffer*, chapter 1. Furthermore, Bonhoeffer himself directly betrays this with regard to

In seeking to continue to lay the foundations for the constructive work of the book, this chapter will argue that looking at Barth's dogmatic work from *Church Dogmatics* II/2 onwards will help in identifying the shared theological concerns of Bonhoeffer and Barth around the issue of religion. Although there were numerous direct comments on religion in Barth's work outside of *Church Dogmatics*,[3] Barth did not engage *directly* with the topic of religion after §17. However, related issues were discussed by Barth, and this chapter will engage with the themes of *promeity* (and *pronosity*) and christocentrism, creation and anthropology, and with paragraph 69 on 'Light and the lights'. Seeing the differing discussions by Bonhoeffer and Barth on religion as representative of the different moods in which their theologies are written around this topic (principally indicative for Barth and principally optative for Bonhoeffer),[4] this chapter will offer no synthesizing account of Bonhoeffer and Barth's parallel paths, but will simply seek to walk alongside them. Rather than a singular definition of religionless or anti-religious theology, the chapter will, therefore, end by giving a provisional summary of formative motifs that will guide the constructive theology which follows this historical engagement.

PROMEITY AND CHRISTOCENTRISM

Charles Marsh's excellent engagement with Barth and Bonhoeffer helpfully asserts that 'Bonhoeffer's theology is possible only in view of Barth's revolution in theological method.'[5] Marsh sees the distinction between Barth and Bonhoeffer as depending on the distinction between the primary and secondary objectivity of God.[6] This is the distinction between 'God in his triune life as such (primary objectivity) and God as he comes to us in the revelation of Jesus Christ (in his secondary objectivity).'[7] Marsh identifies Bonhoeffer's approach to theology as being one which ultimately concerns secondary objectivity: 'Bonhoeffer wants

---

II/2: in a letter dated 13 September 1942, Bonhoeffer mentions having read the second main section of II/2 (on 'The Command of God), but not yet the first; certainly, it is the second half with which Bonhoeffer most engages in his Ethics. Bethge also helpfully reminds us that Bonhoeffer does not comment on CD II/2. See Bethge, *Dietrich Bonhoeffer*, p. 746.

3   For example, Barth writes such things about religion as: 'I hate the word' (Letter to Prof. Herbert Kubly, Basel, 16 July 1963); it 'may be a private affair, but the work and word of God are the reconciliation of the world with God, as it was performed in Jesus Christ' (EvTheol, p. 111); and that it is the place in which the worst form of godlessness is found (ChrL, pp. 129–30).

4   Cf. Ford, *Self and Salvation*, p. 257, n. 41; albeit between the optative and the indicative, not the vocative and the indicative on the particular topic of religion.

5   Marsh, *Reclaiming Dietrich Bonhoeffer*, p. ix.

6   Marsh asserts this as the primary and secondary objectivity of revelation. However, I am accepting the correction of Hunsinger, 'Review of Charles Marsh, *Reclaiming Dietrich Bonhoeffer: The Promise of His Theology*'.

7   Marsh, *Reclaiming Dietrich Bonhoeffer*, p. viii.

to interpret all reality as part of the rich tapestry of God's promeity.'[8] However, as Marsh makes clear, for Bonhoeffer, this engagement in secondary objectivity is crucially dependent upon and presupposes Barth's engagement with primary objectivity. Certainly, Marsh's engagement is subtle and helpful in terms of Bonhoeffer's engagement with Barth's theology before *Church Dogmatics* II/2. One may wish, however, to supplement Marsh's reading of Barth on primary and secondary objectivity by pointing to Barth's active engagement with the relation of God's primary and secondary objectivity in his consideration of God as the one who 'loves in freedom',[9] and in his work in the first volume of *Church Dogmatics* on revelation.[10] For Barth, indeed, it is important that discussion of the perfections of divine loving precede discussion of the perfections of divine freedom:

> the most doubtful feature of [this kind of] conception of God [is] that God is first and properly the impersonal absolute, and only secondarily, inessentially and in His relationship *ad extra* the personal God of love with attributes of wisdom, justice, mercy, etc. But this sequence corresponds neither to the order of revelation nor to the nature of the being of God as known in His revelation. In God's revelation, the disclosure of God is in fact the first and the last, the origin and the end, of the ways of God.[11]

Barth is hardly a theologian simply of so-called primary objectivity. This being said, an evolutionary progression does take place in Barth's theology, which sees Barth take a more deeply christocentric approach in his work, and an engagement with *Church Dogmatics* II/2, and all that follows, might well give further credence to Marsh's suggestion that these two theologians be treated in closest proximity. Not only does Bonhoeffer build upon and presuppose Barth's work on primary (and one might also add, secondary) objectivity, but Barth himself focuses increasingly on secondary objectivity in his work from *Church Dogmatics* II/2 onwards.[12] Clearly, this cannot be an argument about direct influence of Barth on Bonhoeffer, whose life was cut so short, but it is important to the ongoing discussion of the relationship between Barth and Bonhoeffer's works for the communities of scholarship which follow after them.

---

8   Ibid., p. viii.

9   CD, II/1, §§28–31. Marsh does recognize this secondary objectivity as being present, but sees it as less intense than in Bonhoeffer.

10   Secondary objectivity is addressed throughout, but it is notable, for example that CD I/1, §8: 'God in His Revelation' precedes §9: 'The Triunity of God'.

11   CD II/1, p. 349.

12   Appearing before McCormack's seminal work on the importance of CD II/2 to Barth's theological method, it is hardly surprising that Marsh does not attend to these themes, and the following is in no way a critique, but rather an extension of his argument in light of new research. See McCormack, *Karl Barth's Critically Realistic Dialectical Theology*.

Barth's reworking of the doctrine of election in II/2 marks one of the most radical and exciting pieces of theology in the past 500 years. Placing the doctrine of election within the doctrine of God, Barth radically re-describes election, and breaks his continuity not only with Calvin but also with Augustine in the radical departure from the tradition that he makes.[13] In doing this, Barth emphasizes almost beyond measure the *promeity* (and *pronosity*)[14] of God's election, an election in which God determines God's being in God's freedom. Following and refining a move made by Pierre Maury,[15] Barth advocates a christological approach to the doctrine of election,[16] in which Jesus Christ is both the subject and the object of election. Crucially for Barth, however, this is contained within the doctrine of God.[17] It is God's being which Barth is concerned to discuss in discussing election. He begins the first paragraph of the book thus:

> The doctrine of election is the sum of the Gospel because of all words that can be said or heard it is the best: that God elects man; that God is for man too the One who loves in freedom. It is grounded in the knowledge of Jesus Christ

---

13 There has been much written in recent years on the relationship between election and the immanent trinity with regard to this move. This argument is not directly pertinent to the one being made here, and therefore – for sake of space – entry into it is avoided. For an overview of this discussion, see Bruce McCormack, 'Grace and Being: The Role of God's Gracious Election in Karl Barth's Theological Ontology', in *Cambridge Companion to Karl Barth*, ed. John Webster (Cambridge: CUP, 2000); Bruce McCormack, 'Seek God Where He May Be Found: A Response to Edwin Chr. Van Driel', *Scottish Journal of Theology* 60, no. 1 (2007); Paul D. Molnar, *Divine Freedom and the Doctrine of the Immanent Trinity: In Dialogue with Karl Barth and Contemporary Theology* (Edinburgh: T&T Clark, 2002); Kevin W. Hector, 'God's Triunity and Self-Determination: A Conversation with Karl Barth, Bruce McCormack and Paul Molnar', *International Journal of Systematic Theology* 7, no. 3 (2005); Edward Chr. van Driel, 'Karl Barth on the Eternal Existence of Jesus Christ', *Scottish Journal of Theology* 60, no. 1 (2007); George Hunsinger, 'Election and the Trinity: Twenty-Five Theses on the Theology of Karl Barth', *Modern Theology* 24, no. 2 (2008); Bruce McCormack, 'Election and the Trinity: Theses in Response to George Hunsinger', *Scottish Journal of Theology* 63, no. 2 (2010); and Paul T. Nimmo, 'Barth and the Christian as Ethical Agent: An Ontological Study of the Shape of Christian Ethics', in *Commanding Grace: Studies in Karl Barth's Ethics*, ed. Daniel L. Migliore (Grand Rapids: Wm. B. Eerdmans, 2010), pp. 221–7.

14 There is a degree of difficulty here in terms of the language used. I am using the term *promeity* because of its use in Bonhoeffer studies. More directly appropriate to Barth might well be the term *pronosity*: see Chapters 5 and 6 of this book. Given Bonhoeffer's critique of individualism, *pronosity* is also probably a more accurate term for his mature work. However, the terms in this book are used interchangeably to emphasize the being of God for the world.

15 CD II/2, pp. 190–4.

16 This is a move which is already beginning to be seen in a very early form in Barth's 1924–25 lectures at Göttingen (e.g., GD, pp. 468 & 470). This early attempt does not contain the thoroughness of CD II/2, nor does it contain the simultaneity of Christ as elected and electing.

17 On this point, see Colin Gunton, 'Karl Barth's Doctrine of Election as Part of His Doctrine of God', *Journal of Theological Studies* 25, no. 2 (1974); McCormack, 'Grace and Being'; and Eberhard Jüngel, *God's Being Is in Becoming. The Trinitarian Being of God in the Theology of Karl Barth. A Paraphrase*, trans. John Webster (Edinburgh: T&T Clark, 2001).

because He is both the electing God and elected man in One. It is part of the doctrine of God because originally God's election of man is a predestination not merely of man but of Himself. Its function is to bear basic testimony to eternal, free and unchanging grace as the beginning of all the ways and works of God.[18]

Thus, for Barth, election denotes not only the being of God but also the relationship between God and humanity. It is a relationship which is formed from the decision 'in God's self-determination and resultant determination of man' in which God is who God is.[19] This primal relationship belongs to the doctrine of God, which needs to include all God's works *ad extra*. In articulating his doctrine of election, Barth is prepared to depart from the tradition precisely because the Bible responds to human questions about who and what God is by directing humanity to Jesus Christ, and in Christ one sees God's movement towards His people. In seeing Jesus Christ, one sees God, and in Jesus Christ one has to do with the electing God. Thus, to know who the electing God is we need to look to Jesus Christ and the people of God enclosed with Him;[20] and to know what it is to be elected by God, one needs to look only to Jesus and those people who are enclosed in Him.[21] The doctrine of election needs to be placed within the doctrine of God, therefore, since

> He [God] wills to be and actually is God, in the mystery of what takes place from and to all eternity within Himself, within His triune being, God is none other than the One who in His Son or Word elects Himself, and in and with Himself elects His people.[22]

That God wills to be God for us in Jesus Christ is a self-determination of the self-electing God to be for humanity. Barth's doctrine of election seeks by this to demonstrate that it is both *God* who is for us, and God who is *for us*.

Unlike for Thomas and others,[23] for Barth the election of Jesus Christ is not simply passive and confined to the human nature but active and includes the divine. Radically, Barth states that election is:

> the being of Christ in the beginning with God, the act of the good-pleasure of God by which the fulness of the Godhead is allowed to dwell in Him, the covenant which God made with Himself and which is for that reason eternal, the oath which God sware by Himself in the interests of man.[24]

---

18   CD II/2, p. 3.
19   CD II/2, p. 52.
20   CD II/2, p. 54.
21   CD II/2, pp. 58–9.
22   CD II/2, p. 76.
23   Barth also discusses Calvin and Coccejus.
24   CD II/2, p. 107.

The active election of Christ is the basis of God's *promeity* and *pronosity*, which Barth advocates God has had from all eternity:

> before all created reality, before all being and becoming in time, before time itself, in the pre-temporal eternity of God, the eternal divine decision as such has as its object and content the existence of this one created being, the man Jesus of Nazareth, and the work of this man in His life and death, His humiliation and exaltation, His obedience and merit. It tells us further that in and with the existence of this man the eternal divine decision has as its object and content the execution of the divine covenant with man, the salvation of all men.[25]

It is almost impossible to imagine a stronger assertion of God's being for humanity than this. It was this turn, indeed, which marked the basis for Barth's ability later in life to reflect on his theology under the title of 'The Humanity of God'. For Barth, there is an eternal humanity about the very nature of God, a humanity which is the grounds and basis for our humanity.[26]

Furthermore, within this election of Jesus Christ, there is an overwhelmingly positive election of our humanity. While Barth is characterized in so much theology as being a theologian who uttered *Nein!* at every conceivable theological juncture, there is a positive affirmation of humanity by God in his doctrine of election. Indeed, God elects rejection for Himself because He is so deeply for human beings:

> In so far, then, as predestination does contain a No, it is not a No spoken against man. In so far as it does involve exclusion and rejection, it is not the exclusion and rejection of man. In so far as it is directed to perdition and death, it is not directed to the perdition and death of man.[27]

These are the things humanity deserves, and God did not have to act in this way, but in His grace in election He elects to be for human beings. In electing, however, God not only elects fellowship with humanity for Himself, but also elects fellowship with Himself for humanity.[28] It is the church (and in a related way Israel)[29]

---

25 CD II/2, p. 116.
26 For more on this theme, see my *Barth, Origen, and Universal Salvation*, chapter 2.
27 CD II/2, p. 166.
28 CD II/2, p. 168.
29 On Barth on Israel, see Katherine Sonderegger, *That Jesus Was Born a Jew: Karl Barth's 'Doctrine of Israel'* (Pennsylvania: Pennsylvania State University Press, 1992); Mark Lindsay, 'Dialectics of Communion: Dialectical Method and Barth's Defense of Israel', in *Karl Barth: A Future for Post Modern Theology?*, ed. Geoff Thompson and Christiaan Mostert (Adelaide: Openbook, 2000); Eberhard Busch, 'Indissoluble Unity: Barth's Position on the Jews During the Hitler Era', in *For the Sake of the World: Karl Barth and the Future of Ecclesial Theology*, ed. George Hunsinger (Cambridge and Grand Rapids: Wm. B. Eerdmans, 2004); Clement Chia, 'Is Barth a Supercessionist? Reconsidering the Case in the Historical Context of The Nazi Jewish Question', paper presented at the

which reveals what God chooses for humanity in His election of humans – His self-giving love, Himself as Brother and King.[30] This being for humanity is not simply a being for the church, but is primarily a being for all people: 'What takes place in this election is always that God is for us; for us, and therefore for the world which was created by Him, which is distinct from Him, but which is yet maintained by Him.'[31] This being for humanity precedes any other work of God. It is the eternal determination of God's being in relation to the world, regardless of human response or of human sinfulness. Barth puts this emphatically as follows:

> In Jesus Christ He has chosen man from all eternity as His own, for life in His kingdom, to be a member of His people, His possession. In Him He has bound Himself to us, before He bound us to Himself, and before we bound ourselves to Him. In Him He has decided Himself for us before all our decisions, before we recognised ourselves as His servants, His unprofitable servants indeed, before ever He forgave us our sins and called us to a new obedience. In Him, the everlasting Son, He has recognised us as His servants from all and to all eternity. In Him He has loved us, and we are those who are loved by Him.[32]

For Barth after *Church Dogmatics* II/2, it is difficult to imagine how he could not be understood to be concerned (like Bonhoeffer) with dominantly christocentric concerns (referred to by Marsh as an intense secondary objectivity). Indeed, recent research on the theme by the likes of McCormack seems to suggest that these very categories break down for Barth. If religionlessness is to some degree about emphasizing the *promeity* of God, rather than speculative engagement in discussions of inner-trinitarian life and classical metaphysics, then one sees in Barth a resolutely christocentric emphasis on God's nature as being for humanity.[33]

CREATION AND ANTHROPOLOGY

Bonhoeffer lived before Barth's four-part doctrine of creation (which is around twice as long as his doctrine of revelation) was written.[34] Despite its length, it

Society for the Study of Theology (Leeds, 2006); and Glenn Chesnutt, 'The Theological and Political Ramifications of a Theology of Israel', in *New Perspectives for Evangelical Theology: Engaging with God, Scripture and the World*, ed. Tom Greggs (Abingdon: Routledge, 2010).

30　CD II/2, p. 211.

31　CD II/2, pp. 25–6.

32　CD II/2, pp. 736–7.

33　On the nature of Barth's christocentrism, see Marc Cortez, 'What Does It Mean to Call Karl Barth a "Christocentric" Theologian?', *Scottish Journal of Theology* 60, no. 2 (2007). This is of particular note in light of assertions that the distinction between Bonhoeffer and Barth is that Bonhoeffer is christocentric in approach and Barth is trinitarian.

34　It is helpful to note at this juncture that Barth wrote, but decided (for unknown reasons) not to publish, a paragraph originally intended to form a part of his doctrine of creation entitled 'God and the

seems that in many ways this volume of *Church Dogmatics* has remained one of the most understudied aspects of Barth's theology. Crucially, in this volume one finds an affirmation of the world long before the highly popularized account of Barth's saying 'yes' in 'The Humanity of God'.[35]

Barth's paragraph 42 is entitled 'The Yes of God the Creator'. In this chapter, he advocates that creation is a benefit, something which carries with it God's Yes. Barth affirms creatureliness, worldliness:

> even the creature does not merely exist, but does so as the sphere and object of the covenant, as the being to whom God has devoted His good-will and whom He has destined to share in the overflowing of His own fulness of life and love. To be a creature means to be determined to this end, to be affirmed, elected and accepted by God.[36]

Indeed, he can write: 'To be a creature means to be prepared for the place where His honour dwells.'[37] While Barth wishes to protect himself from any movement into natural theology, he nevertheless sees a limited and indirect witness to the Creator at work in creation. This witness is described thus:

> It shines primarily and essentially in its own light. If the created world shines, it does so in reflection of this light. But the light of revelation shines even where the created world itself is without light because the same God who gives it light at one point refuses it light at another, willing to reveal Himself here but to conceal Himself there. God is free to deal in this way with creation. It is still His work and witness, though His silent witness.[38]

Creation has a definitive and good purpose for Barth, though he is more than aware of the negative and miserable side of creation.[39] However, in God's grace

---

Gods', which was to be the first section of §42, originally intended to be entitled 'The Creator and His Revelation'. This work is not readily available (except as scanned documents on CD-ROM), and it is impossible to know the reason why it was not included in CD, or indeed not published elsewhere by Barth. While it will be referred to at a later stage of this book, discussion in this chapter is limited to Barth's published work. For more on 'God and the Gods', see Wolf Krötke, 'A New Impetus to the Theology of Religions from Karl Barth's Thought', paper presented at the Karl Barth Society of North America (Washington, DC, 2006); and Garrett Green, 'Imaginary Gods and the Anonymous Christ: Thinking About the Religions with Karl Barth', paper presented at the Karl Barth on Religion and the Religions Conference, Princeton Theological Seminary (Princeton, 2009).

35   It is this work which is often pointed towards when people seem to suggest that the shifts in Barth's thought (on which this work reflects) only took place at the point of the writing the HoG rather than being a reflection on it. For more on the HoG in relation to the rest of Barth's theology, see John Thompson, 'The Humanity of God in the Theology of Karl Barth', *Scottish Journal of Theology* 29, no. 3 (1976). On the concept itself, see Gunton, 'The Triune God and the Freedom of the Creature', pp. 61–4.

36   CD III/1, pp. 363–4.

37   CD III/1, p. 364.

38   CD III/1, p. 371.

39   CD III/1, pp. 374–5.

He condescends to both the rejoicing and sorrow of creation, and makes it His own, taking to Himself the very contradiction of it and allowing creation's imperfection already to share in God's perfection.[40] Indeed, any No spoken to creation is not for the sake of the No, but rather for the sake of God's Yes to the world.[41] It is from the perspective of this Yes, from the perspective of Jesus Christ, that creation must be understood for Barth:

> in Him [Christ] the created world is already perfect in spite of its imperfection, for the Creator is Himself a creature, both sharing its creaturely peril, and guaranteeing and already actualising its hope. If the created world is understood in the light of the divine mercy revealed in Jesus Christ, of the divine participation in it eternally resolved in Jesus Christ and fulfilled by Him in time; if it is thus understood as the arena, instrument and object of His living action, of the once for all divine contesting and overcoming of its imperfection, its justification and perfection will infallibly be perceived and it will be seen to be the best of all possible worlds.[42]

This is the strongest affirmation of creation from the perspective of Jesus Christ. In the words of Hauerwas, 'Barth was trying to help his readers acquire the skills necessary to see that all that is, is so by God's grace.'[43]

Furthermore, Barth is also positive about humanity,[44] again from the perspective of Jesus Christ. For Barth, the basic characteristic of real human beings is that, as covenant partners of God, they are able to participate in Jesus' life as one who lives for God and for other humans. Barth discusses this determination of humanity in §45 of *Church Dogmatics*. Although humans are blighted by sin, they are nevertheless created with the determination of becoming covenant partners with God, as the true human, Jesus, shows. Jesus Christ demonstrates that real humans are for and not against God, are covenant-partners of God, and are determined by God for life with God.[45] An anthropology based on christology determines that Barth can state: 'If the divinity of the man Jesus is to be described comprehensively in the statement that He is man for God, His humanity can and must be described no less succinctly in the proposition that He is man for man, for other men, His fellows.'[46] Jesus' relationships with human beings and his work *propter salutem nostrum* demonstrate that he has a genuine 'fellow humanity', that He is

---

40   CD III/1, pp. 380–5.

41   CD III/1, p. 384.

42   CD III/1, p. 385.

43   Hauerwas, *With the Grain of the Universe*, p. 184.

44   On Barth's anthropology, see Marc Cortez, 'Body, Soul, and (Holy) Spirit: Karl Barth's Theological Framework for Understanding Human Ontology', *International Journal of Systematic Theology* 10, no. 3 (2008).

45   CD III/2, p. 203.

46   CD III/2, p. 208.

the 'man for other men in the most comprehensive and radical sense'.[47] Further-more, Barth argues that it would be impossible for Jesus to be 'for' God were He not 'for' other humans.[48] Indeed, there is for Barth a correspondence not only between Jesus as human being and other humans, but also between God and humanity:

> [W]e ask concerning the image of God in which every part as such has a share; concerning the correspondence and similarity with the essence of God peculiar to humanity as such. If it were not wholly proper to it, how could it be compatible with the essence of God to give Himself to solidarity with man as He has done in making the covenant with Himself the meaning and purpose of its creation and therefore the determination of its humanity, in Himself becoming man in Jesus Christ? For all the disparity, there is here presupposed a common factor, a parity, not merely between Jesus and other men, but, because between Jesus and other men, between God and man generally.[49]

Once again, this is linked to election. Because of God's self-determination to be human in Jesus Christ, there is a 'parity' or correspondence between God and all other humans. For Barth, in terms of theological anthropology, there is no simple 'I' alone, but only ever an 'I' in relation, only ever an 'I' in relation to a 'Thou'. There is no pure and self-sufficient 'I'; this 'I' is always distinguished from and connected to a 'Thou'.[50] Human beings are, therefore, beings in encounter, and being genuinely human involves engaging in this encounter. As Barth somewhat poetically puts it:

> An action is human when a man who must help himself either well or badly also accepts the call for help issued by another and gives his need a place in the determination of his own action. My action is human when the outstretched hand of the other does not grope in the void but finds in mine the support which is asked. It is inhuman if I am content merely to help myself.[51]

For Barth, it is not merely the case that Jesus is the human for others; it is also the case that since Jesus, as God, is this human being for other human beings, other humans are enabled by His work to come to be able to participate in His true humanity.

---

47   CD III/2, p. 212. This is surely a concept which reflects Bonhoeffer's own discussion of Christ in LPP, p. 501.
48   CD III/2, p. 217. Barth discusses in what follows (pp. 218–22) the *analogia relationalis* – a con-cept which mirrors Bonhoeffer's own discussion of the *imago Dei*.
49   CD III/2, p. 225.
50   CD III/2, pp. 244–74.
51   CD III/2, p. 264.

⊗ ...re further developed in the second part volume of Barth's doc-
...iliation. Although for Barth there can never be a direct relationship
...: unique humanity of Christ and our humanity, Barth's discussion of
...iumanity is worthy of note.[52] This discussion has implications not only
...:ological anthropology but also for Barth's doctrine of God. In this, one is
a. .: to detect a doctrine of God which, in Jesus Christ, recognizes no distance
between God and humanity:

> the sovereignty of God dwells in His creaturely dependence as the Son of
> Man, the eternity of God in His temporal uniqueness, the omnipresence of
> God in His spatial limitation, the omnipotence of God in His weakness, the
> glory of God in His passibility and mortality, the holiness and righteousness
> of God in His adamic bondage and fleshliness-in short, the unity and totality
> of the divine which is His own original essence in His humanity.[53]

Here, one can see the humanity of God – in the incarnate Jesus Christ, who defines
the very nature of God's eternity, omnipresence, glory, holiness and righteousness. The incarnation of Christ determines that humanity – His humanity – is
glorified and worthy of praise. Barth writes:

> It is, therefore, a matter of knowing and glorifying and loving and worship-
> ping God in His humanity. From God, in His action, this humanity, too,
> acquires and has a glory and dignity and majesty which those who know and
> glorify and love and worship Him cannot possibly overlook, but the grateful
> acknowledgment of which is rather included in all the knowledge and honour
> and love and worship addressed to Him.[54]

This is not, however, to say that humanity possesses these things in and of itself,
or that one can abstract from this discussion of Jesus' particularity any generalized anthropological principle:

> As God cannot be considered without His humanity, His humanity cannot be
> considered or known or magnified or worshipped without God. Any attempt
> to treat it *in abstracto*, in a vacuum, is from the very first a perverted and
> impossible undertaking. As Son of Man, and therefore in human form, Jesus

---

52 For an excellent discussion of the humanity of Christ in Karl Barth's theology, see Paul Dafydd
Jones, *The Humanity of Christ: Christology in Karl Barth's Church Dogmatics* (London: T&T Clark,
2008); and Paul Dafydd Jones, 'Karl Barth on Gethsemane', *International Journal of Systematic Theology* 9, no. 2 (2007). An older and less detailed account can be found in Stuart McLean, *Humanity in
the Thought of Karl Barth* (Edinburgh: T&T Clark, 1981).

53 CD IV/2, p. 86.

54 CD IV/2, p. 102.

Christ does not exist at all except in the act of God, as He is first the Son of God. Where He is not known as the latter, He cannot really be known in His humanity as abstracted from the divine Son as its Subject.[55]

Nevertheless, human beings can participate not only passively but also actively in Christ's humanity.[56] His life and humanity has an effect on *all* human beings:

[T]he case of all men is advocated and conducted by this One, all men being included in this One in the covenant as it is perfectly maintained and restored on both sides. There is no one, therefore, who does not participate in Him in this turning to God. There is no one who is not himself engaged in this turning. There is no one who is not raised and exalted with Him to true humanity. 'Jesus lives, and I with Him.'[57]

This participation, furthermore, is not only salvific in manner; participation also possesses an ethical dimension. Because of Jesus' fellow-humanity, there is a determination for the rest of humanity to be turned to other humans also:

He is wholly the Fellow-man of us His fellows; wholly the Neighbour of us His neighbours; wholly the Brother of us His brothers; the Witness, Teacher, Doctor, Helper and Advocate given as a man to us men. In the actualisation which it has found in Him humanity means to be bound and committed to other men. In Him, therefore, man is turned not merely to God but to other men.[58]

Human beings in Christ are turned towards other human beings. As the one for other humans, Jesus orientates those who truly participate in His humanity back towards other humans.

---

55   CD IV/2, p. 102.

56   On participation, see Adam Neder, *Participation in Christ: An Entry into Karl Barth's Church Dogmatics* (Louisville: Westminster John Knox, 2009); Greggs, *Barth, Origen, and Universal Salvation*, pp. 31–4 and 43–8; George Hunsinger, 'A Tale of Two Simultaneities: Justification and Sanctification in Calvin and Barth', in *Conversing with Barth*, ed. John C. McDowell and Mike Higton (Aldershot: Ashgate, 2004), pp. 76–9; Bruce McCormack, 'Participation in God, Yes, Deification, No: Two Modern Protestant Responses to an Ancient Question', in *Denkwürdiges Geheimnis: Beiträge Zur Gotteslehre. Festschrift Für Eberhard Jüngel Zum 70. Geburtstag*, ed. Ingolf U. Dalfterth, Johannes Fischer and Hans-Peter Grosshans (Tübingen: Mohr Siebeck, 2004); Jeannine Michele Graham, *Representation and Substitution in the Atonement Theologies of Dorothee Sölle, John Macquarrie and Karl Barth* (New York: Peter Lang, 2005), pp. 318–20 and 396–7; and Paul T. Nimmo, *Being in Action: The Theological Shape of Barth's Ethical Vision* (London: T&T Clark, 2007), pp. 100–2, 173–9 and 152–3.

57   CD IV/2, p. 271.

58   CD IV/2, p. 432.

Barth's presentation of Jesus Christ, as the human for other humans, clearly parallels Bonhoeffer's thought, as does glimpsing something of God's divinity in Christ's humanity. As Bonhoeffer writes in his outline for a book:

> Jesus only 'is there for others.' Jesus's 'being-for-others' is the experience of transcendence! Only through this liberation from self, through this 'being-for-others' unto death, do omnipotence, omniscience, and omnipresence come into being. Faith is participating in this being of Jesus. (Becoming human [Menschwerdung], cross, resurrection.) Our relationship with God is no 'religious' relationship to some highest, most powerful, and best being imaginable – that is no genuine transcendence. Instead, our relationship to God is a new life in 'being there for others,' through participation in the being of Jesus.[59]

As the model of our own humanity, one is able to see in Christ an existence focused on others, rather than on personal salvation or on religious ritual. The very person of Christ does away with religion not only in who He is, but also in the necessary reframing of the doctrine of God that the incarnation brings about, and in the re-orientation of humans away from individualism and towards co-humanity.[60]

LIGHT AND LIGHTS AND SECULAR PARABLES OF THE KINGDOM

Bonhoeffer's criticism that Barth did not develop his critique of religion into positive theological engagements, with no discussion of religionless theological concepts or non-religious approaches to the Bible, finds its response in Barth's constructive discussion of 'the Light and the lights' and 'the secular parables of the Kingdom' in *Church Dogmatics* IV/3, §69.[61] It is perhaps in this paragraph that we glimpse the closest Barth comes to offering an optative account of his theological indicatives of §17. Indeed, according to Charles Marsh, Bonhoeffer was Barth's primary inspiration for this part paragraph,[62] and the themes addressed

---

59   LPP, p. 501.

60   On the latter point, see Elizabeth Kent, 'Embodied Evangelicalism: The Body of Christ and the Christian Body', in *New Perspectives for Evangelical Theology: Engaging with God, Scripture and the World*, ed. Tom Greggs (Abingdon: Routledge, 2010).

61   For a more detailed discussion of this paragraph, see Thompson, 'Religious Diversity, Christian Doctrine and Karl Barth', pp. 11–18; the excellent discussion of this theme in Hunsinger, *How to Read Karl Barth*, pp. 234–80; and Glenn Chestnutt, 'The Secular Parables of the Kingdom', paper presented at the Society for the Study of Theology (Leeds, 2006).

62   Marsh, *Reclaiming Dietrich Bonhoeffer*, p. 27, albeit I am not sure that the evidence fully stacks up for this point.

within this section of Barth's work certainly respond theologically to many of the concerns that Bonhoeffer raised from his prison cell.[63]

Barth's discussion takes place within his discussion of Jesus' prophetic office. Barth discusses how Jesus Christ lives as both Lord and Servant, which he defines as 'the absolutely solid co-existence between the Creator and His creature, between God and man, to which we have so far confined our reference.'[64] This determination, furthermore, has a purpose: 'Jesus Christ does not live for Himself. His divine-human existence as divine-human act . . . is not an end in itself.'[65] For Barth, the effects of this prophetic work of reconciliation are almost immeasurable for theology:

> Even the formal and general truth must be considered that God and man are in any case bound and live together. As Jesus Christ lives, God and man live in this conjunction. We do not have God here and man there; God is the God of man and man the man of God. This is the epitome of the whole order of creation. This order, too, has its dignity, validity, power and persistence in the fact that Jesus Christ lives. But it has its content and fulness in the fact that the life lived by Jesus Christ is the life of grace, that it is the life of the Saviour.[66]

As Saviour, Jesus is the one attested in scripture as having lived, and (crucially) also as the one who continues to live: His history was one which took place in order that His history might continue to take place. In faith, the believer lives because of the fact that Jesus Himself lives (and not vice versa).[67] It is as this living one that Jesus 'shines out' and 'illuminates'.[68]

Barth develops his exposition of this theme by considering concretely the application of the definite article to Jesus' title of *the* light of life. For him, this means positively that Jesus is the light of life 'in all its fulness', and negatively that there is 'no other light of life outside or alongside His, outside or alongside the light which He is.'[69] This latter statement determines that the singularity and uniqueness of Jesus' being the light of life can never be undermined by any suggestion that there may be other lights of life, even if of lesser status, to the one that Jesus himself possesses and is.[70] None of this, however, aggrandizes the Christian: 'The statement that Jesus Christ is the one Word of God has really nothing whatever to

---

63 It also has its place in a discussion of the theologization of a critique of religion as Barth sees the need to protect the discussion from falling victim to the critique of Feuerbach; see CD IV/3, pp. 72–85.

64 CD IV/3, p. 41.

65 CD IV/3, p. 41.

66 CD IV/3, p. 43.

67 CD IV/3, pp. 44–5.

68 CD IV/3, p. 46.

69 CD IV/3, p. 86.

70 CD IV/3, p. 87. Barth compares this to Muslim and Jewish understandings of Jesus.

do with the arbitrary exaltation and self-glorification of the Christian in relation to
other men, of the Church in relation to other institutions, or of Christianity in relation to other conceptions.'[71] By virtue of this christocentricity, Barth is able to
affirm that this radical exclusivity of Christ's prophetic office relativizes the place
of the Christian religion: 'the criticism expressed in the exclusiveness of the statement affects, limits and relativizes the prophecy of Christians and the Church no
less than the many other prophecies, lights and words relativized and replaced by
it.'[72] Looking to Christ and affirming His unique status brings with it a reduction
of the status of the church and of Christianity as much as it reduces the status of
any other word. While Barth is happy to affirm that there is 'direct witness to Jesus
Christ in the words of the prophets and apostles',[73] he goes on to assert that recognizing the one Word of God does not mean that 'in the Bible, the Church and the
world there are not other words which are quite notable in their way, other lights
which are quite clear and other revelations which are quite real.'[74] Furthermore,
Barth continues:

> Nor does it follow from our statement that every word spoken outside the
> circle of the Bible and the Church is a word of false prophecy and therefore
> valueless, empty and corrupt, that all the lights which rise and shine in this
> outer sphere are misleading and all the revelations are necessarily untrue.[75]

For Barth, on the basis of Christ's prophetic office, there are other words outside
of the preached word of the church and outside of the words of the Bible, which
are true prophecy – words which exist in the outer sphere of creation in which the
universality of Christ's message is also heard.

Barth unpacks the meaning of this assertion, discussing the relationship between
these other words and the one Word of God. According to him, these words are
true and genuine prophecy when they are 'in the closest material and substantial
conformity and agreement with the one Word of God Himself and therefore with
that of His one Prophet Jesus Christ.'[76] However, there remains the need for these
words, even as true words, to distinguish themselves from Jesus Christ, and Barth
recognizes the difference there is between them and the one Word of God in Jesus
Christ. Nevertheless, according to Barth, 'it must have pleased the Word of God

---

71   CD IV/3, p. 91.
72   CD IV/3, p. 91. Cf. Hunsinger, *How to Read Karl Barth*, p. 244: 'The confession of Jesus Christ
as the Word of God . . . has nothing to do with an arbitrary self-glorification of Christianity, the church,
or the Christian. It is strictly a christological statement . . . As such it does not entail any exaltation of
the Christian over the non-Christian, but rather an important bond between them. For the statement
confronts the Christian and non-Christian alike with "the one truth superior" to them both.'
73   CD IV/3, p. 96.
74   CD IV/3, p. 97. Hunsinger, *How to Read Karl Barth*, p. 245: 'All human words as such are relativized by the Word and thus joined in a certain solidarity.'
75   CD IV/3, p. 97.
76   CD IV/3, p. 111.

to allow itself to be in some sense reflected and reproduced in the words of these men. This Word must have demonstrated to these men and their words the grace of its real presence.'[77] These words are not responsible for their own capacity to say anything of the one Word of God; only the Word of God brings about this function of bearing testimony to Him.[78]

Barth uses the existence of parables in the New Testament as the basis and authority of his discussion of these words, and further argues that the existence of such true words are events which have always been perceived in the proclamation of the Old and New Testaments.[79] Indeed, Barth even advocates that the Christian community, too, utters such 'secondary forms of the Word of God'.[80] Outside the Christian community, there are, however, also parables of the kingdom, through which Jesus speaks. Barth states:

> [T]he community which lives by the one Word of the one Prophet Jesus Christ, and is commissioned and empowered to proclaim this Word of His in the world, not only may but must accept the fact that there are such words [through which the Word speaks] and that it must hear them too, notwithstanding its life by this one Word and its commission to preach it.[81]

It is necessary, therefore, for the church to recognize that there are words which correspond to the Word spoken outwith the walls of the community of the church. Furthermore, for Barth these words from the secular world can genuinely address the community of the church. According to him,

> We can count on it as and because we come from the resurrection of Jesus Christ, from the revelation of the humiliation of God's own Son to human sin and perdi-tion as this has been crowned by God the Father, from the revelation of man's exaltation to living fellowship with God as this has been achieved in the person of the Son, in short, from the revelation of the reconciliation of the world with God effected in Jesus Christ. It was to the One who, in virtue of His revelation in His resurrection, was and is and will be the Reconciler, that the history of Israel moved, and the prophets of Israel, and later the apostles, bore witness. It is in Him as this Reconciler of the world that the community believes.[82]

Here, one may see some degree of connection with Barth's christocentric doctrine of election: 'In Him there has taken place the co-ordination of the whole world with God in disclosure, condemnation, yet also remission of the sin of man. He

---

77 CD IV/3, p. 111.
78 CD IV/3, p. 112.
79 CD IV/3, p. 113.
80 CD IV/3, p. 113.
81 CD IV/3, pp. 114–15.
82 CD IV/3, p. 116.

has taken over the rulership of the world.'[83] In affirming that Jesus Christ is the one who was and is and is to come, Barth develops the implications of this thus:

> [W]e recognise and confess that not we alone, nor the community which, following the prophets and apostles, believes in Him and loves Him and hopes in Him, but *de iure* all men and all creation derive from His cross, from the reconciliation accomplished in Him, and are ordained to be the theatre of His glory and therefore the recipients and bearers of His Word. In the very light of this narrower and smaller sphere of the Bible and the Church, we cannot possibly think that He cannot speak, and His speech cannot be attested, outside this sphere.[84]

This is not, however, any form of natural theology, but instead the self-impartation of the triune God. From both the secular world and from the church, 'Jesus Christ can raise up extraordinary witnesses to speak true words of this very different order.'[85] Barth does not consider the existence of a whole world of non-believers to be any limitation to Christ's sovereignty: 'For we must not forget that, while man may deny God, according to the Word of reconciliation God does not deny man.'[86] Because of this, for Barth (who grounds the basis of his argument on scripture), '[e]ven from the mouth of Balaam the well-known voice of the Good Shepherd may sound, and it is not to be ignored in spite of its sinister origin.'[87] Barth utilizes the image of Jesus as the Word of God being the centre of a circle, yet he sees that centre as constitutive of the whole periphery.[88] He argues that it is necessary for Christians to be prepared to see the sovereignty of God at work in spheres outside of the church, whether or not Christians can understand this: even secular occurrences can be 'segments of that periphery concretely orientated from its centre and towards its totality, as signs and attestations of the lordship of the one prophecy of Jesus Christ'.[89] In advocating this case, Barth notes that even in the church it is as a result of the miraculous grace of God, which is greater than all of the ineptitude of the church, that true words are spoken in ecclesial settings, and wonders whether it might be on the basis of the same miracle that the words are spoken outside of the church as well.

Barth then turns to language of Christ being the light of life, and the existence of lesser lights. Barth is clear that Jesus Christ was, is and will be the one, true and only light of life. However, the one light relates to particular and individual lights

---

83   CD IV/3, p. 116.
84   CD IV/3, p. 117. Cf. here, Hauerwas, *With the Grain of the Universe*.
85   CD IV/3, p. 118.
86   CD IV/3, p. 119.
87   CD IV/3, p. 119.
88   CD IV/3, p. 122.
89   CD IV/3, p. 124.

which exist in history, in a qualified sense, offering words and even truth.[90] These are true only in relation to Jesus Christ. But as the theatre of the glory of God, with its basis on the election of Jesus Christ, one can state that

> the creaturely world, the cosmos, the nature given to man in his sphere and the nature of this sphere, has also as such its own lights and truths and therefore its own speech and words. That the world was and is and will be, and what and how it was and is and will be, thanks to the faithfulness of its Creator, is declared and attested by it and may thus be perceived and heard and considered. Its witness and declaration may be missed or more or less dreadfully misunderstood. But it is given with the same persistence as creation itself endures thanks to the faithfulness of its Creator.[91]

This is the case regardless of whether humans recognize this matter and regardless of human sin. The truth and basis of these lights are found in Jesus Christ:

> [B]y the shining of the one true light of life, by the self-revelation of God in Jesus Christ, they are exposed and characterised as lights, words and truths of the created cosmos, and therefore as created lights in distinction from this one light. Yet as such they are not extinguished by this light, nor are their force and significance destroyed.[92]

While they certainly do not bring as much brightness as the one light of Jesus Christ, the lights nevertheless provide illumination for the creation.[93] These lights are not revelations strictly, as no faith is needed to grasp them; they are instead 'only an obvious and almost inevitable perception'.[94] They are lights in which, however, the light of Christ is reflected.[95]

Barth is clearly determined not to fall back into what he perceives to be the old traps of natural theology. However, he does desire to find the correct way in which to speak of the *logoi* of the world, which have their basis only in the *logos* who is Jesus Christ.[96] His work on the parables of the kingdom and the light of the life and the lesser lights seeks to find a way in which to affirm the world's own being as a place in which truths of God can be given. This is a long way from any possible 'positivism of revelation'. In the world, one can discover something of God.

---

90 CD IV/3, pp. 135–6.
91 CD IV/3, p. 139.
92 CD IV/3, p. 139.
93 CD IV/3, p. 141.
94 CD IV/3, p. 143.
95 CD IV/3, p. 153.
96 CD IV/3, p. 159.

PROVISIONAL SUMMARY: MOTIFS IN RELIGIONLESSNESS

Having outlined presentations of Barth and Bonhoeffer on the engagement in theologizing the critique of religion, what features is it possible to note from the preceding chapters for this theology in order to take them forward into formative discussion? The following are suggestive motifs that will prove recurrent themes in the discussions that follow in Parts II and III of this book.[97]

A theology which takes the critique of religion seriously will in the first instance be (1) *radically christocentric*. In seeking to understand who God is, it will necessarily look to Jesus Christ, and seek to learn from Him. In doing this, such a theology will seek to affirm the humanity of God rather than any perceived innate divinity in humans. It will be a theology that realizes that the veil is truly rent, and God is most visibly seen, in the dead human corpse of the human who died for other humans, hanging on a cross. Jesus Christ, as one who stood in opposition to religious authorities and rulers, as the one who was never a member of a priestly class and never created a priestly class,[98] and as the one in whom there is no longer any distance between God and humanity, will be the governing rule of a theology which takes the critique of religion seriously. Revelation will be understood not simply as a 'thing' in relation to Him, but as the act and event of God by which He is known to individuals and communities by the power of the Spirit.

Through this radical christocentrism, this theology will be (2) *christocentrically world-affirming*. In realizing that Jesus Christ is God's eternal Yes to creation as something other than Himself, and in realizing that this Yes is the beginning of all of God's works and ways, a theology which takes the critique of religion seriously will affirm the world in its worldliness as the creation of God, the blueprint of which finds itself in God's eternal self-election in Jesus Christ. Far from any hint of dualism, this theology will recognize the implications for the world of God self-determining Himself to be human in the person of Jesus Christ. As another distinct from Him, creation is the self-willed expression of God's desire to be for another. Creation in all of its variety and particularity must be seen as having its determination in the eternal will, decree and overflowing love of God to be for

---

97   'A theology that follows Bonhoeffer's inspirations in reading the "signs of the times" and in seeing the theological diagnosis of the religious situation as a central element of the theological task cannot simply repeat Bonhoeffer's diagnosis of *his* time and apply it to *our* time as if nothing had changed. Rather, it seems to be much more in keeping with the spirit of Bonhoeffer's theology to attempt a careful description of the phenomena and to try to assess them theologically' (Schwöbel, '"Religion" and "Religionlessness"' in *Letters and Papers from Prison*: A Perspective for Religious Pluralism?', p. 176). In having described and learnt from Barth and Bonhoeffer on religion, this book now seeks to consider how their writing can aid the current times. The motifs listed below seek to be pieces which will aid the building of a bridge between the circumstances of Bonhoeffer and Barth and those of today.

98   For an interesting discussion of this theme, see Herbert Haag, *Clergy and Laity: Did Jesus Want a Two-Tier Church?* (London: Burns and Oates, 1998).

another, personified in the second person of the trinity, who bears the name of Jesus Christ. Because of this, there can be no singular prioritization of those who are religious or of the church since God wills and elects *all* creation, and in His work of reconciliation overcomes the negative aspects of created existence.

A theology which takes the criticism of religion seriously will also be orientated on (3) *God's promeity and reconciliatory work and nature*. God is not simply for the world in a general or abstract manner, but is for the world in the works of creation, reconciliation and redemption. This is not, however, to fall back into a preoccupation with personalized and ego-orientated expressions of salvation. Rather, it is to recognize God's work of reconciling the whole of creation in Christ, the *Pantokrator*. Rather than an engagement in speculative and abstract games regarding the nature of God, a religionless expression of Christian theology will seek to emphasize the God who is known by His acts and events for all creation. This determines that, even in its brokenness and sinfulness, creation is the creation which God wills ultimately to redeem, rather than ultimately to destroy. God's Yes to creation is always louder than any No He might utter to aspects of fallen creation.

This theology seeks to articulate (4) a *pneumatological realness*, emphasizing the work of God the Spirit in relating the ways and works of God to creation, human communities and individuals. The event of the giving of the Spirit is the basis of all discussions of the reception of the revelation of God, and it is only as a dense expression of this reception that the church has its being. The church is the place in which the Spirit may be deeply at work, but the Spirit who blows wherever He wills cannot simply be bound to the church. *Extra muros ecclesiae*, the Spirit is also at work, relating creation to God, and enabling humans to participate actively in God's ways with the world. This is not to say that a theology against religion has a place for natural theology, as if God could be known apart from God's self-revelation, but it is to say that the power of the Spirit is such that the miracle of revelation can take place in which ever way God chooses. Wherever one can perceive the fruits of the Spirit, one can imagine the operation of the Spirit being present in the world. This is not as a result of various religious expressions, as if these condition the Spirit into being present, but is rather as a result of the multiply dense presences of the Spirit acting in creation. The 'realness' of this aspect of this kind of theology rests in its this-worldliness. Realizing that God humbles Himself to engage with creation, it is necessary to affirm the particularity of creation even in the acts and events of the work of God the Spirit. The Spirit works within creation in order that creation and God can remain fully and respectively creation and God, while still uniting the two to each other.[99] The Spirit enables creation to be the creation it was always intended to be, rather than

99   On the radical dedivinization (*radikale Entgötterung*) of the world and the operation of the Spirit in respect of this, see Hart, *Regarding Barth*, pp. 11–17.

removing those who seek to live an 'otherworldly' life from creation. There is no establishment of a religious ideal in this theology, but only of a pneumatological reality within the particularity of human and creaturely existence. This theology, therefore, (5) preserves *created, human and historical particularity*.

There will be (6) a certain degree and affirmation of *mystery* in this theology. This is not a mystery which signifies a groping after answers in the darkness, or a filling of the chasms of human ignorance with the letters G-O-D. Rather, it will be a mystery grounded in the majesty and otherness of God the Creator. While the concept of God can be used to plug ever decreasing gaps of knowledge with a *deus ex machina*, the overpowering glory of God is such that His brightness is blinding, and ever more glorious and worthy of praise. As a result of this, a theology which takes seriously the critique of religion must be a theology which is (7) fiercely *anidolatrous* in its articulation of God. God cannot be confused with a simple idol of human religiosity nor the projection of human desires and ego. The true Godness of God is such that God should not be confused with either a spatial localizing of an idol or a human religious imagining of a metaphysical concept.[100] God cannot be identified with a space or a community in which God might be presumed to be, but is affirmed as the God of all the world, who is the Creator and therefore beyond all human imaginings.[101] This means that theology should not confuse God with religion, with the implication that one can see lines of continuity between Christianity as a religion and other faiths as well: like Christianity, these faiths, too, belong to the category of religion, and the nature of God relativizes Christianity no less than it does these other expressions of religionists.

This theology is a theology, therefore, which is (8) *unwilling to engage in articulating binaries*. It is unwilling to draw lines too sharply around the boundaries of the church (in which God is seen as present) and all else in the world (in which, somehow, He is not). Instead, taking seriously the critique of religion will mean that theology (9) *cannot so neatly differentiate between secular and sacred spaces*, but must recognize the one Lord Jesus Christ, the incarnate Son of God, who does not take the flesh of an institutional priest but simply of a human being. This Jesus did not engage in creating religious binaries,[102] nor indeed in creating a religion, but engaged in breaking down many of these divisions, mixing with women, the ritually unclean, Samaritans, and ordinary women and men in their daily lives. He told stories about such ordinary lives (about shepherds and lamp stands and lost

---

100　Cf. Schwöbel, 'Theology', *Cambridge Companion to Karl Barth*, ed. John Webster (Cambridge: CUP, 2000), p. 26: 'The "beyond" of God is not the "beyond" of the mind.'

101　For an excellent recent articulation of the doctrine of *creatio ex nihilo* in relation to the doctrine of God, see John Webster, 'Trinity and Creation', *International Journal of Systematic Theology* 12, no. 1 (2010), though one should note that this moves significantly away from Barth's theology in CD II/2.

102　On the issues of salvation and eschatology, in which it might seem that Jesus did create sharp binaries, the reader is directed to Chapter 5 of this book.

coins) to tell people about God. A theology which takes the critique of religion seriously must be one that is thus concerned with life in all its fullness, not only content to meet people in their religious spheres or in moments of existential weakness, but concerned to meet people in the fullness of their lives, and to deal with (10) the *whole person*.

Some words of Bonhoeffer seem apposite to conclude this section of the book. He writes simply but arrestingly: 'Jesus calls not to a new religion but to life.'[103] It is this calling of Jesus to life that a theology which seeks to follow the trajectories of Bonhoeffer and Barth with regard to the critique of religion should seek to follow. In the following two parts of this book, it is this calling to life, in conjunction with the motifs outlined above, that will be considered in a formative and constructive religionless Christianity in relation to a complexly secular and pluralist world.

---

103   LPP, p. 482.

Part II

DOCTRINE AFTER CHRISTENDOM:
SECULARISM, SALVATION AND
THE CHURCH

Chapter 5

SAVIOUR OF ALL: SOTERIOLOGY AGAINST RELIGION

The Enlightenment's preoccupation with individualism and its advocacy of personal choice brought with it a religious preoccupation with salvation as an eternal and individual self-preservation.[1] Religious pluralism (intra- and inter-religiously) has provided conditions in which there is a choice of religious self expression, and this choice is often expressed as a decision based upon a body of knowledge to which one assents.[2] Assent to this knowledge then brings with it particular benefits, which are contingent on the choices made. This approach is particularly identifiable in pietistic forms of church expression (across all denominations) in which individual relationship with God has the primary and determining factor of bringing with it the benefits of salvation. In its worst form, religious expression becomes the ultimate assertion of ego, as a self-preserved, individual entity to be immortalized, and the practice of religion becomes a practice aimed at self-preservation, comparable to the pre-occupation of Western society with anti-aging devices and techniques: a regular dose of religion becomes the botox injection for the soul. As a result of this, religious practitioners are seen as being inward facing, self-interested and self-motivated, and religious practice is aimed at preservation of the ego of the religionist, still willing to damn the other (either a religionist of another tradition or a non-religionist) to not receiving the benefits of her particular religious group. Examples of this thinking abound in presentations of Christianity.

---

1   On faith and individualism, see Kent, 'Embodied Evangelicalism: The Body of Christ and the Christian Body'. Also worthy of note here is Thiselton's comment: 'The Enlightenment and post-Enlightenment philosophical discussion of grace . . . transposed Augustine's varied writings into the formulation of an abstract, generalized, theological doctrine' (Anthony C. Thiselton, *The Hermeneutics of Doctrine* (Grand Rapids: William B. Eerdmans, 2007), p. 8). One might alternatively trace these tendencies back to the Reformation itself; see, for example, Martin, *Reflections on Sociology and Theology*, p. 121.

2   It may well be this which explains the high proportion of evangelicals in the United States: as a country without a state religious affiliation, the conditions for Christian pluralistic proliferation are well set, with the result that expressions of faith which emphasize the very *choice* of religion are allowed to flourish in the societal conditions. This compares to the European system in which, until relatively recent times, the principle of *cuius regio, eius religio* reigned supreme.

They are present in the type of preaching which presents the choice of Christianity as bringing with it the benefit of personal self-preservation. Missionary expressions of Christianity are often aimed at this bringing in of others for the benefit of eternal life:[3] often mission events (even those with a social justice focus) also hope to create converts as – if not a direct – an indirect consequence of the activity, a point that preoccupations with numbers in the congregation only serves to underline.[4] Simply looking at posters outside of churches with slogans aimed at inducing some form of choice demonstrates this point: 'If your religion won't bring you to church, it won't get you to heaven'; 'Free coffee; ever lasting life; yes, membership has its privileges'; or 'Jesus – your get out of hell free card'.

The dominant presentation of Christian faith is fixed in its binary and separationist framework. Traditionally, Christian theology has presented a category of people who are inside to God's salvific plan, determined by some form of choice expressed sacramentally, piestically or charismatically;[5] and a second category of humanity which is excluded from this, resulting either in an eternal preservation in hell, or in annihilation.[6] Despite the vast array of different forms of expression of this binary approach to salvation, including discussions around the pious who have never heard the gospel and children who die in infancy,[7] the overarching theme present in each of the expressions of them is the issue of personal and individual self-preservation for one group of people in comparison to annihilation, non-receipt of God's blessings, or everlasting torture for the other section of people. The insular and self-orientated nature of much religious belief is not difficult to identify. Feuerbach surely need not make his case strongly.

In societies now marked by a religious and non-religious pluralism, the need to discuss faith in this way is very much a contemporary phenomenon. From

---

3   This is no less the case in so-called 'fresh expressions' of Christianity, which continue to work within a binary, and for all of its world-affirming discourse, largely works on the basis of finding mechanisms to get people 'inside' in order to see church growth: they are heavily mission-orientated, and betray in that way the binary logics which underlie them, even in their reimagining and broadening of who the insiders might be. One can see an example of this sort of thinking in John Drane: John Drane, *The Mcdonaldization of the Church: Spirituality, Creativity, and the Future of the Church* (London: Darton, Longman & Todd, 2000); and John Drane, *After Mcdonaldization: Mission, Ministry and Christian Discipleship in an Age of Uncertainty* (London: Darton, Longman & Todd, 2008).

4   This is a theme which is addressed more fully in Chapter 6 of this book.

5   Whether the basis of this separation arises out of a sacramental exclusion or the public confession of a *credo* or (even) speaking in tongues is a secondary issue to the exclusivist separation that exists.

6   On annihilationism and conditional immortality, see John W. Wenham, 'The Case for Conditional Immortality', in *Universalism and the Doctrine of Hell. Papers Presented at the Fourth Edinburgh Conference on Christian Dogmatics 1991*, ed. Nigel M. de S. Cameron (Carlisle: Paternoster, 1992); and George Hunsinger, *Disruptive Grace. Studies in the Theology of Karl Barth* (Grand Rapids and Cambridge: Eerdmanns, 2000), pp. 239–42. Notably, the 1995 Church of England's Doctrine Commission, while rejecting hell, affirmed 'total non-being' in its description of the end point of the non-believer.

7   Such as in Nigel M. de S. Cameron, 'Universalism and the Logic of Revelation', in *The Best in Theology*, Vol. 3, ed. J. I. Packer (Carol Stream, Illinois: Christianity Today Inc., 1989).

Constantine's adoption of Christianity as the religion of Rome until the twentieth century,[8] there was a dominantly homogenous religious culture for people, who themselves lived lives marked by a localism surrounded by people of the same faith. Where there was religious variance, this was more commonly intra-religious (most obviously at the time of the Reformation),[9] and it was usually met by an aggressive (and, as in the case of the wars of religion and the crusades, violent) clash of exclusivisms in order to preserve the dominant mono-religious culture of any given state or continent. As a result of this situation, most people were not, until relatively recent times, confronted with the reality of religious or non-religious others.[10]

This dominantly homogenous situation brings with it important theological implications for binary and separationist expressions of salvation. Worshipping in a culture in which there is only one religious tradition, or in which one's interaction takes place within only one religious tradition, determines that an engagement with those outside of the tradition is, if not altogether impossible, a relatively exotic non-issue: it is easier to damn the vague idea of a person than the person who lives next door. A danger exists in transposing theology expressed within a dominantly religiously mono-cultural setting to a pluralist setting that a theology aimed at upholding or increasing the intensity of practice for the homogenously religious faithful is directed at those outside of that community, with whom it was not primarily, originally or concretely concerned: rather than being about the practitioners of the said religion, such theology comes to regard practitioners of another or no religion. Furthermore, when attending to theologians who work within a homogeneous religious setting, one can notice that, even within the stark binary presentations that they offer, a wider hope does exist. For example, while Calvin was always reticent about predicting the number of the elect, even his smallest estimates vastly outstripped any possibility of election being confined to

---

8   Morwenna Ludlow notes that discussion of universal salvation has tended to take place outside of the homogeneous domination of Christianity in any given society; see Morwenna Ludlow, *Universal Salvation: Eschatology in the Thought of Gregory of Nyssa and Karl Rahner*, ed. Maurice Wiles (Oxford: OUP, 2000), p. 8. On the history of universal salvation more broadly, see Richard Bauckham, 'Universalism: A Historic Survey', *Themelios* 4, no. 2 (1978); Morwenna Ludlow, 'Universalism in the History of Christianity', in *Universal Salvation? The Current Debate*, ed. Robin A. Parry and Christopher H. Partridge (Carlisle: Paternoster, 2003).

9   Clearly, there were also inter-religious clashes, most famously surrounding the Holy Land and the clash of Christian and Muslim empires.

10   Even in intra-religiously heterogeneous settings, which were not uncommon following the Reformation, communities of one denomination or another arose, often with different school and education systems. As the situation in Northern Ireland demonstrates (albeit perhaps to an extreme), it was not unusual to live in an intra-religiously pluralistic setting but live, socialize and be educated only with members of one's own denomination. On the shift in the British religious situation, see Grace Davie, *Religion in Britain since 1945* (Oxford: Blackwell, 1994).

the Reformed of Geneva.[11] Indeed, one of Calvin's primary motivating factors in his disagreement with Rome was that, for him, there could be no straight forward parity between the visible and the invisible church:[12] who could know what number of members of the invisible church there were? This approach of recognizing the broader hope in relation to the primary invisibility of the elect has continued (though, no doubt for pastoral reasons quite quietly)[13] throughout the Reformed tradition. Even A. A. Hodge, in the six points regarding heaven that he believed can be known in the present,[14] lists as number five:

> Although heaven can only be entered by the holy, yet such, we are assured, is the infinite provision made for human salvation, and such the intense love for human sinners therein exhibited, that the multitude of the redeemed will be incomparably greater than the number of the lost. My father [i.e. Charles Hodge], at the close of his long life spent in the defence of Calvinism, wrote on one of his conference papers, in trembling characters, a little while before he died, 'I am fully persuaded that the vast majority of the human race will share in the beatitudes and glories of our Lord's redemption.'[15]

Not only, therefore, is it inappropriate to interject the assumptions of the theology of a religiously homogeneous society onto today's pluralistic setting, but it is also important to recognize that even in what one might expect to be the most binary expressions of Christian theology, the hope and expectation that exists for those outside the religiously homogeneous society is indicative of a wider ripple of hope beyond the religiously 'acceptable'.

In articulating a theology against religion in the contemporary world setting, it would be helpful, therefore, to move beyond religious articulations of self-preservation in discussions of salvation. This is not to say that the Christian *Heilsgeschichte* should not play the central role it has done in theological discourse.[16] Rather, it is to say that in articulating a soteriology in the contemporary setting, theology must be alert to the trappings of religion, and prepared to

---

11   See John T. McNeill, ed. *Calvin Institutes of the Christian Religion* (Louisville: Westminster John Knox, 2006), pp. 47, 61 and 868.

12   Cf. ToC, pp. 177–86 & 200–1.

13   On the way in which pastoral concerns affect the preaching of universalism, see Tom Greggs, 'Exclusivist or Universalist? Origen "the Wise Steward of the Word" (Commrom V.1.7) and the Issue of Genre', *International Journal of Systematic Theology* 9, no. 3 (2007).

14   A. A. Hodge, *Evangelical Theology: A Course of Popular Lectures* (London: Banner of Truth, 1976), pp. 399ff.

15   Ibid., p. 401. I am grateful to Dr Steve Holmes for alerting me to this point.

16   In this way, the universalism advocated in this chapter is 'Christian' rather than 'pluralistic' universalism. See Trevor Hart, 'Universalism: Two Distinct Types', in *Universalism and the Doctrine of Hell. Papers Presented at the Fourth Edinburgh Conference on Christian Dogmatics 1991*, ed. Nigel M. de S. Cameron (Carlisle: Paternoster, 1992).

critique religion's effect on Christian articulations of the reconciling work of God for the whole world. Theology should not identify salvation with a select section of the religious in society, but should instead see salvation as being God's reconciling of the *world* to Himself. A soteriology against religion is one seen in the work of Christ as expressed in Colossians:

> For in him all the fullness of God was pleased to dwell, and through him God was pleased to reconcile to himself all things, whether on earth or in heaven, by making peace through the blood of his cross.[17]

In this chapter, just one possible attempt at outlining a soteriology against religion will take place, surrounding the idea of Christ as saviour of all. In advocating this, the chapter will examine universal salvation as a potential version of a non-personalized salvation which still nevertheless takes the salvific work of Christ to be the centre point of theological speech. The victorious work of Christ will be considered as the basis for this universalized approach to the doctrine of salvation. The chapter will then go on to consider the way in which certain themes associated with salvation and eschatology should be considered, looking particularly at the co-sinfulness of all humanity, repentance, demythologizing hell and attending to the present.

UNIVERSAL SALVATION AS A NON-PERSONALIZED VERSION OF SALVATION

In Bonhoeffer's letter of 5 May 1942, he seeks to define what he means by interpreting in a religious sense. He suggests the following:

> It means, in my opinion, to speak metaphysically, on the one hand, and, on the other hand, individualistically. Neither way is appropriate, either for the biblical message or for people today. Hasn't the individualistic question of saving our personal souls almost faded away for most of us? Isn't it our impression that there are really more important things than this question (– perhaps not more important than this *matter*, but certainly more important than the *question*!?)? I know it sounds outrageous to say that, but after all, isn't it fundamentally biblical? Does the question of saving one's soul even come up in the Old Testament? Isn't God's righteousness and kingdom on earth the centre of everything? And isn't Rom. 3:24ff. the culmination of the view that God alone is righteous, rather than an individualistic doctrine of salvation? What matters is not the beyond, but this world, how it is created and preserved, is given

---

17   Col. 1.19–20.

laws, reconciled, and renewed. What is beyond this world is meant, in the gospel, to be there *for* this world – not in the anthropocentric sense of liberal, mystical, pietistic, ethical theology, but in the biblical sense of the creation and the incarnation, crucifixion, and resurrection of Jesus Christ.[18]

While salvation itself, Bonhoeffer proffers, is immensely important, the preoccupation with personalized and individualized salvation is problematic, along with metaphysical presentations of salvation.[19] To interpret the Bible religiously, for him, is to interpret it in a way which associates its message with the preoccupation with the continued existence of the individual. The question arises, however, as to how it is that one can offer an account of Christian theology which recognizes that salvation (the *matter* itself) is the most important issue for the person of faith, but that the preoccupation with saving one's soul (the *question*) is not as important. The answer to this question might be found in a version of theology which recognizes God as the saviour of all of the world, rather than simply some chosen, special, individual and religious few.

A theology which takes universal salvation as the basis for a soteriology against religion must, however, as Bonhoeffer indicates, arise out of the central narrative of the Christian tradition: 'the biblical sense of the creation and of the incarnation, crucifixion, and resurrection of Jesus Christ.'[20] To decrease the emphasis on individual salvation is to articulate a more (and not less) Christian articulation of salvation, as the emphasis shifts from whether the person is inside or outside God's salvific purposes to the very nature of God's work of reconciling the world to Himself: a christocentric account of salvation shifts the focus from an anthropocentric view of God's work, which makes salvation contingent upon the choice or intellectual assent of human beings, and makes God properly the subject of salvation. In relation to an articulation of salvation which does not emphasize continued egoism, one is brought away from self-interested religious presentations of salvation and back to a truly theological focus, appropriate to the God to whom salvation belongs.[21]

This theme is one which occupies Barth's discussions of salvation as well. Barth's primary concern is the person and work of Jesus Christ, in which humans share. His doctrine of election refocuses the electing work of God onto the one elect, Jesus Christ, in whom humanity's election has its foundation, basis and hope. In Jesus Christ's humanity, our humanity is elect from and to all eternity. Election, for Barth, is therefore the basis of the Gospel. It is love in its most glorious forms, in God's condescending, patient, free, overflowing grace.[22] For Barth, there is only one who

---

18   LPP, pp. 372–3, emphasis original.
19   The concern over a metaphysical interpretation of salvation underlies the concern that Barth has in his engagement with Berkouwer; see CD IV/3, pp. 173–80. A more detailed discussion of this engagement and its significance follows below.
20   LPP, p. 373.
21   Rev. 7.10.
22   CD II/2, p. 10.

is rejected, since Jesus self-elects to bear the rejection and condemnation that humanity deserves. Therefore, Barth is able to state that election 'is not a mixed message of joy and terror, salvation and damnation. Originally and finally it is not dialectical but non-dialectical.'[23] Radically redescribing the doctrine of election, Barth does not divide human beings into two religious categories of the elect and the reject, and God's work of salvation into two works (one of gracious saving and the other of holy damnation), but seeks to present a doctrine of election which is altogether Yes:[24] the doctrine of election is always and altogether gospel for Barth.[25]

This christocentric realigning of the doctrine of election has universal implications for all of humanity.[26] Barth writes of Christ: 'His election is the original and all-inclusive election; the election which is absolutely unique, but which in this very uniqueness is universally meaningful and efficacious, because it is the election of Him who Himself elects.'[27] Focusing on the original election of Jesus Christ, and by that on God's saving will and purposes, allows the theologian to be open to the breadth of God's grace, and to the wideness of God's mercy. Emphasizing the particularity of Jesus Christ, and seeing salvation as properly His, allows for an appreciation of the universal scope of salvation.[28] This is made overtly clear by Barth in various of his writings:

If we see Him, we see with and around Him in everwidening circles His disciples, the people, His enemies and the countless millions who have not yet

---

23   CD II/2, p.13.

24   CD II/2, p. 13.

25   CD II/2, p. 10. For more on this topic in relation to the nature of God, see Chapter 4 of this book.

26   One may wish to extend this to speak of all of creation. In emphasizing the human Christ as in the first place a creature (before moving on to speak of His specificity as a human being), one can find the space to speak of Christ as *Pantokrator* of all creation and not only of humanity. I am grateful to David Clough for these insights, and the reader is referred to David Clough, *On Animals: Systematic Theology* (London: Continuum, forthcoming).

27   CD II/2, p. 117.

28   On Barth and universalism, see Berkouwer, *Triumph of Grace*; Joseph D. Bettis, 'Is Karl Barth a Universalist?', *Scottish Journal of Theology* 20, no. 4 (1967); Tom Greggs, ' "Jesus Is Victor": Passing the Impasse of Barth on Universalism,' *Scottish Journal of Theology* 60, no. 2 (2007); Oliver Crisp, 'On Barth's Denial of Universalism,' *Themelios* 29(2003); Oliver Crisp, 'On the Letter and Spirit of Karl Barth's Doctrine of Election: A Reply to O'Neil', *Evangelical Quarterly* 79, no. 1 (2003); John Colwell, 'The Contemporaneity of Divine Decision: Reflections on Barth's Denial of Universalism', in *Universalism and the Doctrine of Hell. Papers Presented at the Fourth Edinburgh Conference on Christian Dogmatics 1991*, ed. Nigel M. de S. Cameron (Carlisle: Paternoster, 1992); Greggs, *Barth, Origen, and Universal Salvation*, esp. chapters 2 and 4; Paul T. Nimmo, 'Election and Evangelical Thinking: Challenging Our Way of Conceiving the Doctrine of God', in *New Perspectives for Evangelical Theology: Engaging with God, Scripture and the World*, ed. Tom Greggs (Abingdon: Routledge, 2010), pp. 34–5; and Oliver Crisp, 'I Do Teach It, but I Also Do Not Teach It: The Universalism of Karl Barth (1886–1968)', in *"All Shall Be Well": Explorations in Universal Salvation and Christian Theology, from Origen to Moltmann*, ed. Gregory MacDonald (Eugene: Wipf and Stock, 2010).

heard His name. We see Him as theirs, determined by them and for them, belonging to each and every one of them.[29]

When one looks to Christ, one sees around Him the many with whom He engaged, and who looked to Him for help. These comprise not only the disciples who follow Jesus but also the Romans, the tax-collectors, the ritually unclear, the lepers and the prostitutes – in short, the religiously unsavoury. As one who lived for them, in His resurrection, He continues to live for the seeming outsiders today. To fail to recognize the breadth of God's grace and to confuse faith with a process which simply has the goal of gaining the *benefia Christi* runs the danger, for Barth, of confusing the salvation of one's soul with the goal of Christian vocation. To focus on the good and earnest desire for personal salvation can lead to unhelpful Christian tendencies:

> [T]hen another conclusion might so easily be drawn, namely, that that which concerns and affects and reaches me, my gracious visitation and salvation, the saving of my soul, and to that extent my reception, possession, use and enjoyment of the *beneficia Christi*, is the only thing which is relevant, essential and important in the goal of vocation, that this goal, and therefore my standing at the side of God, consists absolutely and exclusively in my Christian being, possession and capacity. Is this a false deduction from the classic answer which now occupies us? The fact remains that it has not infrequently been drawn, and not by the worst of people. The fact also remains that from it – who knows? – perhaps even more pregnant deductions (e.g., along the lines of Feuerbach) might well be drawn in respect of the total conception of Christianity.[30]

To focus on personal salvation can lead one to the religious notion that it is one's Christianity (one's religion) that saves, and that self-preservation of individual humans is the essence of the purpose of the good news. Indeed, Barth writes of the 'egocentricity by which Christians are threatened, and indeed to a large extent dominated and not just threatened, when the personal experience of salvation as such is regarded as the principle and essence of Christian being.'[31]

In order in part to counteract this Protestant propensity towards the individual, a further interesting feature of Barth's discussions of salvation is the priority that is always given to the community over the individual. Thus, *Church Dogmatics* II/2, §34 concerns 'The Election of the Community', and only in §35 is Barth concerned with 'The election of the individual'. Similarly, in Barth's Doctrine of

---

29   CD III/2, p. 216.
30   CD IV/3, pp. 563–4.
31   CD IV/3, p. 570.

Reconciliation, the order of discussion is always humanity in general, then the community and then the individual.[32] As Barth writes:

> [T]he *pro nobis* and the even more comprehensive *propter nos homines* will not
> be submerged and disappear in the *pro me*, but in and with the *pro me* they will
> necessarily be given the same degree of honour. . . .   In and with the *pro me*,
> Jesus Christ the Lord of the community and the Saviour of the world will assert
> Himself as the subject of the *pro me*. Only in the light of its object can the faith
> in which the individual becomes aware and certain of his own justification be
> the faith of the community and a faith which is open and addressed to the world.
> . . .   In this light, in the light of its object, it will always be enclosed by, as it
> encloses, that twofold We-faith. In it it will have its catalysator, as it is itself its
> catalysator. It will necessarily be preserved from the subtle egoism which would
> be proper to it as an abstract I-faith. But only in the light of its object![33]

The benefits of Christ 'for me' exist only because they are 'for all' (*propter nos homines*). And even when we speak of the individual, it is the community which takes priority: 'Our confession of faith in God's work accomplished in Him [Christ] states that it was done *pro nobis*, and only so also *pro me*.'[34]

There is the danger with this prioritization of the community (while no doubt better than the prioritization of the individual) that it could suggest a return to a binary articulation of God's work in its most religious form: the church is the only presence of God's work, and to receive this work, one needs to be religiously attached to the church. Indeed, Barth suggests that history demonstrates that 'the pious egocentricity of the individual must always broaden out into at least a kind of collective egocentricity.'[35] However, to read Barth's discussion in this way is to fail to see the purpose and reason for the seeming prioritization of the community (indeed, it is also to fail to see Barth's true prioritization of the objective reconciling work of God for all humanity). For him, the community of the faithful takes priority simply as a *witness* to the world of God's love and reconciliation.[36] The church does not find itself more deserving of God's love, but is the recipient of God's love because of His love for all of the world. The purpose of the community is to testify to the love of God for all of the world:

> As witnesses they have to repeat what God Himself has first said to them. This
> is the task laid upon them in their calling and to be discharged with their

---

32   See CD IV/1, §§59–61, cf. 62, cf. 63; IV/2, §§64–6, cf. 67, cf. 68; IV/3, §§ 69–71, cf. 72, cf. 73.

33   CD IV/1, p. 756.

34   HoG, p. 51.

35   CD IV/3, p. 570.

36   For more on the category of witness, see Chapter 6 of this book.

whole existence. This is the point of their particular existence. This makes them what they are in distinction from all others. Whatever else they may be, and especially their being, capacity and possession graciously granted as their particular experience of salvation, the ethos especially required of them, and all that they might have to undergo in the way of particular suffering – all this depends upon and stands under the common sign of the fact that they are entrusted with this declaration and message and have to discharge this commission. They are witnesses.[37]

'Witness' carries with it different connotations to 'missioner'. A witness witnesses to a reality that already is, while a missionary seeks to bring inside the fold one who is understood to stand outside of it in reality. For the Christian, the activity of the church is to witness to the reality of God's salvation, not to act in such a way as to suggest that it believes that it can cause that salvation by bringing another (either by power or by guilt) onto the side of the false salvific divide on which the Christian believes she stands.[38] This has tremendous implications for evangelization of the religiously 'incorrect':

> the goal of missions is not to convert heathen in the sense of bringing them to a personal enjoyment of their salvation. Neither at home nor abroad can it be the work of the community to convert men. This is the work of God alone. When God does convert a man by His call, then he does, of course, come to personal salvation, but supremely and decisively he becomes a witness in the world. Hence the goal of the missionary work of the community must be to attest to the heathen the work and Word of the God who, as He has created them by His call, wills to make them, too, His witnesses, and to equip them as such.[39]

The role of the church in engaging with those who are of different faiths or none is not to seek to convert them: God alone can do that. Where a person does convert, it is not primarily for the purpose of personal salvation, but to join those others who witness to the reality of God's reconciliation of the world in Christ. God is not, therefore, in this way pushed to the boundaries of which Bonhoeffer speaks, where the message of the church exploits 'human weakness' around

---

37   CD IV/3, p. 576.
38   One should note, therefore, that the words 'mission' or 'missionary' in the quotations from Barth that follow should be understood in terms of witness as described: the mission of the church for Barth is to witness. Here, it is necessary to affirm Wittgenstein's mantra that one should not ask for meaning but for use: the issue is not the presence of the words 'mission' or 'missionary' by Barth, but the way in which the words are used.
39   CD IV/3, p. 876.

themes such as death.[40] Nor can the church engage in any imperialistic role of 'civilizing'. Nor can it push at national boundary lines for its own political ends. As Barth states, 'missionary work among the nations cannot take the form of mastering and ruling, but only of serving, both in its commencement and its continuation.'[41] Witness does not allow the simple sense that there might be a geopolitical border across which God dare not tread, with the damned on one side and saved on the other: witness is a witness to the reality of the God already there on the other side.

Does, then, this mean universal salvation, a doctrine ostensibly anathematized in 553CE?[42] It certainly means that one should be open to this, as scripture itself is.[43] Barth's words on this topic are wise:

It would be well, in view of the 'danger' [of universalism] with which the expression is ever and again seen to be encompassed, to ask for a moment, whether on the whole the 'danger' from those theologians who are forever sceptically critical, who are again and again suspiciously questioning because they are fundamentally legalistic, and who are therefore in essentials sullen and dismal, is not in the meantime always more threatening among us than that of an unsuitably cheerful indifferentism . . . One thing is sure, that there is no theological justification for setting any limits on our side to the friendliness of God towards man which appeared in Jesus Christ – it is our theological duty to see and to understand that as even greater than we had done before.[44]

Far more worrying than issues surrounding universal salvation are those issues that concern the desire to damn or condemn the religious outsider of another or of no faith. Clearly for them, the issue of salvation will be less significant than it is for the Christian,[45] but for the Christian for whom salvation is central to their understanding of the world, there is the concern of how to see these others. If salvation is seen merely as the end of a legalistic or religious contract that a believer takes out with God,[46] then the whole capacity to glimpse the nature of God's grace is lost. Rather than seeing itself as a religiously acceptable section of

---

40   LPP, p. 366.

41   CD IV/3, p. 876.

42   In fact, the anathematization of *apokatastasis* was primarily in connection with the idea of the pre-existence of souls. One should note that the word *apokatastasis* is used in scripture in Acts 3.21.

43   See, for example, I Cor. 15.22; Col. 1.19–20; Phil. 2.9–11.

44   HoG, p. 50.

45   Salvation is obviously a dominantly Christian concern.

46   I am thinking particularly here about my own Arminian Evangelical context in which, at times, piety and 'praying the believers' prayer' can be seen in this way.

humankind, the church should understand itself as the provisional (and broken) representatives of the good news to all the world.[47]

For Bonhoeffer, this concern is true also. Even in the confines of his prison cell, Bonhoeffer is drawn to the work of Irenaeus on *recapitulatio* (*anakephalaiosis*),[48] and to Ephesians 1.9–10: 'He [God] has made known to us the mystery of his will, according to his good pleasure that He set forth in Christ, as a plan for the fullness of time, to gather up all things in Him, things in heaven and things on earth.' Bonhoeffer refers to this teaching as 'a magnificent and consummately consoling thought'. According to him, this doctrinal formulation means

> Nothing is lost; in Christ all things are taken up, preserved, albeit in transfigured form, transparent, clear, liberated from the torment of self-serving demands. Christ brings all this back, indeed, as God intended, without being distorted by sin.[49]

Bonhoeffer returns to the theme of universal salvation at a later stage of his confinement, in his poem 'Christians and Heathens'.[50] In this, the distinction between the Christian and the pagan is not presented as being in terms of salvation or damnation, but is suggested in terms of the preparedness of the Christian to stand by God in the world in which God in Christ is prepared to suffer. Bonhoeffer suggests in the poem that God offers salvation to all:

> God goes to *all* people in their need,
> fills body and spirit with God's bread,
> goes for Christians *and heathens* to Calvary's death,
> and forgives *them both*.[51]

---

47   '[W]hat else is the existence of this special race of men than the mirroring – certainly everywhere obliterated and obscured and all too often with the continuity broken – of the humanity of God, whose kindness to men goes so far as to call and waken some, many of these, as provisionally representing the rest and as His messengers to them for His worship, for His praise and service?' (HoG, p. 51).

48   While this doctrine does not necessarily lead to universal salvation, Bonhoeffer's interpretation of it (which follows) is certainly suggestive of this direction. Certain commentators have interpreted Irenaeus in the same way: see John Hick, *Evil and the God of Love* (London: Macmillan, 1966), chapter 10. On dualism in Irenaeus, see Ludlow, *Universal Salvation*, pp. 30–1; and Tom Greggs, 'Irenaeus and Augustine on the Problem of Evil Reconsidered', *New Theologian* 14, no. 2 (2004).

49   LPP, pp. 229–30.

50   LPP, pp. 460–1. For a detailed discussion of this poem, see Bernd Wannenwetsch, ' "Christians and Pagans": Towards a Trans-Religious Second Naivité or How to Be a Christological Creature' in *Who Am I? Bonhoeffer's Theology through His Poetry*, ed. Bernd Wannenwetsch (London: T&T Clark, 2009).

51   LPP, p. 461, emphasis added.

The work of Christ's salvation knows no religious boundary, and in this context the existence of the church is as a provisional representation of all of humanity.

THE CENTRALITY OF JESUS AS VICTOR

A major problem for Christian universalism is that it can present itself as a principle rather than a hope.[52] When professed as a principle rather than as a hope, universalism becomes precisely the kind of metaphysically orientated speech about salvation which Bonhoeffer critiques as religious. A version of universalism which presents itself as a principle runs the danger not only of an overwhelming christomonism, but also of obliterating human particularity, the place for faith and the importance of ethical decision. This is a charge that was levelled at Barth by Berkouwer: 'Barth's solution of the universalism of the triumph of election unavoidably brought him into difficulty with the meaningfulness of the horatatory kerugma and of human decision in the area of history.'[53] In the terms of the present chapter which seeks to articulate a soteriology against religion, one might be concerned that an overwhelming triumph of the principle of grace, worked out on the basis of God's decision in eternity, removes the possibility for genuine human, historical and worldly particularity. The principle of universalism may take on a religious tone as magical as the worst superstitious excesses.

However, Barth tackles this point directly in response to Berkouwer's presentation of Barth's theology.[54] Barth observes that 'Berkouwer has undoubtedly laid his finger on an important point.'[55] Barth's concern, however, is focused on the book's title, which Barth feels – to do justice to his work – should be replaced with the title 'Jesus is Victor'.[56] In this excursus, it is interesting to observe that Barth never overtly rejects (nor does he mention) universalism. What he rejects are some of the *implications* that Berkouwer draws from this, not the positively objective universal soteriology itself. His discussion with Berkouwer does not remove the emphatically positive ultimate message of the eternal election of Jesus Christ, but clarifies the sense in which this is to be understood – most determinately *in Jesus Christ and in His victory*.

---

52 On this point, see helpfully the discussions of this theme in J. C. McDowell, 'Learning Where to Place One's Hope: The Eschatological Significance of Election in Barth', *Scottish Journal of Theology* 53, no. 3 (2000); and J. C. McDowell, *Hope in Barth's Eschatology: Interrogations and Transformations Beyond Tragedy* (Aldershot: Ashgate, 2001).

53 Berkouwer, *Triumph of Grace*, p. 296. This theme is recurrent throughout Berkouwer's exposition.

54 The following exposition is a slightly rewritten version of a section of an earlier article. For the full version of this argument, the reader is directed to Greggs, ' "Jesus Is Victor": Passing the Impasse of Barth on Universalism'.

55 CD IV/3, p. 173.

56 CD IV/3, p. 173.

First, Barth advocates that his work is not underlined by a christological *principle*.[57] There is nothing worse to Barth's *Nachdenken* mode of theology.[58] The making of the person of Christ into a principle leads to Christ wrongly being understood as a 'mighty executive organ of the divine will of grace',[59] and this gives truly christological thinking only a secondary position. Thus, for Barth, not even grace can be used as a principle through which to see all else: election takes place in Jesus; it is in a person and not in a principle that humanity is elected. The *Gnadenwahl* (God's grace in electing humanity) must be understood through the person of Christ, not the person through the *Gnadenwahl*.

Secondly, Barth asserts that in Jesus one deals with a free person and His free act that cannot simply be grasped 'in the sense of conceptual apprehension and control.'[60] Jesus is not an *in abstracto* engaged in a battle with evil *in abstracto*, but is a living person in whom one can have unlimited confidence. Certainly, Barth concurs with Blumhardt that the superiority of Christ over His opponent can only end in Christ's triumph: this is decided from the very start because 'the One who is the First will also be the Last.'[61] However, again, this is not to replace *the person of Jesus* with a principle. It is not in the principle of grace, but in this real human that humanity is elected.

This does not, thirdly, deny the reality of evil,[62] an accusation that can be levelled at universal salvation. Barth continues to be emphatic in his assertion that it is only through 'Jesus is Victor' that one can understand the nature and reality of evil. Admitting that he has taken his terms from outside scripture, Barth still claims he has used insights from the Bible in shaping his doctrine. In speaking of 'nothingness' (*Das Nichtige*),[63] Barth speaks of something which does not exist as God or His creatures do; he speaks of something which has no basis for its being. However, this does not deny evil the existence to which it has no right. Evil has reality in the existence humans give it, but it is to be 'seen in Jesus Christ', and must thus be understood in its 'absolute inferiority' to His victory.[64] This does not deny evil its present reality, but recognizes its ultimate conquest.

---

57   'When Barth uses the word "principle", it connotes nothing less than the theological equivalent of a major industrial accident, if not a nuclear power plant explosion which can no longer be contained within tolerable limits.' (Gerhart Sauter, 'Why Is Karl Barth's Church Dogmatics Not a "Theology of Hope"? Some Observations on Barth's Understanding of Eschatology', *Scottish Journal of Theology* 52, no. 4 (1999), p. 413).

58   On *Nachdenken*, see David F. Ford, 'Barth's Interpretation of the Bible', in *Karl Barth: Studies of His Theological Method*, ed. S. W. Sykes (Oxford: Clarendon Press, 1979), pp. 81–6.

59   CD IV/3, p. 175.

60   CD IV/3, p. 176.

61   CD IV/3, p. 176.

62   CD IV/3, p. 177.

63   See CD III/3, §50 'God and Nothingness'.

64   CD IV/3, p. 178.

Fourthly, Barth addresses the charge that his work removes the historical encounter between God and evil.[65] Barth holds to his belief that '*from the very outset*' God is infinitely greater and stronger than evil. However, one is not to understand this as a principle which dissolves history. It is in the *narrative* of the life of Jesus in God's encounter with the world that this conquest and strength is seen. Rather than removing any sense of history, it is the very history of God's engagement with the world which establishes this conquest: only in the history of Jesus can humanity know God and evil, and the relationship of each to the other. In narrating the life of Christ, one sees that there is no 'easy "triumph of grace" '.[66] Moreover, this is a history and a conflict in which humanity in general must engage. Since it is *Christ's* conflict, neither an easy gain nor an uneasy pessimism can be its end:

Only victory is to be expected in view of its commencement, in view of Jesus, who has already fought the battle. Yet we have this confidence only with the last and bitter seriousness enjoined and demanded by this commencement, by Jesus. Neither hesitant qualifications nor rash or slothful assurance are possible at this point.[67]

It is from this that Barth moves into his discussion of the drama, war and history of the reconciliation, a history into which humanity is drawn.[68]

What, then, has this to say to the issue of universalism in general, and Barth's eschatology in particular? Barth is clearly reinterpreting universal salvation, by carefully removing the negative charges involved with an ultimate salvation of all humanity, while still allowing for and pointing towards that ultimate friendliness of God to all of humanity. Barth rejects universalism because 'universalism' itself can never be the victor: this victory is Jesus Christ's. It is a person and not a principle in whom humanity finds salvation.[69] There is no retreat for Barth from religion into some metaphysical approach to salvation.

Salvation is offered to humanity in its election *in* Christ – the Christ of whom it must be said 'Jesus is Victor.' It is in the eternal decision, and the history and narrative of the life of the incarnate Christ that our salvation takes place. The election

---

65   CD IV/3, p. 179.

66   CD IV/3, p. 178.

67   CD IV/3, p. 180.

68   CD IV/3, pp. 180ff.; cf. IV/2, p. 402.

69   Oliver Crisp has recently objected to this point in Crisp, 'I Do Teach It, but I Also Do Not Teach It: The Universalism of Karl Barth (1886–1968)', pp. 310–12. As well as there being elements of an underlying misconception of my position in this piece, it seems I am criticized by Crisp for doing precisely what Barth has done: Crisp, himself, on the other hand, seeks to impose a framework of metaphysics onto Barth's account from which Barth himself retreats, as is demonstrated in this chapter.

of humanity in Christ means an election in a life, in a person. It is as a result of this that Barth's chapter on 'The Command of God' follows that on election. Since election is the election of a *person*, it is the determination of a person, and therefore the question can arise even within a presentation of universal salvation of human self-determination which corresponds to *this* determination. Election in the *person* of Jesus allows the space for human freedom which a magical (and religious) principle never can. Barth rejects universalism, as he is determined to keep the particularity of the person of Jesus Christ – a particularity which cannot be gained from a principle.[70] John Webster is helpful in allowing one to recognize the room for human freedom that this allows in his discussion of the ethical implications of *enhypostasis*.[71] Because, for Barth, election is in the person of Jesus Christ, 'human reality, and therefore human agency, are *"enhypostatically* real"', drawing their substance from the human reality of Jesus Christ.'[72] This is not to merge the two realities, but to recognize that our humanity exists from and in His. Indeed, against the charge of christomonism, Barth writes:

> It does not mean that Jesus Christ has merged into world-occurrence and world-occurrence into Him, so that we can no longer speak of them as separate things. This would be Christomonism in the bad sense of that unlovely term. What it does mean is that according to the true insight of the people of God the twofold form of world history loses the appearance of autonomy and finality, the character of an irreconcilable contradiction and antithesis, which it always seems to have at a first glance.[73]

World-occurrence and the history of humanity still continue after Jesus Christ,[74] but the contradiction and antithesis is ultimately removed. It is not that reality is dissolved into a greater reality, but rather that the very particularity of the person Jesus provides the basis for the very existence of the 'twofold form of world history', and in that way the very existence of all creaturely particularity.

Furthermore, the emphasis on the particularity of the person of Jesus Christ guards the freedom and sovereignty of God while still allowing for the salvation

---

70   Indeed, Barth cites his allergy to metaphysics as the reason for his rejection of *apokatastasis*: 'His [God's] election and calling do not give rise to any historical metaphysics, but only to the necessity of attesting them on the ground that they have taken place in Jesus Christ and His community' (CD II/2, pp. 417–18).

71   John Webster, *Barth's Moral Theology: Human Action in Barth's Thought* (Edinburgh: T&T Clark, 1998), pp. 88ff. Although *enhypostasis* is not a doctrine Barth uses overtly in his discussion of election, it is used clearly in Barth's thought both before and after the doctrine of election. On *an-* and *enhypostasis*, see CD I/2, pp. 162ff., 216 (*anhypostasis* only); and IV/2, pp. 44–50. See also, Jüngel, *God's Being Is in Becoming*, pp. 96–7.

72   Webster, *Barth's Moral Theology*, p. 89.

73   CD IV/3, p. 713.

74   CD IV/3, p. 714.

of all humanity. Emphasizing the *person* of Jesus allows for a freedom which cannot be espoused in a principle. It is not that God is bound by the Christ-principle, but rather that in His sovereign freedom He *wills* to be this God in *self*-limitation – to be Jesus Christ. It is not that Jesus Christ replaces the religious *decretum absolutum* as a principle: it is that He crowds it out as a person. Barth is clear that God is under no obligation to elect. But in Jesus Christ, one is able to see the mysterious sovereign *will* of God. While one might be concerned that the metaphysical principle of universalism might bind the sovereignty of God, the insistence on the will of God, found in the emphasis on the person of Jesus Christ, underscores God's sovereignty. This is a sovereignty God demonstrates in God's willed decision to be for humanity in the election of Jesus Christ.

Related to both preceding points is the need to understand Barth's doctrine of eternity and time, in which there is no removal of time by eternity.[75] In Barth's theology, God's eternity is more than simply the unity of all times with the goal and purpose of His will. His eternity is not exhausted by this. God's eternity is rather the *presupposition* of this unity. For that reason, Barth speaks of pre-, supra-, and post-temporal eternity, which he believes is a biblical distinction within the unity of eternity in which it is possible to see eternity's positive relationship to time since in it God has the power to exist before, above and after time.[76] All too often, commentators on Barth have failed to see the importance of this distinction and this *positive* relationship of eternity and time. God's eternity is the precondition of temporality, and eternity is not a concept interchangeable with the simple dialectic of time over and against timelessness. Eternity does not obliterate time; eternity allows for it. The simultaneous possession of all time does not mean the dominance of any one time: pre-temporal eternity does not have priority over supra- or post-temporal eternity as many commentators on Barth would have us believe. Rather, it is *simultaneous*. This simultaneity does not remove the integrity of any one moment of time or of eternity, but unites them. To suggest that in Barth all of history is sewn up by universalism is fundamentally to misunderstand Barth's presentation of eternity. To misunderstand eternity is to fail to grasp the particularity involved in the statement 'Jesus is Victor' – a particularity that can never be involved in a principle. It is also to fail to see that there are few theologians who allow for so much time for humanity as

---

75 In addition to the all too brief comments here, see II/1 §31.3; I/2 §14; and III/1 §51. For the most thorough discussion of this topic, see Roberts, *A Theology on Its Way*, esp. chapter 1. In this, Roberts engages in a thorough and fierce criticism of Barth on time, concluding that Barth is ultimately 'ambiguous' and seeing the dissolution of time by eternity in Barth's theory. While Roberts is undoubtedly correct in the emphasis he places on these concepts in Barth's theology and attempts to identify the innermost logics of his work, his overall conclusions cannot be accepted. For a critique of Roberts, see B. D. Marshall, 'Review of Richard Roberts, *A Theology on Its Way? Essays on Karl Barth*', *Journal of Theological Studies* 44 (1993).

76 CD II/1, p. 619.

Barth does. A principle may well dissolve or negate time; the life in time of a human person, Jesus, cannot. Barth rejects a universalism which removes temporality, but this in no way limits the ultimate victory of Christ.

The issue of ultimacy requires further comment in relation to these themes. In dealing with the *eschaton*, one is dealing with that which is ultimate; in dealing with human history, one is faced with that which is penultimate. Barth finds room for the freedom of humanity and the continued existence of history and world occurrence through his use of this concept. He rejects a universalism which does not allow for this distinction, but he still allows what is ultimate to be ultimate. It is this way that one is to understand the existence of the Christian. Christianity and faith in the present is not an ultimate decisive factor, but a 'preliminary sign of this end'.[77] Moreover, this sign is one 'not only in anticipation of its own awaited completion but also in anticipation of what is truly and finally purposed in what God has done and revealed in Jesus Christ, namely, the liberation of all men.'[78] Penultimacy allows the room for human freedom in history. This is a history which is real and valid in its penultimacy. In it is the room for faith; just as in it is the room for rejection, condemnation and unbelief. But these are not ultimate. The ultimate is this: 'Jesus is Victor.'

Seeing salvation as a participation in the victory of Christ crowds out both an egocentric view of salvation as self-preservation, and a magical religious principle of universalism which removes particularity, freedom, contingency, time and – ultimately – humanity. In this way, both of Bonhoeffer's concerns about religious interpretation being concerned with personal salvation and metaphysics might begin to be overcome.

RELATED THEMES

Given the preceding discussion of the importance of redescribing soteriology in the present generation, the theological import of moving away from an over-emphasis on individual and personal salvation, and the need to understand this historically and particularly in the person of Jesus, it would be wise to discuss some associated themes related to a soteriology against religion. These will be focused around the co-sinfulness of all humanity,[79] reconceiving repentance, and demythologizing Gehenna and attending to the now.

---

77   CD IV/3, p. 675.

78   CD IV/3, p. 675.

79   For a more detailed exposition of this theme, see Tom Greggs, 'Beyond the Binary: Forming Evangelical Eschatology', in *New Perspectives for Evangelical Theology: Engaging with God, Scripture and the World*, ed. Tom Greggs (Abingdon: Routledge, 2010); and Tom Greggs, 'Pessimistic Universalism: Rethinking the Wider Hope with Bonhoeffer and Barth'.

The co-sinfulness of all humanity

Part of the way in which one can observe the failings of a soteriology based on a religious categorization of saved and damned comes in terms of the continued sin that exists in Christians. Bonhoeffer addresses this theme in his doctoral thesis, *Sanctorum Communio*. In discussing the existence of the community of saints within the community of sinners, Bonhoeffer challenges Christians to consider their roles in bringing sin into the world, and their co-responsibility for sin in the world. Rather than simply grouping people into saints on one side and sinners on the other, Bonhoeffer recognizes the complexity that is associated with the exist-ence of the church in the world. Realizing the severely limited quality of Christian faithfulness determines the need to reconsider the capacity of theologians to see Christians singularly as those saved from sin: sin continues in the Christian, who in this way is bound to the non-Christian in co-sinfulness. According to Bonhoeffer,

> The culpability of the individual and the universality of sin should be under-stood together; that is, the individual culpable act and the culpability of the human race must be connected conceptually.[80]

Every human being is found wanting, in Bonhoeffer's account, for any sin. This is because no human being is different in principle from Adam, the first sinner. By virtue of this, all human beings are in effect also Adam.[81] This does not determine, however, that sinners are not responsible for their individual acts of sin. The reverse is to some degree true: present day individual humans are responsible with Adam (and all other humans) for the sin that is in the world. The Christian who sins is co-responsible for the sin of the non-Christian, and for the sin of Adam: in this way, Christians stand in closest connection with all other human beings, as perpetrators of sin.[82] Thus, the church stands under the judgement of sin, which is only replaced eschatologically.[83] The continuance of any sin whatsoever, for Bon-hoeffer, determines that all of humanity is tarnished by sinfulness. Salvation and sanctification do not place the members of the church in any different a position. For Bonhoeffer, it is not so simple as to see a religious group freed from sin and a non-religious group standing under it. This determines that, while Bonhoeffer does think it is necessary not to forget the Bible and the tradition's discussions of a dual eschatological outcome, he can write:

> We must not speak of a dual outcome . . . without at the same time emphasiz-ing the inner necessity of the idea of apocatastasis . . . On the one hand, the

---

80   SC, pp. 110–11.
81   SC, p. 115.
82   SC, p. 116.
83   SC, p. 124.

concept of the church, as Christ's presence in the world which calls for a decision, necessarily demands the dual outcome. The recognition that the gift of God's boundless love has been received without any merit would, on the other hand, make it seem just as impossible to exclude others from this gift and this love.[84]

Indeed, it is this argument which, for Bonhoeffer, is the strongest argument for universal salvation: being responsible for bringing sin into the world, the Christian stands alongside the non-Christian, and continues to need God's gracious salvation.[85]

To accept such an unwillingness to categorize humans into religiously acceptable and religiously unacceptable human beings brings with it a fundamental shift in attitude towards those who do not share in faith, or those whom one finds difficult from the perspective of salvation and damnation. No longer can these others be seen as damnable sinners; instead they are seen to be fellow humans – tainted by sin as Christians are, but beloved of God as Christians are also.[86] In focusing on God's gracious self-giving in Jesus Christ, the Christian's focus can shift from being religiously pure or set aside to being centred on other human beings. Barth captures this well when he writes:

[T]he power of the revelation of the salvation accomplished for each and all on Golgotha consists in the fact that they are brought, and brought into, the peace which was there concluded in their name, so that they can consider and respect and to that extent have it even in the midst of strife. When this power is at work, man can no more imagine that on the frontier of his life he is confronted by an enemy whom he can meet only in a pitiful submission to his merciless rule or with a defiant shout of freedom. When this power is at work the One with whom he has to do, as a brother of Jesus Christ, is God as his Father. Nor need he see in his fellows only those who constantly disturb the peace, so that his only course is either to avoid them, or resist them, or at very best tolerate them. On the contrary, he now finds that these men are unmistakeable and undeniable, if sometimes very doubtful and difficult, brothers of Jesus Christ and therefore his own brothers.[87]

---

84   SC, pp. 286–7.
85   For discussion of this in relation to ecclesiology and to pharisaism, see Chapter 6 of this book.
86   Indeed, the opposite may be the case: the situation of the Christian might be more perilous. Lindbeck writes, for example: 'the beginning of damnation, of deliberate opposition to God, is possible only within the church, within the people of God: Jesus pronounced his woes (and wept) . . . over the cities of Israel, not those of the Gentiles.' (George A. Lindbeck, *The Nature of Doctrine: Religion and Theology in a Postliberal Age* (Philadelphia: Westminster, 1984), p. 59).
87   CD IV/2, p. 314.

It is in this way that there is an ethical determination for the Christian regardless of the wealth of salvific benefits offered to all of humanity. The role of the church is not to be a separate religious society, but an organization which exists entirely for the sake of others – God and fellow humans.[88] When it does this, it can become 'the place where in Christocratic brotherhood the crown of humanity, [which] names man's co-humanity, can become visible . . . [and] the humanity of God is recognised.'[89]

Reconceiving repentance

A shift in the way in which one understands salvation will bring with it the need to reinterpret the way in which one can understand repentance. To do this, however, is not to shy away from the biblical message, but to think more fully from within it. As Barth points out,

> We certainly do not have in the Bible stories of conversion such as that which Augustine recorded in his autobiography, or the numerous legends of the saints stimulated by Augustine in the Middle Ages, or the Christian portraits of which the first half of the 19th century was so particularly fond, or the testimonies given in gatherings of the Salvation Army and Moral Rearmament by those who at first were not interested in personal salvation, then sought it in the wrong place and finally sought and found it in the right place. There can be no contesting the significance of an experience like that of Luther in the cloister. But where do we find even the remotest likeness to it in the Bible?[90]

The conversion experience deeply rooted in the Christian faith and *psyche* (deeply significant as it is) does not find a clear and direct parallel in the text of scripture. However, there is in the gospel accounts a call to 'repent'.[91] How, then, is this repentance to be understood?

Bonhoeffer addresses this question directly in his *Letters and Papers*. Concerned to advocate that being Christian does not mean being 'religious in a certain way' but being a human,[92] Bonhoeffer defines repentance (*metanoia*) as follows: 'not thinking of one's own needs, questions, sins, and fears but allowing oneself to be pulled into walking the path that Jesus walks, into the messianic event, in which Isa. 53 is now being fulfilled!'[93] Bonhoeffer goes on to describe this being

---

88 For further unpacking of this, see Chapter 6 of this book.
89 HoG, p. 52.
90 CD IV/3, p. 571; cf. pp. 585 and 592. Indeed, even with regard to Paul, Barth states that '[h]is personal salvation was no doubt very dear to him, but it was only secondary' (IV/3, p. 591).
91 Mk 1.14–15, and parallels.
92 LPP, p. 480.
93 LPP, p. 480.

caught up in Jesus Christ in a variety of ways, advocating that there is a plurality of forms of Christian discipleship in the New Testament: classical versions such as the story of Zacchaeus, but also stories which do not involve 'converted sinners', such as the centurion of Capernaum, Jairus, Joseph of Arimathea, the women at the tomb and others.[94] Bonhoeffer is concerned with what he terms clerical 'prying into the sins of others in order to catch them out',[95] and points out that Jesus did not make people into sinners in order to save them, but simply engaged with people as they were: 'When Jesus made sinners whole, they were real sinners, but Jesus didn't begin by making every person into a sinner. He called people from their sin, not into it.'[96] For Bonhoeffer, repentance does not mean turning away from sin, but primarily turning towards Christ; the former is likely to be contained within the latter, but the latter takes priority. It is not that repentance makes people into religious beings, but rather that it orientates people (in their wholeness) back onto Christ. As Bonhoeffer arrestingly puts it, 'the "religious act" is always something partial, whereas "faith" is something whole and involves one's whole life. Jesus calls not to a new religion but to life.'[97] An interpretation of repentance within a discussion of soteriology against religion must prioritize the wholeness of a human being, who by turning towards Christ turns simultaneously towards God and fellow humans.

Demythologizing Gehenna and attending to the now

Just as it is necessary to reconceive the way in which we might speak of repentance, as a result of taking seriously the criticism of religion, so too it is necessary to think about the way in which to understand the apocalyptic imagery of hell. While there are certainly texts in the Bible which seem to suggest a universal salvation (such as I Cor. 15.22; Col. 1.19–20; Phil. 2.9–11; and I Tim. 2.4–6), there is nevertheless a separationist tenor to much of scripture. Much of the contemporary use of separationist

---

94   This plurality of approaches to repentance seems highly apposite for the gospel narrative. At the very start of Jesus' public ministry, Mark records that Jesus proclaimed repentance throughout Galilee. However, never again are those words recorded on Jesus' lips. When the disciples are sent out by Jesus, we are told that they preached that people should repent (Mk 6.12), but Jesus never uses the term Himself beyond the first chapter. It seems sensible, therefore, to see all else that follows in Jesus' public work as an outworking of this proclamation with Mk 1.14–15 functioning as some kind of sub-heading. The nearness of the Kingdom of God and the command to repent and believe the good news is the ministry of Jesus in a nutshell. Therefore, if we are to understand this proclamation, then we must look through the rest of the story to see *how* Jesus proclaimed repentance and belief, and what he meant by it. Only in reading the stories that follow these verses as examples or types of Jesus' proclamation can we understand what He meant by these words, and only in that can we understand how to interpret them today.

95   LPP, p. 456.

96   LPP, p. 450.

97   LPP, p. 482.

imagery certainly owes more to Milton and Dante than it does to Jesus Christ. However, there is in the New Testament, and particularly in Jesus' eschatological discourses, a clear discussion of the existence of hell, albeit one should be careful not to import into these images the pictures painted by the Mediaevals. The primary word for hell used in the New Testament is the word '*Gehenna*'. This word is used 13 times in the New Testament (over half of these occur in Matthew's gospel).[98] Yet, it is important as a contemporary reader to be alert to the fact that for the original listeners to the gospel there was significance to *Gehenna* which we all too easily lose. On the south side of Jerusalem existed the Valley of Hinnom, which in Hebrew is '*Ge Hinnom*' from which *Gehenna* is derived. This was seen as a place of unrighteousness associated with the idolatry of Manasseh and the human sacrifices of Molech. For the listeners to Jesus and the early Jewish gospel communities (hence the focus of the material in Matthew), the message about *Gehenna* would have been understandable in terms of a literal place.[99] For them, the discourse would have been seen as one based on imagery concerning the Valley of Hinnom, rather than a physical place called *Gehenna* after death. To interpret the imagery of hell in this manner, as an image indicative of unimaginable distance from God (an existential state) based upon the worst physical place that the audience might be able to imagine, allows this image to stand alongside the more universalized salvific passages pointed to above:[100] one cannot simply see separation as the message of scripture and universalism as non-scriptural. There is clearly a need to allow both sets of texts to stand side by side, and to seek to interpret one through the other. Prioritizing the universalist passages, and seeing the passages on hell as contextual imagery related to an existential distance from God for those in the present facing death helps to maintain these two traditions in scripture together.

Furthermore, in the seemingly most harrowing of these stories, it is not always clear on which side of the divide the 'religiously acceptable' find themselves. This adds a tremendous level of complexity into any simple binary approach. In Jesus' parabolic use of the imagery of the sheep and the goats (Mt. 25.31–46), it is important to note that the sheep think they are goats and the goats think that they are sheep: there is on each side of the eschatological divide the expectation to be in the other camp. The religious self-categorization of one body of people confident

---

98   The other word used for 'hell' in the New Testament is 'Hades'; this is used ten times.

99   In this way, I disagree with the (albeit excellent and informative) presentation of Gregory MacDonald, *The Evangelical Universalist: The Biblical Hope That God's Love Will Save Us All* (London: SPCK, 2008), pp. 144–5. The book offers, however, a useful overview of the complexities of the biblical material surrounding these themes.

100   In the words of Boring regarding separationist and universalist passages in the New Testament: 'As propositions, they can only contradict each other. As pictures, they can both be held up, either alternatively or, occasionally, together, as pointers to the God whose grace and judgment both resist capture in a system, or in a single picture' (M. Eugene Boring, 'The Language of Universal Salvation in Paul', *Journal of Biblical Literature* 105, no. 2 (1986), 292).

of their salvation in comparison to another has nothing to do with the eschatological determination of the people in this parable: quite the reverse, the religious seem to be those who are sent to damnation.[101] The defining aspect of this judgement is the degree to which humans engage in co-humanity:

> Then the righteous will answer him, 'Lord, when was it that we saw you hungry and gave you food, or thirsty and gave you something to drink? And when was it that we saw you a stranger and welcomed you, or naked and gave you clothing? And when was it that we saw you sick or in prison and visited you?' And the king will answer them, 'Truly I tell you, just as you did it to one of the least of these who are members of my family, you did it to me.'[102]

Eschatological judgment is associated with the present way in which one deals with other human beings.

For a soteriology against religion, this focus on present co-humanity is central. For Bonhoeffer, 'one only learns to have faith by living in the full this-worldliness of life.'[103] In this way, the Christian is to abandon any attempt at becoming religious, and must focus on this world. He describes this shift to 'this-worldliness' as follows:

> living fully in the midst of life's tasks, questions, successes and failures, experiences and perplexities – then one takes seriously no longer one's own sufferings but rather the suffering of God in the world. Then one stays awake with Christ in Gethsemane. And I think this is faith . . . [104]

Living in the world, and being concerned with fellow humans as brothers and sisters of Christ is the concern of the blessings of salvation. This concern is greater than any continued individual or institutionalized egocentrism.

CONCLUSION

In seeking to articulate a soteriology against religion, one does well to think about what it is from which one is saved. The narrative of the fall in Genesis 3 offers us

---

101   Cf. Christopher Rowland, 'The Lamb and the Beast, the Sheep and the Goats: "The Mystery of Salvation' in Revelation", in *A Vision for the Church: Studies in Early Christian Ecclesiology in Honour of J. P. M. Sweet*, ed. Markus Bockmuehl and Michael B. Thompson (Edinburgh: T&T Clark, 1997), who not only considers this passage but also separationist discourses in Revelation. On these themes, see also Greggs, 'Beyond the Binary: Forming Evangelical Eschatology'.

102   Mt. 25.37–40

103   LPP, p. 486.

104   LPP, p. 486. I do not want to enter here into the topic of the passibility or impassibility of God. Instead, I understand this language (and its parallels in Bonhoeffer) to be language concerned with christology primarily (God suffering in Jesus Christ) rather than theology proper (God suffering).

a glimpse of the essence of all human sinfulness: the desire to be as God rather than to allow God to be God. It is with this that the serpent tempts the human: 'you will be like God' (v. 5). The danger exists that, in our soteriological discussion, we too can – even in seeking to be freed from sin – seek to be like God. Seeking to displace God's role as judge, the church can so often seek to offer eschatological judgements over the appropriate level and kind of religiosity of groups of people and of individuals, seeking to identify the difference between good and evil, for self-preservation and anticipated divine preference. A soteriology against religion, however, should seek to understand salvation as the process of humanization – God's restoring of humanity to its proper place (anticipated for all eternity by God and yet in prospect for humanity). Rather than seeing salvation as divinization,[105] a theology against religion should see salvation as humanization:[106] God demonstrates true humanity to human beings in Jesus Christ, but humans (even – and perhaps especially – the pious) wish to make an idol of themselves.[107] In an age in which there is the dehumanizing of those of faiths and world-views different from our own, for the Christian to attend to the present, rather than worrying about her personal benefits in future salvation, might be a wise way to approach the doctrine of salvation in a complexly secular and pluralist setting. Emphasizing God's universal salvific purposes, and seeing the outworkings of these in acts of correspondence to the divine act of reconciliation, is the approach to salvation that a theology against religion should take. In being focused, like Christ, on God and on other human beings (rather than being concerned with religious propriety) one may find oneself among the truly humane sheep rather than the religiously expectant goats. It is to the manner in which humans are enabled to become more fully human that this book now turns in its examination of pneumatological ecclesiology after Christendom.

---

105   On divinization and *theosis*, see Norman Russell, *The Doctrine of Deification in the Greek Patristic Tradition* (Oxford: OUP, 2006). However, it should be noted that many doctrines of divinization see *participation* in God as the true goal of humanity: 'a *deified* humanity . . . does not lose its human characteristics', John Meyendorff, *Byzantine Theology: Historical Trends and Doctrinal Themes* (New York: Fordham University Press, 1987), p. 164.
106   Ethics, p. 96: 'human beings are not transformed into an alien form, the form of God, but into the form that belongs to them, that is essentially their own. Human beings become human because God became human.'
107   A helpful discussion of the issues surrounding Christian theological anthropology can be found in the recent book by Janet Martin Soskice, *The Kindness of God: Metaphor, Gender, and Religious Language* (Oxford: OUP, 2007), esp. pp. 37–9.

Chapter 6

POST-CHRISTENDOM ECCLESIOLOGY

The decline of church attendance in Western Europe has been such that from a position in which the church once held power and influence in individual, local and national lives, it now finds itself almost on the brink of empirical disappearance. An Anglican bishop in Britain recently warned that the Church of England would disappear within a generation, reporting that the falling numbers in Sunday morning congregations is accelerating at around 1 per cent per annum, and that on this basis it is difficult to see the church surviving for more than 30 years.[1] And the Church of England is in one of the strongest positions of the denominations in Britain. The question Bonhoeffer poses to the situation of de-Christianization seems more pertinent today than it even did in the situation in which Bonhoeffer found himself: 'What does a church, a congregation, a sermon, a liturgy, a Christian life, mean in a religionless world?'[2]

Responses to this have, in the words of a scholar from the United States about his own ecclesial situation which is far less desperate than the European one, been marked by 'the hyperactivity of panic. This manifests itself in clutching for any and every programmatic solution and structural reorganization in the desperate hope that survival is just another project or organizational chart away.'[3] Furthermore, where there has been reflection by churches on this situation of de-Christianization in society, it has often led to the determinately countercultural ecclesiologies of the Radical Reformation.[4] Added to the fact that de-Christianization has taken place simultaneously to the growth of religious plurality, it is not simply the case that now less people are going to church: more people are now attending mosques, temples and gurdwaras in societies once divided only by which form of Christian denomination

---

1 Rt Revd Paul Richardson, 'Britain is no longer a Christian nation', *The Sunday Telegraph*, 27 June 2009. For more on church attendance figures and the situation in Europe, see Davie, *Europe: The Exceptional Case*, pp. 6–7; and Davie, *Religion in Britain since 1945*, pp. 46–9.

2 LPP, p. 364.

3 Michael Jinkins, *The Church Faces Death: Ecclesiology in a Post-Modern Context* (New York & Oxford: OUP, 1999), p. 9.

4 David Fergusson, *State, Church and Civil Society* (Cambridge: CUP, 2004), p. 44. Other approaches to this issue which have sought to be tied more firmly to culture have simultaneously been too liberal, imbibing *Kulturprotestantismus*, and have failed to be clear about what distinctiveness the church has.

one chose to worship at on a Sunday. Indeed, perhaps Bonhoeffer's question needs to be rephrased as 'What do a church, a community, a sermon, a liturgy, a Christian life mean in a simultaneously de-Christianized *and religiously pluralist* society?' In this situation, the concerns associated with individual egoism in terms of salvation (see Chapter 5 of this book) run the danger of reforming themselves tribally as communal egoisms: there can all too easily be a replacement of the individual person with the collective identity of the church, but the base concerns are the same. By this is meant that the danger of expressing a favoured soteriological future for a section of society, or a favoured providential position within the world for a singular group with whom God is singularly concerned in a way in which He is not with others lurks behind much discussion of ecclesiology. In the contemporary religious and secular setting, this danger is all too real, and there is a need to discuss issues surrounding ecclesiology with an awareness of the complex societal and global situation in which the church operates. Discussing ecclesiology after Christendom requires significant attention to the situation in which the church now finds itself: in what ways does the church live in, with and for the world of which it is a part, a world marked by pluralism and secularism with regard to religion?

Bonhoeffer unpacks some of the questions arising from his initial discussion of a religionless expression of the church thus:

> How do we go about being 'religionless-worldly' Christians, how can we be *ek-klesia*, those called out, without understanding ourselves as privileged, but instead seeing ourselves as belonging wholly to the world? Christ would then no longer be the object of religion, but something else entirely, truly Lord of the world. But what does that mean? In a religionless situation, what do rituals [Kultus] and prayer mean? Is this where the 'arcane discipline' [Arkandiszip-lin], or the difference (which you've heard about from me before) between the penultimate and the ultimate, have new significance?[5]

It is to these concerns that this chapter wishes to turn in seeking to articulate theologically the nature and purpose of the church in light of the contemporary religious sociological setting. Are we merely a holy remnant by which God announces His judgement against the rest of His creation? Or does the church have no or little role in an age which (while it might believe) very often does not express belief in God in an ecclesial way by belonging to the church?[6]

This chapter will discuss these themes in dialogue with Bonhoeffer and Barth by considering the nature of the church as dynamic and actualistic.[7] It will go on

---

5   LPP, pp. 364–5.

6   See Davie, *Religion in Britain since 1945*, chapter 6, in her discussion of believing without belonging as a description of contemporary societal religiosity.

7   Actualism is a feature that pervades Barth's theology, and is a term which is variously used within 'Barthiana'. For an overview of actualism beyond the parameters of its use in this chapter in relation

to articulate this in terms of the intense and active presence of God's Spirit, before attending to the church's role within and for the world.

DYNAMIC AND ACTUALISTIC ECCLESIOLOGY OF THE SPIRIT

There are various models with which one might proceed in describing the church, and taxonomies of such models are various and variously complex.[8] In his work *Finding the Church*, the Anglican ecclesiologist Daniel W. Hardy sets out a helpful broad analysis of these models of the church, which he describes in a fourfold form: the ontological model (as is found in traditional Roman Catholic ecclesiologies); the mystical model (as is associated with the Eastern churches); the actualist model (as present in Reformed church ecclesiologies); and the historical model (associated with Anglicanism).[9] An Anglican himself, Hardy expounds the historical model in his own work, but his description of the actualist model may find more resonance with anti-religious theology. His description of Reformed ecclesiology is expounded in terms of the church being 'an assembly that is always being reconstituted by the graceful act (election) of God in the Word of God as received in faith.'[10]

This dynamic and actualistic ecclesiological framework is certainly an appropriate description of Calvin's work. Calvin writes that there is no reason 'to pretend . . . that God is so bound to persons and places, and attached to external observances, that he has to remain among those who have only the title and appearance of a church [Rom. 9.6].'[11] It is, therefore, the Holy Spirit of God alone who gives life to the church. The church is properly speaking invisible, as God alone sees it; and empirical and visible expressions of the church exist only in groups constituted by gathering around the Word of God in scripture. This visible and empirical constitution is no guarantee of salvation, however: 'although they put forward a Temple, priesthood, and the rest of the outward shows, this empty glitter which blinds the eyes of the simple ought not to move a whit to grant that the church exists where God's Word is not found.'[12] Indeed, Calvin

---

to ecclesiology, see Nimmo, *Being in Action*, pp. 4–12.

8   See, for example, Avery Dulles, SJ, *Models of the Church* (New York: Doubleday, 1987); and Healey Nicholas M. Healy, *Church, World and the Christian Life: Practical-Prophetic Ecclesiology* (Cambridge: CUP, 2000), chapter 2.

9   Daniel W. Hardy, *Finding the Church* (London: SCM, 2001), pp. 30–4.

10   Ibid., p. 32.

11   McNeill, ed. *Calvin Institutes of the Christian Religion*, 4.2.3, p. 1044. These discussions concern Roman Catholicism polemically. However, outside of that polemic, the dogmatic content remains helpful and can usefully be redirected back to the Protestant church as itself an *ecclesia semper reformanda*.

12   Ibid., 4.2.4, p. 1046.

quotes Augustine: 'many sheep are without, and many wolves are within.'[13] No direct or exact correspondence can be made between the church empirical and the church spiritual and invisible.

Although this form of ecclesiology is sometimes associated with a certain '"purism" of the Word',[14] with the suggestion that only the appropriate expounding of scripture can bring about the constitution of the church, one crucial aspect of this actualistic ecclesiological model is its recognition of the appropriate ordering of doctrines. Ecclesiology is always a subset of pneumatology:[15] the Spirit creates the church at Pentecost, and the creed lists the church's existence under the third article. Put formally one might say that the presence of the Spirit is the *sine qua non* of the church, but the church is not the *sine qua non* of the presence of the Spirit, who in His freedom blows wherever He wills. Ordering the doctrines appropriately helps us to recognize this. It is thus only as an act of the Spirit that the church is brought into being in time, but the acts of the Spirit are not simply the bringing into being of the *ecclesia* in history.

The concern to deal appropriately with the invisibility of the church and with God's act as the basis of the church is one which is found in the theologies of Barth and Bonhoeffer. For Barth, it is clear that the church exists only as an act of the Holy Spirit who enables the community of Jesus Christ to exist: 'The Holy Spirit is the power of God proper to the being of Jesus Christ in the exercise and operation of which He causes His community to become what it is.'[16] That the church's nature is dependent on an act of the Spirit determines, in Barth's words, that its nature is always 'mobile', 'dynamic' and 'historical':

> the being of Jesus Christ to that of His community is not static nor immobile, but mobile and dynamic, and therefore historical. As the act of the Holy Spirit which underlies the existence of the community takes place in the order of the being of Jesus Christ and His community, the latter existing as He exists, so this order of the being of Jesus Christ and His community is the order of grace, the order of the act of the Holy Spirit, the community existing as Jesus Christ causes it to exist by His Holy Spirit.[17]

This dynamism need not bring with it a purism or Puritanicalism as is sometimes the case, but should bring with it a proper recognition of the dependence of the

---

13   Ibid., 4.1.8, p. 1022. For Calvin, however, a church is constituted as a place where the Word is preached and the sacraments are celebrated (ibid., 4.1.9).

14   Hardy, *Finding the Church*, p. 33.

15   For a survey of different ways in which the relationship between the Spirit and the church might be mapped, the reader is referred to John McIntyre, *The Shape of Pneumatology: Studies in the Doctrine of the Holy Spirit* (Edinburgh: T&T Clark, 1997), chapter 8.

16   CD IV/3, p. 759.

17   CD IV/3, p. 759.

church on the work and operation of the Holy Spirit, and not on the basis of any religious ecclesial essentialism. This in turn means that one cannot be too firm about where the boundary of the church lies: 'For all the seriousness with which we must distinguish between Christian and non-Christian, we can never think in terms of a rigid separation.'[18] The inability to identify this boundary exists because the church properly speaking is invisible, a creation of the freedom of the Holy Spirit of God.[19] The church is not a function of the collectivism of religion: indeed, there is no direct evidence that religion is innately social (as its interior and mystical forms demonstrate).[20] And no particular form of religion (whether centred on purity of word or liturgy) can ever be the basis for the presence of the true church – only the basis for something with the semblance of a church. The Holy Spirit alone forms the church in history.

Indeed, scripture itself provides that one should be sceptical about seeing religious affiliation as the basis and determination of the community of God. Barth points in this direction clearly in his discussion of those other people of God (outside of the Jewish community) who are prominent in the text of the Bible. In differentiating between the visible and the invisible church, Barth is able to claim that: 'We can expect this hidden neighbour, who stands outside the visible Church, just because there is a visible Church.'[21] Outside of the walls of the church are those who are nevertheless 'hidden neighbours' of the *visible* church, members of the true and *invisible* church of God. These neighbours have a function for the church:

> individual figures whom we must not overlook . . . also have a present place
> in the redemptive history attested by the Bible. They are strangers, and yet as
> such adherents; strangers who as such have some very important and incisive
> things to say to the children of the household; strangers who from the most
> unexpected distances come right into the apparently closed circle of the divine
> election and calling and carry out a kind of commission, fulfil an office for
> which there is no name, but the content of which is quite obviously a service
> which they have to render.[22]

---

18   CD IV/3, p. 494. This is a theme which will be returned to below and in the chapter on theology of the religions (chapter 8).

19   However, importantly for Barth, it is only from within the context of the visible church that this inability to identify the boundary is known. O'Grady helpfully observes: 'Visibility is so essential to the community that even what it is invisibly must not be sought apart from its being visible, but in it. . . . Ecclesiological docetism is just as impossible as Christological docetism.' (Colm O'Grady, *The Church in the Theology of Karl Barth* (Washington: Corpus Books, 1969), p. 255).

20   SC, p. 128. However, Bonhoeffer's assertion in this section of SC that only the Christian religion is social needs to be rejected (pp. 130–1): it is plainly untrue as simply looking to Islam and *Ummah* or the Jewish community demonstrates.

21   CD I/2, p. 425.

22   CD I/2, p. 425.

Barth lists Balaam, Rahab, Ruth, Hiram, Cyrus, the Magi, the centurion of Capernaum, centurion Cornelius at Cæsarea, the Syro-Phœnician woman, the centurion at the cross with his messianic confession, and the many who shall come from the East and from the West who shall sit down with Abraham and Isaac and Jacob. But for Barth the most significant of all of these figures is the priest of Salem, Melchizedek:

> According to Heb. 5:6f., 6:20, 7:1f., he is the type of Jesus Christ Himself and of His supreme and definitive high priesthood. It is therefore not merely legitimate but obligatory to regard the figure of Melchisedek as the hermeneutic key to this whole succession. It is not on the basis of a natural knowledge of God and a relationship with God that all these strangers play their striking role. What happens is rather that in them Jesus Christ proclaims Himself to be the great Samaritan: as it were, in a second and outer circle of His revelation, which by its very nature can only be hinted at. It must be noted that no independent significance can be ascribed to any of the revelations as we can call them in a wider sense. There is no Melchisedek apart from Abraham, just as there is no Abraham apart from Jesus Christ.[23]

The priestly role of Melchizedek here is significant and ecclesial. While Barth discusses the significance of this enigmatic priestly figure from the perspective of christology, to consider the priest's position pneumatologically may be helpful in establishing the proper ordering of the relationship between the Spirit and the church. The Spirit rests on Melchizedek, making him a priest despite his not being clearly within visible the community of God; it is not his religion or his priestliness (or any priestliness within or without the visible community of God) which determines that the Spirit rests upon him. The church can neither be so assured in its own religiosity to presuppose the Spirit's presence, nor so assured of its singularity as to presuppose the Spirit's exclusivity to it.

For Bonhoeffer, similar concerns also permeate his thought. Bonhoeffer's 'Outline for a Book' includes in it the statement: 'We cannot . . . simply identify ourselves with the church.'[24] This is a problem that he associates with Roman Catholicism and significantly also with the Confessing Church. Similar concerns (though more traditionally expressed) are present in Bonhoeffer's early writings. In these, he is clear that the Kingdom of God is always greater than the church. Even in his most ecclesial writings, Bonhoeffer realizes that the activity of God is always greater than the activity of God within the bounds of the *ecclesia*. He writes, for example:

> The purpose of God's rule is the Realm of God. This Realm includes all those who are predestined; the church, in contrast, includes only those who are elected

---

23   CD I/2, p. 426.
24   LPP, p. 503.

in Christ as church-community (Eph. 1:4; 1 Peter 1:20). Thus the former exists from eternity to eternity, while the latter has its beginning in history.[25]

While Bonhoeffer is concerned that the empirical church receives due consideration in order that reflection on ecclesiology is conducted with due attention to the being of the lived church of believers, he is, even in his earliest work, emphatic that this should not simply be identified with a religious society:

> The empirical church is not at all identical with religious community. Rather, as a concrete historical community, in the relativity of its forms and in its imperfect and modest appearance, it is the body of Christ, Christ's presence on earth, for it has his word. An understanding of the empirical church is possible only in a movement from above to below, or from inner to outer, but not vice versa.[26]

Due ordering of the discussion of ecclesiology is present in this in terms of the category of 'the movement from above to below': we must begin with understanding the church as an act of God and then examining that act, not examining the church and seeking to understand how or why it is that God acts within it.[27] Only in the context of recognizing the church as a community dependent upon God's gracious act is it then possible to reflect on the narrower category of the empirical church. In this narrower reflection, it is then possible to recognize openly and primarily that the latter is always imperfect, incomplete and modest.[28]

What, however, is the significance of this ecclesiological modelling for a theology against religion? This is in the first instance three fold. First, recognizing the proper ordering of theological reflection, and prioritizing pneumatology over ecclesiology, which exists only as a subset of the former, determines that God's Spirit is not institutionalized into a religious prison. The Spirit who is free to blow wherever He wills establishes the church by His gracious act; the church does not determine the presence of the Spirit. This allows for a greater openness to the idea that God is present outside the walls and confines of the church.[29] Secondly, realizing the dependence of the church on the presence of the Spirit,

---

25   SC, pp. 217–18.

26   SC, p. 209. Bonhoeffer goes on to discuss the way in which the church can, following this statement, be understood to be a religious community which is really established by God.

27   This distinction is important with regard to many church growth strategies, or the likes, which seek to create the conditions in the church by which God might be present (or present more powerfully), in contrast to recognizing that the presence of God is the condition for the creation of the church *ex nihilo*.

28   Cf. CD IV/2, p. 621.

29   There is obviously a related issue here of discernment. One may well seek to understand this in terms of the fruits of the Spirit. This theme, and that of the discernment of the presence of the Spirit outside of the walls of the institutional church, is discussed further in Chapter 8 of this book.

who enables the church to proclaim the Lordship of Jesus Christ, guards the church against any purism or idealization of its nature: since the church arises from the gracious act of the Spirit, there is the space for the reality of lived, human contingent life in failed and broken communities; the quality of the community does not determine the presence of the Spirit as the Spirit generates the community. Thus, the church is protected from purism or Puritanicalism, as the Spirit is God's operation with real human beings in real lived contexts and situations in all of their complexity and messiness.[30] The nature of the church as a people gathered and made the *ecclesia* by an act of the Spirit protects ecclesiology from a preoccupation with *form* and reminds the church universal of its primary identity. In this way, avenues for ecumenism are opened which do not rely on the oppressive monotony of sameness and uniformity, but are open to genuine and visible unity in brokenness. Thirdly, prioritizing the work of the Spirit in the establishment of the church provides the church with the possibility of not replacing one religious essentialist ecclesiology with another. Many recent developments in ecclesiology have focused around *how* best to be church, often concerned with the mode of practice that a church group engages in. Dominant in British ecclesial cultures has been the rise of the Emerging Church and/ or Fresh Expressions of Church groups.[31] Working to relate social and cultural movements in society more broadly to modes of being church, these groups have nevertheless worked within a framework of asking *how* best to be church, rather than seeking primarily to identify the operative and dynamic work of the Holy Spirit. Their ecclesial framework is no different from other essentialist models of church; and their ecclesial framework is definitively from below to above, seeking to locate in physical and spatial communities the presence of God, and to get people on the 'inside' of a (modified but substantially defined notion of) church in which the visible takes prioritization over God's invisible and universal acts.[32]

Having discussed the nature of the church as an operation of the Holy Spirit, it is now possible to discuss the nature of the church in relation to believers before going on to discuss its nature in relation to the world.

---

30 Cf. 'An overweighting of the christological as against the pneumatological determinants of ecclesiology together with an overemphasis on the divine over against the human Christ has led to a "docetic" doctrine of the church', Colin E. Gunton, 'The Church on Earth: The Roots of Community', in *On Being the Church: Essays on the Christian Community*, ed. Colin E. Gunton (Edinburgh: T&T Clark, 1989), p. 65.

31 For more on these groups, see, for example, Eddie Gibbs and Ryan K. Bolger, *Emerging Churches: Creating Christian Community in Postmodern Cultures* (Grand Rapids: Baker Academic, 2005); and Graham Cray (ed.) *Mission-Shaped Church: Church Planting and Fresh Expressions of Church in a Changing Context* (London: Church House, 2004).

32 See, for example, Drane, *The Mcdonaldization of the Church: Spirituality, Creativity, and the Future of the Church*; Drane, *After Mcdonaldization: Mission, Ministry and Christian Discipleship in an Age of Uncertainty*.

CHURCH AS COMMUNITY OF
INTENSITY AND ACTIVISM

In Bonhoeffer's *Ethics*, he identifies a problem:

> This belonging together of God and the world that is grounded in Christ does
> not allow static spatial boundaries, nor does it remove the difference between
> church-community and world. This leads to the question of how to think about
> this difference without falling back into spatial images.[33]

Indeed, Bonhoeffer sees this as a religious problem, in which by fighting for space,
the church becomes a 'religious society' or a 'cult'.[34] An emphasis on the actualistic nature of God's operations with His church is one way to overcome this problem – a problem which to some degree is innate to all religious speech which seeks
(unhelpfully) to differentiate secular and sacred spaces. As an act of the Holy Spirit,
the church is established as a community of the intensive presence of God for
active participation in His service and for His purposes. The Spirit who is present
extensively in the world dwells intensively with particular communities in time for
the service and performance of God's will.[35] The church is not, therefore, a place in
which one might think of a binary dividing line from the world. It is, instead, the
people in which the presence of God, which in God's omnipresence cannot be
spatially limited, dwells in intensity by the power of His Spirit in a community in
time. This people is thus enabled to proclaim the Lordship of Jesus Christ, and to
participate in God's salvific and redemptive work for all creation. Bonhoeffer
states: 'The church-community is separated from the world only by this: it believes
in the reality of being accepted by God – a reality that belongs to the whole world.'[36]
There is a temporality to this operation of God. Not an essentialized and eternal
institution, the church is a temporal people in which the actualization of God's
eternal purposes takes place in the present by the Holy Spirit.[37] Thus, as Bonhoeffer
advocates, '[i]n order for the church . . . to build itself up in time, the will of God
must be actualized ever anew, now no longer in a fundamental way for all people,

---

33   Ethics, p. 68.
34   Ethics, pp. 63–4.
35   Language of 'intensity' and 'extensity' is borrowed from Hardy, *Finding the Church*. For more
on the dynamic operations of the Spirit and the Son in salvation in relation to God's universal and
particular works, see Greggs, *Barth, Origen, and Universal Salvation*, esp. chapters 5 and 7.
36   Ethics, pp. 67–8.
37   Cf. SC, p. 139. As Gunton puts it, 'Sometimes it has appeared that because a *logical* link has been
claimed between the Spirit and institution, the institution has made too confident claims to be pos-
sessed of divine authority. The outcome . . . has been too "realised" an eschatology of the institution,
too near a claim for the coincidence of the Church's action with the action of God.' Gunton, 'The
Church on Earth: The Roots of Community', p. 61.

but in the personal appropriation of the individual.'[38] This is a calling for individuals to participate in the community which is not extensively and universally operative, but intensively and particularly determined as a vocation for some: 'the vocation of man is a particular and unique event in God's encounter with man which is as such a history, the occurrence and coming into being of a relationship which does not exist always, everywhere and from the very first. Not all men, therefore, are called as such.'[39]

The calling and active engagement of the church is, therefore, a particular calling upon some people to an active participation in the work of God in the present. It is in the context of the church community that this calling is exercised and fulfilled. As Bonhoeffer states, '[w]e experience our election only in the church-community, which is already established in Christ, by personally appropriating it through the Holy Spirit, by standing in the actualized church.'[40] While this experience is itself the result primarily of God's activity, it is hardly less real for that. The experience of election is not a mere and passive assent to a body of knowledge, but an active recognition and engagement in the movement of God towards humanity.[41] Barth is worth quoting at some length here:

The invocation of God by Christians is the subjective, or, as one might simply say, the human factor and element in this history and these dealings. We remember that it is due only to the free grace of God that as there can be dealings with God at all, so there can be the special dealings between God and these men, the history of their encounter, the concrete intercourse and exchange between them, a living relation in which not only God acts but these specific people may and should be truly active as well. The grace of God is the liberation of these specific people for free, spontaneous, and responsible cooperation in this history. In his free grace God purges himself from the base suspicion that he is an unchangeable, untouchable, and immutable deity whose divine nature condemns him to be the only one at work. By God's free grace these people are not marionettes who move only at his will. They are given the status of subjects who are able and willing to act, able and willing to do what is appropriate to them in dealing with him, able and willing to call upon him as the Father of Jesus Christ and therefore as their Father and also as the Father of all men.[42]

---

38   SC, p. 143.
39   CD IV/3, p. 483. Albeit, it is necessary to keep in mind Barth's comments on IV/3, p. 491 also.
40   SC, p. 143.
41   Cf. Stanley Hauerwas, *Hannah's Child: A Theologian's Memoir* (London: SCM, 2010), p. x: 'I do not put much stock in "believing in God." The grammar of "belief" invites a far too rationalistic account of what it means to be a Christian. "Belief" implies propositions about which you get to make up your mind before you know the work they are meant to do . . . I am far more interested in what a declaration of belief entails for how I live my life.'
42   ChrL, p. 102.

The Spirit frees individual humans to participate actively in a community of God's gracious and intensive presence in and for the world.

The nature of this active engagement can be seen in terms of a differentiation between the work of sanctification that has already taken place *de iure* in Jesus Christ, and that which takes places *de facto*. This purpose of this *de facto* participation is 'the revelation of the sanctification of all humanity and human life as it has already taken place *de iure* in Jesus Christ.'[43] The church has a purpose directed not towards its own end, but one for the sake of the world (see below). As the 'all' of humanity moves towards this goal, so, writes Barth,

> Christianity, or Christendom, is the holy community of the intervening period; the congregation or people which knows this elevation and establishment, this sanctification, not merely *de iure* but already *de facto*, and which is therefore a witness to all others, representing the sanctification which has already come upon them too in Jesus Christ.[44]

The distinctive role for the church, therefore, in God's ultimate salvific purposes for creation is the active engagement in God's ways with the world. There is, thus, a realization of the ontological (for the whole world) in the ontic (for the church).[45] As a member of the church, the Christian is made free by the Spirit and undertakes to engage actively in faith in Christ, obedience to Christ and confession of Christ.[46] This active engagement in God's work will always run the threat of falling into sin (and is already, indeed, an engagement in God's activity by sinners), but the purpose of the church is always to point beyond itself and its present broken and worldly provisionality.[47]

It is in this active engagement in the Christian life that one can find the necessary unity of the Spirit and the word in the church. As the Spirit dwells with intensity on the community of the church, so the church is freed beyond its own parameters. Those who hear God's word are now enabled to proclaim that message as well, repeating what God has already spoken to them. For Barth, the biblical witness testifies that those whom God calls, He commands to speak:

> As God speaks His Word to these men in and with what He does, and as He is heard by them, He gives them the freedom, but also claims and commissions them, to confess that they are hearers of His Word within the world and

---

43   CD IV/2, p. 620.
44   CD IV/2, p. 620.
45   This theme is discussed by Graham, *Representation and Substitution*, pp. 318–20; and in detail in Neder, *Participation in Christ*.
46   CD IV/3, p. 544.
47   CD IV/3, p. 623.

humanity which has not heard it but for which His work is dumb, and in this way to make the world and humanity hear. This is their *raison d'être*.[48]

The Spirit who enables the Word of God to be heard in communities of His intensive presence calls those communities to engage extensively in proclaiming God's salvation to the world which God has created, saved and will redeem. In Bonhoeffer's words: the church 'must tell people in every calling [Beruf] what a life with Christ is . . . It will have to speak of moderation, authenticity, trust, faithfulness, steadfastness, patience, discipline, humility, modesty, contentment.'[49] It is this activity to which the Spirit calls *some* in the world for the world. As Bonhoeffer's words demonstrate, however, this activity is not a preaching which is associated with any purism of the Word, but a preaching with our whole lives of the presence of the Spirit by the fruits He produces: it is more active than simple proclamation-reception; it involves wholeness.

However, when the church feels assured that it is created and formed by the Holy Spirit as a community of intensity and activism, the need once again to turn the critique of religion back upon itself (even in a church's self-perceived purist form) returns. The nature of the church as an event dependent upon the action of the Holy Spirit cannot itself be essentialized into some version of ecclesial purism: the church's very nature as dynamic and actualistic requires a constant alertness to the need to turn the critique of religion back onto itself and its own religiosity even in its quest to be a community formed by the dynamic and actualistic presence of the Spirit. A church against religion can never believe that it has arrived. The point is not that altars must be stripped, but that the very activity of stripping altars is as likely itself to arise from religious desires expressed in ecclesial essentialist forms as the activity of building the altar in the first place.[50] Turning the critique of religion back onto the church which seeks to follow this path

---

48 CD IV/3, p. 576.

49 LPP, p. 503; cf. Ethics, pp. 396–9.

50 One of the best examples of the point that is trying to be made here comes from C. S. Lewis' *The Screwtape Letters* in which the senior devil addresses his nephew with the following point: 'I warned you before that if your patient can't be kept out of the Church, he ought at least to be violently attached to some party within it. I don't mean on really doctrinal issues; about those, the more lukewarm he is the better. And it isn't the doctrines on which we chiefly depend for producing malice. The real fun is working up hatred between those who say "mass" and those who say "holy communion" . . . And all the purely indifferent things – candles and clothes and what not – are an admirable ground for our activities. We have quite removed from men's minds what that pestilent fellow Paul used to teach about food and other unessentials – namely, that the human without scruples should always give in to the human with scruples. You would think they could not fail to see the application. You would expect to find the "low" churchman genuflecting and crossing himself lest the weak conscience of his "high" brother should be moved to irreverence, and the "high" one refraining from these exercises lest he should betray his "low" brother into idolatry. And so it would have been but for our ceaseless labour.' C. S. Lewis, *The Screwtape Letters: Letter from a Senior to a Junior Devil* (London: Collins, 1942), pp. 84–5.

away from religion is the critical point: when one thinks one has arrived at avoiding religion as a church, the likelihood is that one has precisely essentialized some form of ecclesial purism which prevents the church from recognizing its dependence on the free activity of the Holy Spirit. The church must avoid the arrogance of believing its form is anything other than that of the broken body in which the Spirit freely chooses to act intensively.[51] There can be no absolute and sharp dividing line between the church and the world both because of God's freedom to work outside the bounds of the church, and because of the church's own broken and failed form – even if that form is an attempted enactment of the avoidance of religion.[52]

CHURCH: A COMMUNITY WITHIN THE WORLD

It is important, moreover, in recognizing this intensive work of God's Spirit as being the basis of the church's existence that one does not confuse this intensity of God's presence with a spatial exclusivity of God's presence as if God were not present elsewhere in the world. The purpose of the church is not to become a reclusive sect separated from the world but to dwell deeply and fully within the world.[53] While the Holy Spirit sanctifies and makes holy (from without) the community and individuals, this is not done by separating humanity into camps of sanctified and sinners, and engaging only with those whom we perceive as the former. Not only does the gospel message tell of a Jesus who ate and drank with sinners and tax collectors, but it also tells of a Jesus who transformed those categories. Jesus condemned the religiously puritanical Pharisees and suggested that tax collectors and prostitutes would precede them in their entry into the Kingdom of God.[54] The church must be a place, therefore, which stands with and within the world, not against it.

   Even in the very community identifiers of the church in its sacramental order, the unity of the church with the world is found. The symbols through which God

---

51   This is, I believe, the point at which the presentation of ecclesiology here differs from those of the Radical Reformation as much as from those of Roman Catholicism. Both prioritize the visibility of the church, and do not turn the critique of religion back onto themselves. This is particularly the case in ecclesiologies of the Radical Reformation, which have too great a confidence in the visible church (even in its stripped back form). I have far less confidence in the capacity of the church to 'arrive', or the capacity to draw as sharp a dividing line between church and world. In this way, while I have personal sympathy with the ecclesiologies of the likes of Yoder, I am nervous of the quest for the 'pure' church and the ecclesial essentialism in contrast to the world which underlies such approaches.

52   This parallels (ecclesially) the arguments in Chapter 5 on continued existence of sin in the believer and the broader hope of salvation.

53   There are dangers not only in sects which separate themselves from the world, but also in radical ecclesiologies which appear at times to shun engagement with secular powers and society.

54   There is an interesting discussion of the Pharisees in Ethics, pp. 309–15.

initiates and sustains the members of His church are not ones which remove the church from the world, but are ones which bind the church to the world. Water is itself the very basic necessity of life for all humanity (indeed, all creatures), and it is by this basic reality that a person is made a member of the people of God, Father, Son and Holy Spirit. The same degree of ordinariness is present in the sacred meal of the Christian church, the Lord's Supper. At the Lord's Table, we are not offered the 'special' elements of the Passover meal – the Passover lamb or the bitter herbs – but we are presented with the body of Christ in the most universal of food substances, bread, and his blood in the normality and 'everydayness' of wine. These elements of grace bind us to the world, as well as to the other members of the church. Furthermore, in the eschatological dimension of the Lord's Supper, the church is also bound to the Kingdom in which the many shall come from East and West to feast with Abraham, Isaac and Jacob. While these symbols of initiation and community membership present in themselves a unity of believers to one another,[55] as those baptized into the community of faith and sustained by the consumption of the bread and wine as the body and blood of Christ, these very sacramental elements not only bind Christians to one another but also, in the simplicity and ordinariness (one could say, in the secularity) of the signs God has chosen of bread and wine and water, to the very created order and to the ordinariness of everyday life in which God's Spirit is at work. Indeed, there is a degree to which the church is the place which demonstrates true sociality with the world, as opposed to any anti-social religious expression of individual or collective egoism. As Barth puts it:

> Solidarity with the world means that those who are genuinely pious approach the children of the world as such, that those who are genuinely righteous are not ashamed to sit down with the unrighteous as friends, that those who are genuinely wise do not hesitate to seem to be fools among fools, and that those who are genuinely holy are not too good or irreproachable to go down 'into hell' in a very secular fashion.[56]

Genuine piety and faith involves deep sociality with the world, not a collective egoistical separation from the world.[57]

---

55 The importance of unity for the sacraments was present in the church from earliest times. See, for example, I Cor. 11.19; *Didache* 9, 'As this broken bread, once dispersed over the hills, was brought together and became one loaf, so may thy Church be brought together . . . '; and Ignatius Mag. 7.2, Tral. 7.2 and Phd. 4. (Translation taken from Maxwell Stamforth and Andrew Louth, *Early Christian Writings: The Apostolic Fathers* (London: Penguin, 1987)).

56 CD IV/3, p. 774.

57 Clifford Green discusses this in terms of Bonhoeffer's christology in SC thus: 'The new humanity of Christ, socially concrete in the church, is presented in the third act of the drama of all humanity from creation (primal community), through fall (broken community), to reconciliation. This Christology and ecclesiology, therefore, is concerned with the rehabilitation and renovation of genuine

As has already been discussed, it is significant to note that the direction of Barth's writing is always from the world to the community to the individual, and therefore our capacity to understand God's being *pro me* (even in the collective *pro me*) exists only within the context of God's being radically and firstly *pro nobis*.[58] This has profound effects on expressions of the community: 'The solidarity of the community with the world consists quite simply in the active recognition that it, too, since Jesus Christ is the Saviour of the world, can exist in worldly fashion, not unwillingly nor with a bad conscience, but willingly and with a good conscience.'[59] There is thus a need for the church to stand on the side of the world, and not simply against it. This involves community engagement with the world, a deep sociality with the non-Christian:

> as those who are called we are constrained to be absolutely open in respect of *all other men without exception*, exercising towards them the same openness as that in which alone, because the event of our calling can never be behind us in such a way that it is not also before us, we can see and understand ourselves as those who are called. If our assertion has the validity which it can have only as grounded in Jesus Christ and therefore in the work and Word of God, then we cannot view any man only in the light of those factors, e.g., the corruption of his mode of life, the perverted and evil nature of his actions, the untenability of the ideas and convictions expressed by him, which obviously seem to characterise, and in very many cases do actually characterise him, as one who is not called, as non-Christian, unchristian and even anti-Christian.[60]

The church is not, therefore, a community whose concern is its own religion and self-preservation apart from and separate to the world. It is, instead, by the Holy Spirit a community of Christ with and in the world.[61] As such, the church is 'the society in which it is given to men to be under obligation to the world. As they know it, and are united in solidarity with it, they are made jointly responsible for it, for its future, for what is to become of it.'[62] To be the church is not simply to be on the side of the world, but to be in part responsible for the world.

The reason for this commitment to the world, and connection to it, arises from the provisional and representative nature of the church. The church's only real

---

humanity for all people. Christ is the Kollektivperson of the new humanity, superseding Adam as the Kollektivperson of the old humanity. Bonhoeffer's thinking is the very opposite of sectarian exclusivism; it moves, like Paul and Irenaeus, on the level of universal humanity.' Green, *Bonhoeffer: A Theology of Sociality*, p. 53.

58   CD IV/3, p. 496.
59   CD IV/3, p. 774.
60   CD IV/3, p. 493.
61   Cf. Ethics, pp. 96–7, in which Bonhoeffer differentiates a community that reveres Christ (religiously) and one in which Christ takes form.
62   CD IV/3, p. 776.

role is to be a provisional representation of all of humanity in the time before the eschaton – an expression of hope for all humanity which is justified in Christ. It is this which is the church's purpose and meaning in the world.[63] The church's direction is pointed towards the end in these end times, but this is not an end which will see the church's glorification. The end is one which will see the church's own end:

> [T]he end-time is the time of the community. It does not have it and its exist-
> ence in it merely for its own sake. As we have seen, it cannot be an end in
> itself. It has it for God, who is so very much for us men that He will not have
> it otherwise than that before He has finished speaking His last Word some, and
> even many, should already be for Him. And it has it for the world in order that
> as a provisional representation of the justification which has taken place in
> Jesus Christ it may be the sign which is set up in it, which is given to it, which
> summons it, in order that it may be to it a shining light – a feeble and defective
> but still a shining light – until the dawning of the great light which will be the
> end of all time and therefore of this end-time, the coming Jerusalem in which
> Rev. 21[22] tells us there will be no more temple because the Almighty God will
> Himself be its temple. The Christian community will then have rendered its
> service.[64]

Far from an everlasting religious community,[65] the apocalyptic community will need no temple as God will be the temple, and all of humanity will share in this eschatologically fulfilled community.

Given this eschatological direction to the nature of the church (an eschatological direction which will see its fulfilment in there being no need for the church), the church's nature is such that it is directed towards its end. The purpose of the church is thus not to seek to glorify itself, but to seek to serve the world by speaking of and demonstrating the justification and sanctification awaiting all humanity. While the distinction already discussed between *de iure* and *de facto* participation exists, this is not eternally determinative. Instead, Barth continues in his discussion of this distinction by stating of the church's representative function in relation to the *de facto* the following:

> This representation is provisional. It is provisional because it has not yet
> achieved it, nor will it do so. It can only attest it 'in the puzzling form of a
> reflection' (1 Cor. 13[12]). And it is provisional because, although it comes from
> the resurrection of Jesus Christ, it is only on the way with others to His return,

63   CD IV/1, p. 727.

64   CD IV/1, p. 739.

65   'An inescapable characteristic of the Church is . . . that as part of creation it, too, is finite and contingent.' Gunton, 'The Church on Earth: The Roots of Community', p. 67.

and therefore to the direct and universal and definitive revelation of His work as it has been accomplished for them and for all men.[66]

This provisionality does not mean that divine work is not done effectively and genuinely within the church,[67] but it does mean that the church is not the only community destined for eternal salvation as one religious sect in distinction from all other religious or non-religious sects. The church is, instead, representational of all humanity, and it is the task of representation with which the church is charged. The church is thus 'savingly necessary', but as a demonstration of God's present (and not simply past or future eschatological) saving work each day:[68] 'For the Jesus Christ who rules the world *ad dexteram Patris omnipotentis* is identical with the King of this people of His which on earth finds itself on this way and in this movement.'[69] However, this movement is a 'fitting of the Christian community for the provisional representation of the universal scope (concealed as yet) of the person and work of Jesus Christ.'[70] Indeed, the sin into which the church is constantly in danger of falling is precisely that of 'trying to represent itself rather than the sanctification which has taken place in Jesus Christ; of trying to forget that its existence is provisional, and that it can exist only as it points beyond itself'.[71]

Bonhoeffer engages in similar reflections to Barth's on provisional representation in terms of his categories of the ultimate and the penultimate, categories indeed which Bonhoeffer thinks may have special relevance to his reflections on religionless Christianity and the church.[72] While the context of Bonhoeffer's discussion of the ultimate and the penultimate is ethical, the implications of his thought may well bear fruit (as he thought it might) for ecclesiological reflections after Christendom. Bonhoeffer is deeply concerned with a Christianity or a theology or ethics which fails properly to attend to the simultaneity of the ultimate and the penultimate. Prioritizing one or other of these, advocates Bonhoeffer, leads to one of two extreme resolutions (extreme because they set the ultimate and the penultimate up as oppositions) – either the radical approach or the approach of compromise.[73] The radical solution attends only to the ultimate, seeking to break free from all that is penultimate;[74] the opposite solution of compromise attends

---

66   CD IV/3, pp. 620–1.
67   CD IV/3, p. 621.
68   CD IV/3, p. 621.
69   CD IV/3, p. 622.
70   CD IV/3, p. 623.
71   CD IV/3, pp. 622–3.
72   LPP, p. 365.
73   Ethics, p. 153.
74   Ethics, p. 153.

only to the penultimate, breaking with the ultimate.[75] Bonhoeffer neatly summarizes these positions as follows:

> Radicalism hates time. Compromise hates eternity.
> Radicalism hates patience. Compromise hates decision.
> Radicalism hates wisdom. Compromise hates simplicity.
> Radicalism hates measure. Compromise hates the immeasurable.
> Radicalism hates the real. Compromise hates the word.[76]

For Bonhoeffer, the only true relationship between these two positions can rest in the person of Jesus Christ, the incarnation of God in human flesh.[77] However, his perspective on the ultimate and the penultimate may well prove useful in thinking of the church as created *ex nihilo* as the Body of Christ in the present by an act of the Spirit. The danger of the church understanding itself as a radicalized community set against the world is precisely the danger of a religious church community which sees itself as God's presence on earth in opposition to all of the rest of the world (indeed, Bonhoeffer himself sees this as pharisaical);[78] this negative engagement fails to recognize the provisionality of the church in the present, as a community orientated towards its end when God shall be all in all. Indeed, Bonhoeffer hints at these concerns even in his earliest writings:

> [A] society and a community relate differently to time. If we describe the temporal intention of a community as reaching the boundary of time [grenzzeitlich], that of a society would be timebound [zeitbegrenzt]. Because of the eschatological character of community, which it shares with history, the deepest significance of community is 'from God to God'.[79]

However, the danger of compromise also lurks within an ecclesiology which fails properly to understand the church's representative function, or else its nature as an intensive community of the act of the Holy Spirit of God. The church is within and with the world, but it is not simply the same as the world, and as Barth puts it, *absolute* tolerance of the non-Christian would not take the non-Christian seriously. Again, Bonhoeffer's earliest writings display these kinds of concerns: 'only in faith do human beings know the being of revelation, their own being in the church of Christ, to be independent of faith.'[80] The world

---

75 Ethics, p. 154.
76 Ethics, p. 156.
77 Ethics, pp. 155–9.
78 Ethics, p. 156.
79 SC, p. 101.
80 AB, p. 118.

and the church constitute a differentiated whole, not an undifferentiated one.[81] For the church to exist within and with the world involves the church existing for the world as well.

This existing within the world for the world is precisely a non-religious engagement in ecclesiology, and a fitting expression of ecclesiology in a post-Christendom era. There is something deeply significant in what Bonhoeffer calls the 'structural being-with-each-other [Miteinander] of church-community and its members, and the members acting-for-each-other [Füreinander] as vicarious representatives':[82] this deep sociality recognizes the inter-connection of human beings, and (rather than being set against those one sees as other) is deeply engaged in being for others. In Bonhoeffer's early work (from which the preceding quotation is taken) this 'being for' is orientated towards others within the church. However, as his thought develops, so too does the extent to which this 'being for' is a determinative feature of the church for the world:

> The concept of vicarious representative action [Stellvertretung] defines this dual relationship most clearly. The Christian community stands in the place in which the whole world should stand. In this respect it serves the world as its vicarious representative; it is there for the world's sake.[83]

As with Barth, this 'being for' is an existence orientated on those outside the walls of the church,[84] in a manner which breaks the introverted and communally egotistical self-imaged idols of the church's creating. Being for the world involves the church prioritizing the serving of others over its own benefits, even to the point of cost to itself or self-sacrifice. In an age in which the church in the West is increasingly small (at least in the European context), the need to attend to the nature of the church within the world as for the world is pressing. Here, emphasizing the Reformation doctrine of the priesthood of all believers takes on new importance.[85] At a time when the church and the society of which the church is a part are no longer the same, and therefore when individual and clerical priests are not able to be vicarious for society at large, the whole community of the church is now more than ever needed to be the vicarious representatives of Christ in the world. How this is so is suggested in the next section of this chapter.

---

81   Cf. CD IV/3, p. 826.

82   SC, p. 191.

83   Ethics, p. 404.

84   This point provides the foundation for the engagements which follow in Chapters 7–9 of this book.

85   Jinkins notes: 'The church as sign cannot merely point to or signify itself (self-representation) without losing its existence as sign. But the church's existence as sign conveys more than justification; the church signals God's continuing priestly event of sharing God's life with humanity' (Jinkins, *The Church Faces Death*, p. 83).

CHURCH: A COMMUNITY FOR THE WORLD

Religion is not as innately communal as is often presumed: the mystic and ascetic often climb to religious heights through solitude and introversion; and even the most communal of religious groups often exercise intra-sociality for the preservation and survival of the communal ego. Bonhoeffer recognizes how these tendencies are related to a movement away from God and other human beings, and towards self-alienation and religion. The matters interrelate:

> Human beings have torn themselves loose from community with God and, therefore, also from that with other human beings, and now they stand alone, that is, in untruth. Because human beings are alone, the world is 'their' world, and other human beings have sunk into the world of things . . . God has become a religious object, and human beings themselves have become their own creator and lord, belonging to themselves.[86]

In light of such a description, it is not surprising, therefore, that Jinkins argues, '[i]ronically the church is most attractive when it pursues its vocation unconcerned with its own survival.'[87] The concern for others beyond the collective ego of religion allows that the existence of others is not merely an existence of other human beings within one's own self-created world, in which one's self-created God also exists. The church's vocation is, therefore, communion with God found by not belonging to oneself (individually or collectively), but found instead in the sociality that the act of the Spirit brings about. This vocation of the church is its existence for the sake of the world, and not for the sake of itself. Being a community determined to be for the world itself presupposes a depth of sociality to enable a reaching beyond its own communitarian bounds. This, too, is an act of the Holy Spirit: the Spirit who dwells intensively in the church, pushes the church beyond its own walls into the extensity of the world. Put otherwise, one might say that, while faith and hope are gifts to be desired, the gift of love is the greatest to be desired because of its orientation on the other. Barth asserts this emphatically:

> The work of the Holy Spirit in the gathering and upbuilding of the community (*C.D.*, IV, 1 § 62 and IV, 2 § 67) cannot merely lead to the blind alley of a new qualification, enhancement, deepening and enrichment of this being of the community as such. Wonderful and glorious as this is, it is not an end in itself even in what it includes for its individual members. The enlightening power of the Holy Spirit draws and impels and presses beyond its being as such, beyond all the reception and experience of its members, beyond all that is

---

86 AB, p. 137.
87 Jinkins, *The Church Faces Death*, p. 32.

promised to them personally. And only as it follows this drawing and impelling is it the real community of Jesus Christ.[88]

As is demonstrated in the person of Jesus Christ, God is not simply for Himself, but for the world.[89] As the community of witness to Jesus Christ, which is brought about by the Holy Spirit, the church cannot simply be an end in itself. The task of the church, instead, is to be sent into the world within which and with which and for which it exists. The church's orientation is not to be focused on itself as a pure religious community, but on the world which is no less really God's creation than the church is. Thus far in this chapter, it might seem that there has been little discussion of the church being for God. However, it is in this very being for others that the church is for God, that it executes the purpose for which God has created it, and that it fulfils the task God has set it. In the church's reaching beyond itself to the other in love, the church is enabled by the Spirit to participate in mutual love of God the Holy Trinity. In being for others, the church is enabled genuinely to be for God.

Although one should use spatial language with a degree of caution, Bonhoeffer's discussion of these themes is helpful:

> The space of the church does not, therefore, exist just for itself, but its existence is already always something that reaches far beyond it. This is because it is not the space of a cult that would have to fight for its own existence in the world. Rather, the space of the church is the place where witness is given to the foundation of all reality in Jesus Christ. . . . The space of the church is not there in order to fight with the world for a piece of territory, but precisely to testify to the world that it is still the world, namely the world that is loved and reconciled by God.[90]

According to Bonhoeffer, a church which fights for its own interests rather than those of the world can only ever be a religious society rather than the church of God. The church's role is instead to be for the world, a witness to the world of the reality it already knows.[91] This task of witness is one which Barth sees as being primary to the role and purpose of the church.[92] The vocation of humans is to be Christian, and by this to be witnesses to God's word.[93] This vocation leads the church out towards the world:

---

88   CD IV/3, p. 764.

89   CD IV/3, p. 763.

90   Ethics, p. 63.

91   Ethics, p. 67.

92   In his excellent work on the post-liberal theologians (themselves heavily influenced by Barth), it is the category of witness that Paul DeHart sees as being the heartbeat of the theologies of both Frei and Lindbeck. See Paul J. DeHart, *The Trial of the Witnesses: The Rise and Decline of Postliberal Theology* (Oxford: Blackwells, 2006), esp. chapter 6.

93   One should note that Barth also discusses the lesser lights in §69, and the reader is directed to Chapters 4 and 8 of this book for further reflection.

the Christian is a witness, a witness of the living Jesus Christ as the Word of God and therefore a witness to the whole world and to all men of the divine act of grace which has taken place for all men. Thus in what makes him a Christian the first concern is not with his own person. He is referred, not to himself, but to God who points him to his neighbour, and to his neighbour who points him to God. He does not look into himself, but in the most pregnant sense outwards . . . [94]

The concern of Christians is not for themselves, or their religious purism, but for the neighbours around them. This is because realizing the graciousness of God, the Christian is able to recognize that she exists in the 'most profound solidarity with the great and little sinners' with whom she lives, and to whom she witnesses as most likely 'the first and greatest sinner'.[95] Not only is this the case on an individual level. For Barth, this service of witness is a communal calling: 'The *community* dares to hope in Jesus Christ and therefore it dares to hope for the world.'[96] The church is a community in which there is intensive activity of the Holy Spirit in order that it may witness to the world within which and for which it exists.

For Bonhoeffer, the degree to which the church is for the world as a witness finds new depths in his provocative assertion that the role of the church is to bear the guilt of the world. In this discussion, one might see a creative and contextually appropriate version of the priesthood of all believers in a post-Christendom society. In Bonhoeffer's presentation, it is clear that the church is a minority, but one which should not seek to be a moralistic religious remnant. Bonhoeffer arrestingly writes:

The church is today the community of people who, grasped by the power of Christ's grace, acknowledge, confess, and take upon themselves not only their personal sins, but also the Western world's falling away from Jesus Christ as toward Jesus Christ.[97]

Bonhoeffer develops this idea thus:

With this confession the whole guilt of the world falls on the church, on Christians, and because here it is confessed and not denied, the possibility of forgiveness is opened . . . for there are people here who take all – really all – guilt upon themselves, not in some heroic self-sacrificing decision, but simply overwhelmed by their very own guilt towards Christ. In that moment they can

---

94   CD IV/3, p. 652. See also the discussion of the category of witness in relation to mission in Chapter 5 of this book.
95   CD IV/3, p. 653. This is a theme I have addressed in detail above in the sub-section 'The co-sinfulness of all humanity' in Chapter 5.
96   CD IV/3, p. 720.
97   Ethics, p. 135.

no longer think about retributive justice for the 'chief sinners' but only about the forgiveness of their own great guilt.[98]

In this description of the role of the church, we see a version of ecclesiology entirely at odds with religious approaches: rather than a community identity determined for eternal glorification, one sees a community of the Spirit which is truly enabled to be the body of Christ, bearing the world's guilt and sacrificing itself for the sake of the other. It is here that we see the real self-sacrifice involved for the church which seeks to be for the world. This is a true act in correspondence with the life of Jesus; it is genuinely being within the world for the world.

CONCLUSION

In the situation of post-Christendom, with visibly reduced power and status for the church, the need to think about ecclesiology is pressing. If salvation (from a Christian perspective) is not, as I have argued in Chapter five of this book, simply tied to religious affiliation, the purpose of the church in the world requires rethinking: the normal categories of the church as the setting in which a person may come to have eternal life are no longer appropriate. Barth asks:

Did the Son of God clothe Himself with humanity, and shed His blood, and go out as the Sower, simply in order that He might create for these people – in free grace, yet why specifically for them and only for them? – this indescribably magnificent private good fortune, permitting them to obtain and possess a gracious God, opening to them the gates of Paradise which are closed to others?[99]

The answer to this question of suspect *sacro egoism* is quite determinately '*Nein!*'. The church is not a society that exists for its own purposes or benefit, declaring dividing spatial lines of where God is or is not present, confining God in its own temples and precincts, and establishing itself as a remnant and a moral minority. Its purpose is not religious, but concerns an orientation on the world within which and for which it exists. It is this message which needs to be heard so that liturgies can be transformed in order to praise not an idol but the God of all creation,[100] and so that sermons may begin to share the good news to a post-Christendom world. It is this message which needs to be heard in order that the lives of the saints can demonstrate a wise ordering on God and neighbour. How this good news might relate to the public sphere, and how the church is to be for the world in society is the topic to which this book now turns.

---

98 Ethics, p. 136. When one considers the situation in which Bonhoeffer is writing about the 'chief sinners', the force of what he is saying is even greater.
99 CD IV/3, p. 567.
100 On these themes and worship, see Boulton, *God against Religion*.

Chapter 7

RELIGIONLESSNESS AND PUBLIC SPACE: GENEROUS PARTICULARISM

The decreased power of the church in a post-Christendom society both in terms of numbers and in terms of influence suggests that theological discussion of the relationship between the church and the state would be a wise enterprise in which to engage in this changed societal environment. Indeed, the very fact of a complex and heterogeneous religious situation within states determines that the traditional issue of the relationship between the church and the state cannot simply be thought of or stated in those terms any longer. Rather, it is now considered in terms of the relationship between what the state terms 'the religious' (in the place of the church) and the secular. However, even this raises a complexity. When people of faith are asked by the state or state organizations to identify themselves, there is usually a question or box to fill in which is entitled 'religion'. Despite the movement to the relationship between the religious and the secular in such public discourse, the very answer to the kind of question that the state poses regarding religion from practitioners of faith never involves simply the answer: 'yes' or 'religious'. The response is always deeply particular and specific – an identification with one of a series of particular traditions which the state lists together (Christian, Sikh, Muslim and so on). In a sense, therefore, the problem of the contemporary relationship between the secular and the religious is one which is formed to a degree by the state in response to the de-Christianization or pluralization of political nation states.[1] Church–state relations have been replaced with religious–secular relations in contemporary states, and it is thus necessary to consider theologically the way in which religion operates as a category in discussions of these themes. The category of the religious in political

---

1 Clearly, the state is not the singular cause of this relationship: minimal settlements in the post-Reformation era, to which the birth of secularism can be traced, involved both the churches and the state, and religion was also a category utilized in nineteenth-century Protestant theology. However, we might wish to concur with Bonhoeffer in terms of the fundamental effect of this creation of secular space on the church: 'God's being pushed out of the world, away from public human existence, has led to an attempt to hang on to God at least in the realm of the "personal," the "inner life," the "private" sphere' (LPP, p. 455).

terms is one which is generally formed outside of the specific and individual traditions of faiths. Nevertheless, since the category itself points to the complex situation in which the church now finds itself, in which it must negotiate its relationship to a state which understands itself as secular and yet is also simultaneously a representative pluralist nation (the very fact that causes the state to shape the category religion), it remains an important theological issue to consider. Indeed, failing to attend to this categorical relationship between the secular and the religious will determine that attending to *either* secularism *or* pluralism will always be insufficient, since these two terms are deeply interconnected. This chapter argues that religionless or anti-religious theology is well placed to respond to these issues, and seeks to articulate a theologically sensitive account of the church's relationship to the public square, which might offer potential wisdom with the purpose of healing a broken situation in which there is inadequate and insensitive negotiation of issues surrounding religious–secular relations. At a time when much in politics concerns itself with religious pluralism on a national or global stage, wise approaches to the relationship between politics and so-called religion are surely to be valued and sought.

THE POLITICS OF THE SECULAR

If ever there were need to prove the worth in Wittgenstein's mantra that we should look not for meaning but for use with regard to language, the word 'secular' would undoubtedly offer proof of his point. As well as concerning a decline in numbers attending churches and a decline in active engagement in religious activity within a population, the secular process might also be considered to concern the creation of secular space, which in Western European (and, in a different way, American) terms can be seen generally in the increased separation of the church and state, and in the decline of ecclesial power in the temporal sphere. In his discussions of secularism, the sociologist David Martin points to the concept of differentiation in terms of dealing with this movement: activities that were once focused on the church now find themselves separate from the church and present in autonomous spheres under the control of their own professional experts. This gives rise to secular professions equivalent to services once offered by the church (including psychiatrists, social workers and counsellors), and social and intellectual spheres are released from ecclesiastical tutelage and control.[2] Martin describes this as 'the collapsing of a social frame around which the vines of faith have traditionally been twisted'.[3] The detailed particularities of this process are unpacked by Martin in some of his earlier work. In this, he describes the secular process in a fourfold (but not a unified and singular) manner: first, the decreased power, wealth, influence, range of control and

---

2   Martin, *Reflections on Sociology and Theology*, pp. 237–8.
3   Ibid., p. 239.

prestige of ecclesiastical institutions; second, the decreased frequency, number, intensity and perceived efficacy of religious rituals, customs and practices; third, a movement in the intellectual sphere towards the rationalistic, empirical and sceptical; and fourth, a shift in attitude towards the reverential, charismatic and noumenal.[4] While elements of these trends have no doubt been welcomed by elements of the church, as they protect the church against a singularly other-worldly focus, or a singularly power-based this-worldly focus, these disparate movements have often been programmatically linked together as a single, unified and all-encompassing thesis aimed and targeted at describing a paradigm in which religion no longer has any place.[5] Talal Asad describes this unification as secularism as a 'doctrine'.[6] In this mode, secularism demands a distinction between private reason and public principle, placing of the 'religious' in the category of the private (crucially) on account of the secular.[7] This is a maximal outworking of the secular settlement which was initially formed to be what Quash and Jenkins refer to as 'set of minimal rules or dispositions that allow the working together of the various religious intensities in some sort of political unit for some sort of collective good'.[8] In this maximal outworking, what we see is a form of secularism which claims to be:

> the horizon of civilization, a final truth about humanity that will replace all local traditions, whether cultural, social, political, ethnic or religious in expression. In this way, instead of being simply a court of last resort in the case of disputes between forms of intensity/identity, secularism becomes a rival form, seeking to displace all these various forms of intensity (designated collectively as 'religion') from the public sphere.[9]

In this form, maximal secularism becomes the very thing it was initially meant to prevent. It forms a singular and universal voice, which will not allow others to speak, and which drowns out public religious speech in its belief that its self-created category of 'the religious' belongs only to the private realm. Thereby, secularism becomes detached from the pluralism it was designed to mediate. Rather than being a political tool, it becomes a political agenda.

However, maximal secularism has suffered somewhat from a backlash to its eschatological predictions about religion. Secularization itself has led to 'powerful movements of counter-secularization', most obviously in various forms of religious fundamentalisms that have appeared around the globe.[10] In his own

---

4   Martin, *The Religious and the Secular*, pp. 48–54.
5   Martin helpfully describes this as a placing together of a large number of discrete elements into an 'intellectual hold-all' (ibid., p. 2)
6   Asad, *Formations of the Secular*, p. 1.
7   Ibid., p. 8.
8   Jenkins and Quash, 'The Cambridge Inter-Faith Programme: Academic Profile'.
9   Ibid.
10   See Berger, 'The Desecularization of the World: A Global Overview'.

book on Bonhoeffer's religionless Christianity, Jeffrey Pugh puts it thus: 'Chaos, dead bodies, havoc and the sight of passions inflamed as chants are yelled and gunshots fill the air. And somewhere in the world where these things take place you just know that the name of God, Allah, or Shiva is going to be invoked.'[11] Even in the situation of Western Europe, which remains the exceptional case since it is continuing to evince some form of continued secularization,[12] not only do global politics determine that religious fundamentalism is on the political agenda of the most seemingly secular of countries,[13] but commentators wonder whether the conditions are already set for de-secularization: 'Would there – could there – be a rechurching of Europe? . . . Social space is undoubtedly being cleared. Either there will be a vacuum – something that has never happened before – or a religious nature fills the vacuum.'[14]

A maximal version of secularism has responded to the perceived potential for violence from religious communities by itself becoming violent towards individual faith commitments, and by seeking religious eradication. This has in turn led to a response to extreme secularism of this variety from certain faith communities, and a vicious cycle has followed, as one form of fundamentalist dogmatism reinforces its equal and opposite kind.[15] What one sees, therefore, is not only an intellectual symbiosis of the religious and the secular, but a political symbiosis of the two, which is likely only to become more deeply mutually dependent. If public theology is to do with the public relevance of theological statements,[16] the public situation into which theology speaks is one marked by a complex relationship between the secular and the religious. Speaking supposedly from the side of the category which secularism affirms as religious, theology needs to think from within faith traditions about how to engage in this complex negotiation of the relationship between the community it describes and seeks to form, and the political society in which it dwells more broadly. The imperative to engage with the political state is all the more pressing when it is recognized that for the church so sharp a line between the ostensibly public secular space and the ostensibly private religious space is simply not one which is easy to draw (if it is possible at all).[17] As Barth evocatively reminds us:

> the object of the promise and the hope in which the Christian community has
> its eternal goal consists, according to the unmistakeable assertion of the New

---

11   Pugh, *Religionless Christianity*, p. 69.

12   See Davie, *Europe: The Exceptional Case.*

13   One sees this not only in foreign policy decisions in the Middle East, but also in the radicalization of young Muslims in non-Muslim countries, and even (from the perception of maximal secularists) in the disputes over such issues as the wearing of the *hijab* in France.

14   Martin, *Reflections on Sociology and Theology*, p. 231.

15   Cf. Ford, 'God and Our Public Life: A Scriptural Wisdom', p. 76; and Martin, *The Religious and the Secular*, p. 3 and chapter 4.

16   On the nature of public theology as a discipline, see Storrar and Morton, 'Introduction', p. 1.

17   See the discussion in Chapter 6 of this volume.

Testament, not in an eternal Church but in the *polis* built by God and coming down from heaven to earth, and the nations shall walk in the light of it and the kings of the earth will bring their glory and honour into it . . . [18]

There is, therefore, no such thing as an apolitical church.[19] It needs to be remembered that even Jesus' statement 'render under Caesar that which is Caesar's and render unto God that which is God's' (Mk 12.17) is spoken within a theological framework in which even Caesar himself is understood to be a creation of God, who needs to be justified and redeemed by Him. Again to quote Barth:

> By believing in Jesus Christ and preaching Jesus Christ it [the church] believes in and preaches Him who is the Lord of the world as He is Lord of the Church. And since they belong to the inner circle, the members of the Church are also automatically members of the wider circle. They cannot halt at the boundary where the inner and outer circles meet, though the work of faith, love and hope which they are under orders to perform will assume different forms on either side of the boundary.[20]

Political engagement is necessary for the church truly to be the church. This means that simple binary thinking about the secular and the sacred, a religious realm and a political realm, requires challenging: the church cannot simply accept the external mandate of maximal secularism (or even perhaps its minimal form) either by succumbing to its demands or rejecting it *in toto*. The question is not whether the church should be political, but what the wise way is in which the church should be political, and how it can negotiate its purpose in a complexly pluralist and secular society.

OVERCOMING BINARIES: THE COMPLEXITIES OF INTER-RELATIONSHIP

The acceptance of binary patterns of thinking about these issues runs deeply in politics, the church, the academy and society more generally.[21] Maximal secularism has in many ways become the dominant voice, not in terms of its multilateral acceptance but in terms of its ability to control the agenda of the discussion around

---

18   CCCC, p. 154.

19   CCCC, p. 157.

20   CCCC, pp. 158–9. As Fergusson puts it: 'By emphasizing the universal significance of God's action in Christ from which the polity of the church derives, ecclesial isolationism may be avoided.' (David Fergusson, *Community, Liberalism & Christian Ethics* (Cambridge: CUP, 1998), p. 167).

21   On binary logic (and how to overcome it), see Peter Ochs, *Peirce, Pragmatism and the Logic of Scripture* (Cambridge: CUP, 2004).

these themes. This is not only a potentially but also a genuinely dangerous situation, given that politics at its most elemental form is based on pluralism and the co-existence of people who will invariably have competing agendas. In its extreme form in New Atheism, maximal secularism presents a situation which seeks co-existence by the denial of plurality. Aggressively organized atheist pressure groups, which include those such as the one headed by Richard Dawkins, are tantamount to the suppression of pluralism:[22] they propose a society which in reality is as anti-Muslim, anti-Sikh, anti-Hindu, and so on, as it is anti-Christian. This form of maximal secularism is no tolerant and peaceful society, but a society of oppression, state domination and persecution of religions, and – to employ terms pertinent not only to our age but to the most aggressive attempt in Western Europe at an atheist society, that of France following the Revolution – of terror.[23] The mirror opposite to this form of non-pluralist secularist politics is the non-pluralist politics of fundamentalism. In this religious approach to the world, the possibility of genuine politics (based on difference and pluralism) is also driven out in order that God (who becomes a spatially confined idol in nations and the world) does not have to secede space to secularist atheism or the foreign gods. Like maximal secularism, fundamentalism works with exclusive logic which disallows a place for the other, and sees otherness as a dangerous affront to society.

It is here where one might begin to see the potential fruit that theologizing the critique of religion might bear politically. Put crudely, one might say something like this: simply accepting the critique of religion (as espoused by the likes of Feuerbach and his intellectual heirs, Nietzsche and Marx)[24] leads to an intolerant atheism; refusing to accept the critique of religion leads to fundamentalism. Engaging *theologically* with the critique of religion offers the capacity to engage critically and formatively *from within*. This mode of engagement has the potential to offer a political settlement that does not come at the expense of the displacement of the individual communities of faith, but arises from within the deep particularism of individual faith communities. Recognizing the capacity of the secular strategy to marginalize (and alienate) faith commitment, Charles Mathewes operates within the kinds of logic espoused here: 'If the fundamental problem of modern politics is pluralism, this is a fundamentally religious problem and must be confronted as such.'[25] By engaging with the critique of religion, I propose that problematic elements of religion are identified as such. However, by theologizing with this critique, I seek to offer genuine engagement with the issues at stake at the root of the problems from within the traditions themselves.

---

22   For an example of this mode of thinking, see his recent book *The God Delusion*.

23   As Charles Mathewes puts it: 'To save its cities, Europe destroyed its churches . . . ' Charles Mathewes, *A Theology of Public Life* (Cambridge: CUP, 2007), p. 112.

24   Under the guise of biological-materialism, it seems the critiques of the likes of Dawkins owe their philosophical roots to Marx.

25   Mathewes, *A Theology of Public Life*, p. 111.

The necessity of such theological engagement is made all the more plain when one recognizes that the binaries of maximal secularism and fundamentalism form the extremes of a more deep-seated binary approach. From a religious perspective, the binary possibility that most religious traditions seem to work within in this context is either adaptation to modernity/secularity or rejection of modernity/secularity. Here, Peter Berger's comments are wise: 'As is always the case when strategies are based on mistaken presumptions of the terrain, both strategies have had very doubtful results.'[26] The problematic nature of the position which espouses rejection seems clear enough: its incapacity to engage with the public square arises in its unwillingness to do so for the sake of its own authenticity. But the case of adaptation is also problematic in terms of the relativization of religious particularity to an external norm outside the tradition. Adaptation creates a religious liberalism which is distrusted by those who understand themselves as standing more orthodoxly within a tradition, as the very tradition of which it is a part is subjugated to an external liberal norm.[27] MacIntyre's observations are helpful here: 'liberal theory is best understood, not at all as an attempt to find a rationality independent of tradition, but as itself an articulation of an historically developed and developing set of social institutions and forms of activity, that is, as the voice of a tradition.'[28] For those engaged in adaptation, the tradition of liberalism, therefore, is the particular way in which the particularist religious tradition both presents itself and is read. In this way, what the political setting is offered by the assimilated community is not a mechanism for dialogue between seemingly competing communities in a pluralist framework, but a principled agreement around a secular political norm (a liberal tradition) which receives a more definitive status than the particularity of the tradition which has assimilated to that norm. Not only can liberals not speak with the more conservative co-members of their faith tradition, who distrust them as inauthentic members of their community, but they also cannot genuinely engage in politics, as they work by assimilating themselves to the external norm which is meant as *the mechanism for* dialogue rather than *the terminus to* that dialogue: their assimilation removes the need or basis for genuine politics as secular principles are able to replace or trump the exclusivity and diversity of faith commitments. In response to the challenge of disagreement and difference in a pluralist setting (i.e. in response to politics in its most elemental form), Mathewes is right, therefore, to assert: 'Modern thought in general, and modern theology in particular, is ill-equipped to help us here, as it is committed more to avoiding than to confronting the challenge.'[29] Liberal religious traditions, by assimilating and adapting to secularism, do not break the binary relationship between religion and secularity in the modern world despite what might seem an

---

26   Berger, 'The Desecularization of the World: A Global Overview', p. 3.
27   Cf. Bonhoeffer's comments on radicalism and compromise; see Chapter 6 of this book.
28   MacIntyre, *Whose Justice? Which Rationality?*, p. 345.
29   Mathewes, *A Theology of Public Life*, p. 108.

ostensible solution to the problems outlined. What has resulted, therefore, is in Barth's words an approach which often follows one of two options – 'Pietistic sterility on one hand, and the sterility of the Enlightenment on the other'.[30] Bonhoeffer, too, speaks in similarly binary terms in discussing 'a spiritual exist-ence that takes no part in worldly existence, and a worldly existence that can make good its claim over and against the sacred sector. The monk and the cultural Prot-estant of the nineteenth century represent these two possibilities.'[31] The danger is that the attempt at a purified religion (i.e. the purely sacral/religious), which rejects engagement with the world, leads to a church which is insufficient in being only spiritual; and that an attempt at producing a secular gospel, which concerns human law, creates a deity who is not the Father of Jesus Christ.[32] In this creating of a deity or deifying of the state (and the theory behind it), Barth recognizes the dan-gers of 'making the State a devil'.[33]

Instead, what is needed in the current political setting is an approach which takes seriously particularity and authenticity, and engages from *within* the unique specifi-cities of an individual tradition in order to facilitate a genuinely political society – one of difference and plurality. In Christian theological terms, this is a position which recognizes that innate to Christian theology's engagement with secularity there needs to be a direct engagement with the setting of plurality that underlies secularism. For Christian theology, secular-faith concerns are deeply and inextric-ably linked to inter-faith relations, since secularism is itself an attempt at mediating or coming to terms with a pluralist society. One might say, therefore, that the engage-ment with the secular other is an engagement with the religious other, that secular-ism presupposes and is fearful of. Theologizing the critique of religion provides the basis for one such approach here, in its capacity to engage with individual religious intensity, but (in a political community of difference) to turn its critique back onto itself, and in so doing to be cautious of finding offence in the other. It is to the effects of an anti-religious theology on liberalism that this chapter now turns.

LIBERALISM AND PARTICULARISM

In his book *Christianity in a Secularized World*, Wolfhart Pannenberg asserts:

Christian theology in the secular world must not give up central elements in God's transcendence of the world and in his salvation or allow them to fade

30   CS, p. 105.
31   Ethics, p. 57. Cf. LPP, p. 428: 'The weakness of liberal theology was that it allowed the world the right to assign to Christ his place within it'.
32   CS, pp. 104–5.
33   CS, p. 125. Given this, Barth can hardly be seen, as Raymond Plant suggests, as 'the classic state-ment of the liberal view of the relationship between religious belief and wider political culture' (Raymond Plant, *Politics, Theology and History* (Cambridge: CUP, 2001), p. 201). Indeed, Barth is fierce (as we shall see) in his rejection of the idea of the state as somehow an embodiment of Christian values.

into the background for the sake of assimilation to the secular understanding of reality. On the other hand, Christianity may not be content with just securing the existence of the dogmatic content of the tradition. That would be merely to oppose a counter-world of faith to the secular world, not to bear witness to God as creator and reconciler of this world of ours.[34]

In supporting his position, Pannenberg points to the theology of demythologizing, and advocates that its mistake was not in its engagement with the biblical worldview, but in its disputing that faith in God had any relevance for understanding the world. The concern that needs to be engaged for him, therefore, is how to say something which is deeply and genuinely relevant *to the world* but to the world as seen from within the tradition of the Christian faith.

This move requires more careful navigation than the matter is often given. Jeffrey Stout, for example, advocates 'a form of pluralism, one that citizens with strong religious commitments can accept and that welcomes their full participation in public life without fudging on its own premises'.[35] So far, so good, we might say, given what has been advocated thus far in this chapter. But he continues by stating: 'But I see pluralism primarily as an existing feature of the political culture, not as a philosophical doctrine needing to be imposed on it. Our political culture is already pluralistic in the relevant sense.'[36] What Stout fails to recognize is the difficult relationship of individual 'strong religious commitments' to plurality, and he thus must surely presuppose some degree of assent to liberal versions of faith in this. Stout does not offer due attention to the exclusivist and different claims about the world that are made by individual and particular communities. Dealing (relevantly to the present book) with the charge of atheism, Kendall Soulen makes this point well with regard to ancient theo-politics of religion from the perspective of Roman authority: 'Jews (and later Christians) were atheists – not because they were monotheists, but because they were *exclusive* monotheists.'[37] What Stout fails to recognize is in Mathewes' words: 'The challenge of pluralism confronts theology as both a contingent socio-historical problem and a basic problematic essential to the theological tradition.'[38]

One can see the implications of this point exemplified in Stout's engagement with Barth. Stout speaks of what he sees to be Barth's 'commendable commitment to democracy',[39] and even goes on to assert

---

34 Wolfhart Pannenberg, *Christianity in a Secularized World* (London: SCM, 1988), pp. 56–7.

35 Jeffrey Stout, *Democracy and Tradition* (Princeton: Princeton University Press, 2004), pp. 296–7.

36 Ibid., p. 297.

37 R. Kendall Soulen, '"Go Tell Pharaoh" or, Why Empires Prefer a Nameless God,' *Cultural Encounters* Sample Issue (2005), 9, emphasis added.

38 Mathewes, *A Theology of Public Life*, p. 121.

39 Stout, *Democracy and Tradition*, p. 298. Barth does affirm democracy (e.g. CS, p. 145), but advocates that the members of the church, who are supportive of it, are nevertheless foreigners to it (e.g. CS, p. 146). Stout is hoist by his own Barthian petard here.

It would be a good thing if the relevant parts of Barth's *Church Dogmatics* came to hold a prominent place in the seminary curricula of all the desert faiths. So much the better if voices seeking to democratize religious institutions were heard as well.[40]

That he speaks of Barth as being normative for Jews and Muslims is indicative enough of his failed recognition of the importance of particularity. Why should Barth be the basis of any Muslim, Jewish, or other tradition's engagement with theo-politics? And why should democracy be the norm? Pertinently perhaps, I say this as a democrat myself, and as one deeply committed to inter-faith engagement – a member of the religious left to which Stout points. But more subtly indicative of Stout's failure to attend to particularity is the assumptions he reads into Barth. These assumptions arise from a mode of reading which misses Barth's concern for particularity and assumes certain external, secular and liberal predispositions in Barth which are not there in the way Stout thinks they are.[41] Barth is emphatic, for example, that the Christian should not assert that one political system is *the* political system, the most true or most Christian: 'the Christian community has no exclusive theory of its own to advocate in face of the various forms and realities of political life. It is not in a position to establish one particular doctrine as *the* Christian doctrine of the just State.'[42] This is as true for democracy as anything else. But, and herein lies the rub, Barth's basis for making this claim does not rest at any point in the claims of the liberal state, or in the realities of the historical and contingent situation. Instead, Barth's basis for making the claims arises from the very particularity of his Christian faith which undermines any capacity to confuse this world with the Kingdom of God, or any political principle with Jesus Christ. The rejection of the idea that any system can be identified as Christian is precisely because God does not reveal Himself in this way. In Bonhoeffer's words:

> Christ is not a principle according to which the whole world must be formed. Christ does not proclaim a system of that which would be good today, here, and at all times. Christ does not teach an abstract ethic that must be carried out, cost what it may. Christ was not essentially a teacher, a lawgiver, but a

---

40   Ibid., p. 298.
41   Stout reads democracy into Barth's account, missing at times the important actualistic nature of Barth's mode of thinking. Thus, Stout points to Barth's statement that God can speak through Communism or a flute concerto, and suggests that God clearly can speak through democracy, therefore (ibid., p. 109); however, Barth does not see these things as *in themselves* things through which God normatively speaks (nor does he ever give democracy as an example), but is pointing to God's freedom to reveal Godself however God wills (cf. Chapter 2 of this book). Stout's work is, therefore, at least as much a hardening (albeit in a different purported direction) of Barth's dynamism as he detects is the case in Hauerwas and Yoder (ibid., p. 154).
42   CCCC, p. 160; cf. p. 161.

human being, a real human being like us. . . . God did not become an idea, a principle, a universally valid belief or a law; God became human.[43]

It is the very revelation of God in the person of Jesus Christ which is the basis for a rejection of any individual political system as the godly one (democracy as much as theocracy); it is not an assent to a liberal category to which all else must be subjugated, a category which thereby reduces particularist intensity.

The outworking of this concern for particularity in the church and theology in terms of their engagement with secularity and plurality is, as Quash and Jenkins put it, that there needs to be

> a certain distance from what one might call 'conceptualist' or 'comparative' approaches. By emphasizing common ground between traditions at the outset, these latter approaches consciously or unconsciously reproduce the wider (or second) secular project of seeking a common humanity and public space over and against the particularity of any single faith.[44]

Rather than refusing to reject the possibility of engagement in a pluralist setting, the basis for a genuine engagement with a pluralist society needs to be found on the basis of individual particularism.[45] MacIntyre's perspective is precisely right, therefore, when he states that we need to recover from the Enlightenment

> a conception of rational enquiry as embodied in a tradition, a conception according to which the standards of rational justification emerge from and are part of a history in which they are vindicated by the way in which they transcend the limitations of and provide the remedies for the defects of their predecessors within the history of that same tradition.[46]

A positive engagement with difference should not for intensively and exclusively faithful people be found outside of the traditions of which they are a part: the basis for it can only be found from within those traditions. Part of this may well include seeking 'remedies for the defects of their predecessors within the history of that same tradition', but those remedies again should be found deeply within the tradition from which the discourse arises. Thus, what is required of theology is a particularist approach which presents, as being deeply innate to the particularism from which it arises, a positive openness towards the other in their otherness.

---

43 Ethics, pp. 98–9; cf. p. 231.
44 Jenkins and Quash, 'The Cambridge Inter-Faith Programme: Academic Profile'.
45 Quash and Jenkins engage with this idea in terms of inter-faith under the helpful title of 'interactive particularity'. For more on this issue, see Chapter 9 in this volume.
46 MacIntyre, *Whose Justice? Which Rationality?*, p. 7.

This particularism means that, while recent 'communitarian' approaches to public life have sometimes led to an introversion and separation from society or (in the terms of the previous chapter) a moralist sacral egoism arising from the Radical Reformation,[47] the mode and inclination of the communitarian approach is right. What is required of this approach is a more positive engagement with the world, brought through bringing the critique of religion back onto the church and onto the religious communal and individual self, a move which helps to protect against any remnant or moral minority understandings of the community of the church.[48] Just as Barth's intense christology led him to a more positive assessment of the capacities of knowing God in the world,[49] so the deep particularity of the church's engagement with the plurality of the societies of which it is a part must give rise to a more positive assessment of interaction and engagement with the other, who comes not to be defined as the one whom the Christian is against but the one whom the Christian is for. Engagement with the state and plurality needs to become necessary on the grounds of the particular revelation of God to the world in Jesus Christ, known through the work of the Spirit.

For Barth, the grounds for this engagement are expressed christologically. The state is a christological sphere, but at a lower level than the Christian church.[50] It is notable for him that the Pontius Pilate comes to be a person included in the creed, and it is particularly important to note that he is discussed under the second article.[51] The christological focus of the church leads it outwards to the world which is created through the Logos and reconciled and redeemed by Him also. The state forms the outer circle of which the church is the inner, but the centre of both is the same – the person of Jesus Christ.[52] This means that the state exists as an allegory, correspondence and analogue to the Kingdom of God.[53] It might well be the case that the state does not know who its centre is (a reality known only to the church), but that centre – for the Christian engaging in the political sphere – is still there. The world cannot be given up on prematurely.

ULTIMACY AND PENULTIMACY

One way of helping to articulate this relationship between Jesus Christ and the world is through the helpful discussion Bonhoeffer offers in his *Ethics* around

---

47 I think Fergusson's critique holds true here, but we part company over the degree to which we are able to assess the positivity of the liberal approach. See Fergusson, *Community, Liberalism & Christian Ethics*, p. 8.

48 See the preceding chapter for more on this kind of ecclesiology.

49 Hauerwas, *With the Grain of the Universe*, pp. 158–9.

50 CS, p. 120.

51 CS, p. 114.

52 CCCC, p. 169. We might think here about the effects of theological centering rather than boundedness. On this issues, see Hays, 'Postscript: Seeking a Centred, Generous Orthodoxy'.

53 CCCC, p. 169.

the motifs of the ultimate and the penultimate.[54] This is a distinction which Bonhoeffer sees as being particularly pertinent to his discussion of religionless Christianity,[55] and one might say that it is a way of dealing with the themes that this chapter addresses in temporal rather than spatial terms (as in the concentric rings approach above). Bonhoeffer is concerned with any breaking away of the penultimate from the ultimate. To prioritize the penultimate at the expense of the ultimate leads to compromise (such as that described above with regard to the theological acceptance of the liberal secular settlement which is imposed upon the church from without); to prioritize the ultimate leads to a radicalism such as one detects in versions of Christianity that reject genuine and real political engagement.[56] Simultaneously, both the ultimate and the penultimate are necessary for true Christianity. For Bonhoeffer, a belief in the ultimacy of God's work of justification must not determine that one 'cannot forgive God for having created what is.'[57] But nor can the Christian simply engage in 'accommodation to the point of resignation'.[58]

Bonhoeffer's engagement with these themes takes a decidedly political turn. On the side of remembering the ultimate, Bonhoeffer states:

[I]n Jesus Christ God comes down into the very depths of the human fall, of guilt, and of need, that the justice and grace of God is especially close to the very people who are deprived of rights, humiliated, and exploited, that the help and strength of Jesus Christ are offered to the undisciplined, and that the truth will lead the erring and despairing onto firm ground again.[59]

Such a message could sound like a spiritualization of the gospel – with Christ somehow coming to those whom society sees as weakest in their moments of need with an other-worldly salvation. This is, after all, described as the coming of Christ's grace which must 'finally clear and smooth its own way'.[60] However, none of this means that a practical engagement with people (whoever they are) is precluded by Christ's coming: 'None of this excludes the task of preparing the

---

54 See Chapter 6 on this subject. This is also a theme which is returned to in terms of theologies of the religions and inter-faith dialogue. See Chapters 8 and 9.

55 LPP, p. 365.

56 Ethics, pp. 153–70. Obviously, there is a form of political engagement which is radical (and perhaps connected with the 'Religious Right'). However, the degree to which this is genuinely *political* (in the elemental sense of dealing with competing claims and pluralism, rather than suppressing them) is surely to be questioned.

57 Ethics, p. 155.

58 Ethics, p. 156.

59 Ethics, p. 163.

60 Ethics, p. 162.

way.'[61] It is worth quoting Bonhoeffer on the preparing of the way at some length in order that the power of his words are able to resonate:

> It is . . . a commission of immeasurable responsibility given to all who know about the coming of Jesus Christ. The hungry person needs bread, the home-less person needs shelter, the one deprived of rights needs justice, the lonely person needs community, the undisciplined one needs order, and the slave needs freedom. It would be blasphemy against God and our neighbour to leave the hungry unfed while saying that God is closest to those in deepest need. We break bread with the hungry and share our home with them for the sake of Christ's love, which belongs to the hungry as much as it does to us. If the hun-gry do not come to faith, the guilt falls on those who denied them bread. To bring bread to the hungry is preparing the way for the coming of grace.
>
> What happens here is something penultimate. To give the hungry bread is not yet to proclaim to them the grace of God and justification, and to have received bread does not yet mean to stand in faith. But for the one who does something penultimate, for the sake of the ultimate, this penultimate thing is related to the ultimate. It is *pen*-ultimate, before the last.[62]

What one can see in this quotation is Bonhoeffer's attendance to the reasoning behind and activity of an engagement which is difficult to imagine as anything other than political. This is in itself a reformation and shaping of the political: the public shape of the act will not be identical to the shape of a differently motivated act. In this activity, the engagement with the one who is outside of the faith com-munity concerns an attendance to physical needs and human rights, but the motivation for and activity of the Christian in doing this is entirely internal to the Christian tradition. It is not strictly speaking the preaching of the gospel, but it is attending to the penultimate situation in which the world exists. In this situation of penultimacy, the life of faith is not only the proleptic anticipation of the ultim-ate, but also 'always life in the penultimate, waiting for the ultimate'.[63] Further-more, the penultimate is not only important in its waiting for the ultimate, but is also important in and of itself. Bonhoeffer writes: 'the penultimate also has its seriousness, which consists, to be sure, precisely in never confusing the penulti-mate with the ultimate and never making light of the penultimate over and against the ultimate.'[64] On the basis of the ultimate, attending to the penultimate is cen-tral. On the basis of the ultimacy and finality of Jesus Christ and His work of salvation, engaging in contemporary political settings and being for real human beings is crucial.

---

61   Ethics, p. 163.
62   Ethics, p. 163.
63   Ethics, p. 168.
64   Ethics, p. 168.

For Barth, similar concerns are expressed in terms of the relativization of the state (and the church) by the eschaton. His concern to engage with the state in the present age is grounded on the fact that there will be a heavenly state – a city in which there is no temple (Rev. 21.21). Thus, writes Barth:

> And from Revelation 21 we learn that it is not the real church (*ekklesia*) but the real city (*polis*) that truly constitutes the new age. Or, to put it otherwise, the Church sees its future and its hope, not in any heavenly image of its own existence but in the real heavenly *State*.[65]

The new age is not determined, therefore, by the real church, but by the real city.[66] This means that the Christian church cannot work for or understand itself as the perfect state in the present: the church cannot do this, not on the basis of the good-ness or badness of the state but on the basis of the ultimacy of the heavenly Jerusa-lem.[67] The church also cannot confuse itself with the heavenly state, endowing itself with its predicates in an overly realized way. Instead, it must be remembered that the '*heavenly* State is and remains exclusively the *heavenly* State, established not by man but by God, which, as such, is not capable of realization in this age, not even in the Church.'[68] The church cannot, therefore, exclude itself from political engagement as a state within a state, or a state sitting in judgement over the state. Instead, the church must affirm the city which is to come.[69] However, since the church lives in the anticipation of this heavenly, future state, the church should honour the state in the present, and constantly expect the utmost from it – 'that, in its own way amongst "all men," it will serve the Lord whom believers already love as their Saviour.'[70] The church's role is to remind the state of Jesus Christ, to wit-ness to Him, but not to attempt to force the state to become in the likeness of the Kingdom. Nor can the church confuse itself with this heavenly Kingdom, since even at its best the church is but an *image* of the Kingdom of God.[71] Thus, there cannot be a singularly internally orientated creation of a community which under-stands itself as the creation of an alternative state,[72] nor can there be an externally orientated attempt to transform the state into an alternative or true church. But none of this precludes intense political involvement. Instead, Barth advocates that:

> the resolute intention of the New Testament is brought out still more plainly when it is clear that Christians must not only endure the earthly State but that

---

65   CS, p. 124.
66   CS, p. 124.
67   CS, pp. 122–5.
68   CS, p. 126.
69   CS, p. 157.
70   CS, p. 140.
71   CCCC, p. 168.
72   This is where I part company with MacIntyre and those who follow after him in their rejection of the idea of the nation state.

they must *will* it, and that they cannot will it as a 'Pilate' State, but as a just State; when it is seen that there is no outward escape from the political sphere; when it is seen that Christians, while they remain within the Church and are wholly committed to the future 'city,' are equally committed to responsibility for the earthly 'city,' called to work and (it may be) to struggle, as well as to pray, for it; in short, when each one of them is responsible for the character of the State as a just State.[73]

A simple distinction between this-worldly and other-worldly, which is so central to the basest concerns of the *saeculum*, is simply not possible within a theology set against religion, but a recognition of the complex relations between the heavenly city and the state and the church today must be noted.

THE MARKERS OF PUBLIC THEOLOGICAL ENGAGEMENT OF A THEOLOGY AGAINST RELIGION

In many ways, the theology outlined thus far has had to engage in more background and contextual discussion than the majority of the rest of the chapters of this book up to this point. In part, the reason for this is that the discussions contained herein form a bridge to the discussions in which theology urgently needs to engage in terms of the contemporary political setting in which religion is seen to be a troubling issue in intra- and extra-state relations. The direct engagement with theologies of the religions and inter-faith dialogue will form the following chapters of the book. However, engaging in establishing what this relationship might be, not only in discussion with Barth and Bonhoeffer, but in dialogue with significant contemporary contributors to this debate, has been necessary to lay the foundations on which to build. Beginning to build on this foundation, it is now possible to indicate markers which might be seen to characterize a public theology against religion. These are addressed without discussing any individual and particular matter per se, and with the awareness that the approach of particularism and self-critical engagement already articulated will be the manner in which the engagement will need to take place.

An-idolatrous

The impetus of a theology against religion engaging in the public sphere should take place to some degree from seeking to guard society against idolatry.[74] There is a sense in which this might concern the state's propensity to deify itself,[75] and

---

73   CS, pp. 145–6.
74   Mathewes makes some interesting observations about idolatry in relation to his work and that of Milbank. See Mathewes, *A Theology of Public Life*, p. 125.
75   CS, pp. 124–5.

to seek its own presentation as the just heavenly Kingdom (as one might see, for example, in Communism) or to present itself as an ultimate and true people (as seen perhaps in Nationalism). But, more significantly, the kind of public theology suggested herein should try in the first instance to turn the critique of idolatry back onto itself, back onto the church. The church needs to realize that while it is the community of a specific and particular people, it differs from the state in terms of the extent of its engagement. The church cannot, therefore, make claims upon the state that seek to make the state more like the church. While Barth affirms the close relationship between the state and the church, he nevertheless writes:

> [The] Church cannot itself become a State, and the State, on the other hand, cannot become a Church. It is true, of course, that in principle the Church, too, turns to all men; but it does so with its message of justification and its sum-mons of faith. The Church gathers its members through free individual deci-sions, behind which stands the quite different free choice of God, and in this age it will never have to reckon with gathering all men within itself. The Church must have complete confidence in God, who is the God of *all* men, and must leave all to Him. But the State has always assembled within itself all men living within its boundaries, and it holds them together, and holds them together, as such, through its order . . . [76]

The church should, therefore, see the limits of its own reach: the universal con-cern with all (different) members of the state is to be left to God. The church cannot, therefore, overreach its authority or confuse itself with the totality of the state: any attempt at a Christian state or a theocracy is impossible. Turning the critique of religion back onto itself, the church is made to realize that religion divides whereas the state concerns all humans.[77] This also limits the power of the state, since '[o]nce religion is rooted there [in the state] anything becomes pos-sible in the name of God, even the death and annihilation of others who do not share our particular idea of the absolute. The gods are seldom found on the sides of our enemies after all.'[78] There must be, therefore, a suitable humility in the church's public engagement which recognizes that while God is the Lord of all of the world ultimately, the church most certainly is not.

However, this anidolatrous turn should not be seen as an excuse for doing or saying nothing. The God who cannot be captured in an idol, brought under human control, or confused with a world-view, is nevertheless the God who reveals Him-self particularly. Soulen helpfully observes:

> the Bible makes clear that while God cannot be circumscribed, God can be identified. But note: God is identifiable not because God's namelessness sets

---

76   CS, pp. 131–2.
77   Cf. Pugh, *Religionless Christianity*, p. 80.
78   Ibid., p. 72.

us free to give God names according to our own predilections. Rather, God is identifiable because God reveals God's name to us, and in doing so casts aside all of our self-serving talk of God.[79]

It is on the basis of the particular revelation of God that we affirm His transcendence, the inevitable humility this brings for the church's engagement with the state, and the incapacity of the church to be able to turn itself into a state – not on the basis of a politically conditioned pluralism which affirms God's ineffability for reasons of political and imperial unity.[80]

Outwards orientated

A second feature of a theology against religion engaging in the public square is that the concerns of theology's speech in that place, while humble and not confused with the totality of the state, should always be outwards focused. Religion can all too easily be concerned to employ God for the 'privileging of my tribe, my community, my culture',[81] but an awareness of the dangers of this propensity, and a turning of theological scepticism back onto such religious claims determines a concern for the other for the other's sake. Since the church is not an end in and of itself, but seeks to serve God and thereby to serve humanity,[82] the purpose of the church's engagement in the political sphere is not for its own end or betterment, but for the sake of the other. Thus, writes Barth:

> In the political sphere the Church will not be fighting for itself and its own concerns. Its own position, influence, and power in the State are not the goal which will determine the trend of its political decisions . . . The secret contempt which a Church fighting for its own interests with political weapons usually incurs even when it achieves a certain amount of success is well deserved.[83]

For Barth, whenever the church has engaged in politics for its own claim for public recognition or to serve its own ends, it has 'always been a Church which has failed to understand the special purpose of the State, an impenitent, spiritually unfree Church.'[84] There should never be a special Christian party, therefore, formed for Christian self-interest.[85] In Bonhoeffer's terms, this means that the

---

79   Soulen, ' "Go Tell Pharaoh" or, Why Empires Prefer a Nameless God', 12.
80   Cf. Ibid., 7.
81   Pugh, *Religionless Christianity*, p. 72.
82   CCCC, p. 166.
83   CCCC, p. 165.
84   CCCC, p. 167.
85   CCCC, p. 182. This obviously has considerable implications for the 'Religious Right' and political pressure groups which act on behalf of church interests.

church can never fight for its own space against the world, but should see itself as a place in which witness is given to the foundation of all reality in Jesus Christ.[86] Since the church is formed by the Spirit, and the Spirit offers the capacity for Christians to open up to the crossing of boundaries, this operation of witness opens the church out towards others.[87] However, for Bonhoeffer, even in this witness, there cannot be a totalizing sense of what the church is capable of in the political sphere: '*Are there even Christian solutions* to worldly problems? . . . If one implies that Christianity has an answer to *all* social and political questions of the world, so that one would only have to listen to these answers to put the world in order, then this is obviously wrong.'[88] The church's witness is more than simply a collective articulation of self-righteousness. However, this 'more' in the political sphere is simply a humble sense that the church has something to say about worldly matters, as part of the world itself.[89]

Centred spatiality

Crucially for the purposes of public engagement for the church, a theology against religion denies that there is any capacity to make absolute differentiation between two spaces in the world – one religious, one secular. This book has addressed this theme repeatedly thus far, but the significance of this for the political is important. The capacity to separate rigidly secular and religious spaces determines not only that the church should not simply be involved in what the secularists understand to be private religious engagement, but also that the church's place in the political realm is central to a properly understood notion of pluralism: denial of two spaces does not only affect secular-faith engagement but also inter-faith engagement. Politics over the last decade has demonstrated that the capacity to make such a distinction is limited: after all, much of the call for inter-faith engagement comes from the so-called secular sphere. Recognition of the political aspects of this engagement and also the *theological* significance of pluralism is important for a sensitive engagement in these themes.

   As has also been central to discussions thus far, the lack of sharp distinction between the secular and the religious does not determine that there is no differentiation between the church and the state: they are connected but differentiated. Making these differentiations absolute is impossible, however: provisos in earlier chapters about the nature of the church and the scope of salvation suggest this. The Christian should desire to participate in the reality of God and the world,

---

86   Ethics, p. 63; cf. CCCC, p. 173 and CS, pp. 126–8. For a more detailed account of witness, see Chapters 5 and 6 of this book.
87   Cf. Colin E. Gunton, *The One, the Three and the Many: God, Creation and the Culture of Modernity. The 1992 Bampton Lectures* (Cambridge: CUP, 1993), pp. 182–3.
88   Ethics, p. 353, italics original.
89   Ethics, p. 354.

recognizing that it is for her impossible ever to experience the reality of God without the reality of the world, or the reality of the world without the reality of God.[90] There is no capacity to be Christian without being worldly. Bonhoeffer writes:

> Thinking in terms of two realms understands the paired concepts worldly-Christian, natural-supernatural, profane-sacred, rational-revelational, as ultimate static opposites that designate certain given entities that are mutually exclusive. This thinking fails to recognize the original unity of these opposites in the Christ-reality and, as an after-thought, replaces this with a forced unity provided by a sacred or profane system that overarches them. Thus the static opposition is maintained. Things work out quite differently when the reality of God and the reality of the world are recognized in Christ.[91]

For Christians, Bonhoeffer recognizes the connection, but also crucially the distinction, of each of these spheres. It is this deep connection, however, of the different realms which enables the church to speak regarding worldly matters, and to see the presence of God outwith the bounds of the church.[92]

This is in many ways the outworkings of the soteriology and the ecclesiology espoused in the preceding chapters. For Barth, his capacity to speak positively in terms of the state arises to some degree from an engagement with the doctrine of *anakephaliosis*.[93] The final and universal victory of Jesus includes the powers and the authorities. In this way, the state belongs to Jesus ultimately. However, this does not allow the church to see the state as its tool or even as itself in the present. The ultimate victory of Christ does not remove the distinctions of the Christian and the non-Christian in the present, but it does remove the ultimacy of that distinction and allows for the capacity to affirm creation. The affirmation of creation also allows that the work of God the Spirit need not be confined to the visible church (though this may be a place in which the greatest intensity of God's Spirit is present), and recognizes that God is at work outside of the walls of the church.[94]

Beyond tolerance to Christian virtues

Within the walls of the church, however, there must not be a simple engagement with what might be considered secular virtues for religious communities. Prime among these in the present discourse stands the weak and minimal virtue of

---

90   Ethics, p. 55.
91   Ethics, pp. 58–9.
92   Cf. Fergusson, *Community, Liberalism & Christian Ethics*, pp. 28–9.
93   CS, p. 117. This is also an important theme for Bonhoeffer; see LPP, p. 230.
94   See Chapters 8 and 9 of this book for further consideration of this theme.

tolerance.[95] While tolerance may well pertain to ideas, it does not work well as a concept regarding people. The idea of tolerating a person involves a degree of negativity or even imperialism on the part of the one tolerating: 'We only tolerate those things which we dislike or deplore.'[96] This surely cannot be understood to be a Christian virtue for existence within a society of neighbours of difference. Since the concern of the church in the political sphere should primarily be other human beings (in particular human beings of difference),[97] the theological affirmation of tolerance can only be understood as minimally significant, if significant at all:[98] tolerance finds no place in the narrative of Jesus, as that narrative offers the story of the enactment of the much stronger virtue of self-sacrificial love for the other. Tolerance is a state virtue (that members of the church should have as simultaneously members of the state), but the virtues demanded of the Christian are *more* than that: they are the witness of love and forgiveness.[99] For the Christian, others do not exist in the world, therefore, as aliens and enemies to be despised or at best tolerated, but as the beloved children of God and fellow brothers and sisters of Jesus Christ. These others are to be loved because of God, and not because of any inherent value we attach to them, as Bonhoeffer helpfully advocates: they are real human beings who are to be loved because their being is grounded in the incarnation of God in the person of Jesus Christ.[100] The motivation for this love of the other is, therefore, based in the co-humanity of all human beings who are determined to share ultimately in Christ's humanity. This determination is itself the outworking of God's love for the world. Tolerance has no place, since God does not become human because He tolerates the world but because He loves it.[101]

There is, indeed, even here, a determined link to an anti-religious theology. This is not only in the worldliness of the concerns, and in the focus on the other, but also in terms of the concerns which lead to theology needing to be articulated thus. Bonhoeffer points to the arch-critic of religion, Nietzsche, in terms of his (unknowing) acknowledgement of the spirit of the New Testament in his chiding of a narrowly focused religious notion of who the neighbour is: Bonhoeffer, points out, instead, that the neighbour can be the one who is furthest from us (even Jesus

---

95   Even Barth gives a theological defense of this 'virtue': CD I/2, p. 299.

96   Fergusson, *State, Church and Civil Society*, pp. 74–5.

97   Barth notes that in the political sphere 'the Church will always and in all circumstances be interested primarily in human beings and not in some abstract cause or another' (CS, p. 171).

98   On tolerance, see Fergusson, *State, Church and Civil Society*, pp. 74–93; cf. Fergusson, *Community, Liberalism & Christian Ethics*, p. 164. Fergusson is more positive about tolerance as a virtue than I am, but recognizes some of the complexities involved in the idea for Christian theology.

99   CS, p. 131; cf. CCCC, p. 151.

100   Ethics, p. 87.

101   Instead of categories such as tolerance, those of more Christian significance (such as forgiveness and reconciliation) should be sought, as in the likes of Miroslav Volf, *Exclusion and Embrace: a Theological Exploration of Identity, Otherness, and Reconciliation* (Nashville: Abingdon, 1996).

Himself).[102] This engagement with the neighbour is an affirmation of the world, and a concern for others beyond a concern for the self or the repetition of the self in our religious community:

> The statements in the New Testament regarding Christian action, as well as the Sermon on the Mount, do not grow out of bitter resignation over the irreconcilable rift between the Christian and the worldly, but from joy over the already accomplished reconciliation of the world with God, from the peace of the already accomplished work of salvation in Jesus Christ.[103]

From this perspective, even the most seemingly distant figure is known as being ultimately one who is beloved of and reconciled to God. While the church might be tempted into judgements over individuals or groups, Bonhoeffer reminds us:

> While we distinguish between pious and godless, good and evil, noble and base, God loves real people without distinction. God has no patience with our dividing the world and humanity according to our standards and imposing ourselves as judges over them.[104]

When the church is engaged in judgement-making over individuals, it engages in sin itself.[105] This is not only in the negative sense of judgements against others but in the positive sense of realizing its own piety without turning the critique of religion back onto itself.

CONCLUSION

The above descriptors can only ever seek to offer *directions* and *suggestions* for action. The purpose of this chapter is not to concretize and set standard behaviour for individual circumstances; to a degree that is impossible, since it would itself make the church into some form of theoretical, theocratic state. The motifs and themes addressed in this chapter are not meant to be principles, but stand in opposition to any direct principles. They are, instead, suggested modes of thinking for dynamic and actualistic engagement.[106] However, the suggestions in this chapter will mean that the church should seek to be orientated on the gospel which proclaims good news to the poor and liberty to the captive. If the church seeks the Spirit who will guide and convict the church in terms of its operations

---

102 Ethics, pp. 294–5.
103 Ethics, p. 238.
104 Ethics, p. 84.
105 The reader is also directed here to the discussion of the co-sinfulness of humanity; see Chapter 5.
106 On actualism in this context, see particularly Chapter 6 of this book (cf. Chapters 8 and 9).

in the public sphere, then the Spirit who blows where He wills will determine that what these convictions mean in practice will be difficult to predict. There will, therefore, need to be continual decisions on the part of the church, which will differ between state and state, and between empirical church and empirical church: the relationship of the church to the state will differ in, for example, Nazi Germany in the 1930s and 40s, the Civil Rights Movement in the United States in the 1960s, and the contemporary war against terror.[107] It will be the job of preachers and pastors, and lay men and women, to work out what this means for their own contexts and communities in the living of their lives, as they seek not to be religious people turned in on themselves and concerned with their own salvation and the survival of their churches, but to be people who live wisely and responsibly before God and the neighbours God entrusts to their care.

In seeking to think in a more focused way about these neighbours and others (and particularly those who profess another faith), this book now turns to the so-called religious other. Clearly, as has been articulated thus far, this religious other cannot be separated from the secular other, who to some degree identifies the religious other as such. What follows is not to be understood, therefore, as a different or new conversation, but as a variation on the ongoing conversation around one particular set of people within society, whom society also identifies along with the church as being religious.

---

107 CS, pp. 119–20.

Part III

ENGAGING WITH THE RELIGIONS: PLURALISM AND THEOLOGY AGAINST RELIGION

Chapter 8

A THEOLOGY OF RELIGIONS AGAINST RELIGION

It may seem strange that a Christian theology which seeks to recognize the problematic nature of religion and to assert the need to recognize this in theological speech should engage in seeking to articulate a theology of religions (plural). However, given the interplay that this book has pointed towards with regard to secularity and plurality, the need to consider not only theology's relation to the category of religion but also to the concrete existence of other empirical religions is pressing. In a world situation in which relations between the religions are considered to have dramatic importance on national and international stages, theologians live at a time when it is necessary to serve society by helping it to think more carefully about the relations between those distinct and particular groups that society terms religious. Even if the grouping of religions together is an alien construct that society (as part of its own secular agenda)[1] foists upon individual faith traditions, that these traditions are grouped thus requires theological reflection for a theology which recognizes a need to serve the world. Indeed, with all of the provisos attached to too universalized a notion of religion, the very dependence of Christianity upon Judaism and the overt relationship that the Qur'an asserts to other peoples of the Book is indicative that, at least between the Abrahamic peoples, there is an asymmetrical connectedness of differing traditions to each other.[2] Since modernity, society has spoken of the connection between various discrete individual traditions as 'religion' (a term which had been used previously about the correct ordering of worship and only specifically about the tradition to which the writer was an insider).[3] Inasmuch as this description differentiates the engagement of peoples of different faiths from, for example, Christian engagement with trade unions or charities, and

---

1   Albeit a construct which certain theologians have accepted, and perhaps contributed to: this includes theologians of the nineteenth century who made religion a central category (such as Schleiermacher), and contemporary liberal approaches to the theologies of religions, such as those offered by John Hick.

2   The asymmetrical nature of this connectedness is reflected in the complexity of the term 'Abrahamic' and the different (potentially rival or competing) claims of Abrahamic descent.

3   Jenkins, *Religion in English Everyday Life*, p. 9. One should note that even in the post-Reformation settlements, the engagement was between different expressions of the one religion of Christianity.

recognizes the complexities involved in engaging in reflection on the interrelation of traditions, reflection on other concrete and empirical religious traditions theologically has a place within a theology which seeks to express itself against religion. Within this book, and arising from theological reflections on the critiques of religion, religion has been used thus far as a Christian theological concept which implies a series of problematic self-expressions of the Christian faith (idolatry, self-centredness, inwards orientated piety, self-preservation of the ego etc.). Over and against this, a series of motifs have been identified which seek to aid Christian theological reflection in order that it might become more genuinely theological and more intensely Christian rather than religious – christocentric world affirmation, reconciliation, pneumatological realness and so on.[4] Given this Christian theological *self-*critique of religion, there is much potential for this reflection to provide resources for Christian engagements with those of other traditions. Not only is it the case that, being aware of the plank in our own eye, we are less likely to pursue identifying the speck in the other's, but it is also the case that a reorientation away from our own religious self-preoccupations might well also open us up to more positive engagements with the other.

This chapter questions the approach to theologies of the religions which identify a positive substantialized and universalized connective between traditions which are externally identified as religious. While this book has engaged with religion, it has done so only as a *theological concept meaningful only within a particular theological tradition.* Part of the critique of religion which underlies this book is, in this context, a critique of a positive uniting element that connects all religious traditions to the so-called noumenal or divine.[5] Such a unitary element not only interposes an external category on individual traditions,[6] but also plays down particularity and difference, doing violence to the otherness of the other. Religion becomes the lowest common denominator connector between different traditions, and those who establish this connector often do so in such a way as to identify the unitary element through their own individual preoccupation (in the case of Christianity, normally salvation). In place of such an approach, this chapter advocates a particularist and more dynamic engagement in theologies of the religions, which recognizes the need for differentiation in terms of Christianity's engagement with different faith traditions. The chapter then seeks to identify the effects of the relativization of theological speech by the object on which it reflects. The realization that as Christians we can speak only as religionists (with all of the negative connotations that category holds in this book's account) has significant implications for the way in which theologians might understand their relationship to those of other faiths. The chapter then returns to earlier themes

---

4   See Chapter 4 of this book.
5   This mode of thought is detected in the theologies of the religions of the likes of John Hick. See, for example, Hick, *God and the Universe of Faiths*; and Hick, *An Interpretation of Religion*.
6   Parallels can be found here to discussions in the preceding chapter.

regarding multiple pneumatological intensities (cf. Chapter 6), and also considers the need to engage sensitively in articulating differentiated exclusivisms (cf. Chapter 5), with discussion also of the doctrine of providence and the multiplicity of covenants in scripture. The chapter concludes by pointing to the central import-ance of eschatology for Christian theology. In addressing these themes, the chap-ter seeks to lay foundations for the more directive and practical engagements in the next chapter of this book which concerns inter-faith dialogue.

The fact that little direct engagement exists in Barth and Bonhoeffer on a the-ology of religions determines that this chapter (and the next) will of necessity be more constructive than much of the work that has preceded it. This chapter seeks to draw out the implications of what Barth and Bonhoeffer have to say about reli-gion (as a wholly negative category which is directed *only* at Christianity) for Christian engagement with and thinking about those of other faiths. Drawing from the motifs of a theology against religion, already offered, this chapter seeks to offer insights which might allow Barth and Bonhoeffer's work to be heard at a very different time than their own on an issue which is theologically and politic-ally pressing, and on which bringing to bear their theological acumen might be tremendously beneficial.

Against a Substantialized Theology of Religions

Speaking about religion as a theological category determines that the conceptual meaning of religion is significant only within the specific confines of the theologi-cal discourse in which religion is being discussed. Seeking to articulate a theology of religions does not necessarily remove this specific community context, how-ever, or the specific theological content of the idea of religion for Christian the-ology. Instead, if we see the concept of religion as only applicable to our own community context, then the critical turn which has been advocated thus far is only directed towards ourselves: it is a concept meaningful only within Christian discourse regarding Christianity. In identifying other empirical religions, we are not identifying 'religion' but a group of discrete traditions that somehow stand in relation to Christianity as variously other to it. This lack of a universalized notion of a critique of religion is necessary. What meaning, for example, would a Chris-tian critique of idols have for traditions which worship using idols? Or how can Christian attitudes towards salvation be seen as conceptually normative for trad-itions which are not teleologically ordered or do not have salvation as a central concern? The issue, therefore, is not the application of a Christian self-critique of religion as normative across all traditions of empirical religions, but is rather about seeking to understand the way that a Christian's theological self-critique of religion might be able to offer important theological motifs which facilitate an engagement with those considered to be other than Christian, not simply in a negative denial of

the Christian faith but in a positive ascribing to another tradition commonly identified as religious. George Linbeck's description of his own approach to these themes
is useful. He states that he is

> open to the possibility that different religions and/or philosophies may have
> incommensurable notions of the truth, of experience, and of categorial
> adequacy, and therefore also of what it would mean for something to be most
> important (i.e., 'God'). Unlike other perspectives, this approach proposes no
> common framework such as that supplied by the propositionalist's concept of
> truth or the expressivist's concept of experience within which to compare reli-
> gions. Thus when affirmations or ideas from categorically different religious
> or philosophical frameworks are introduced into a given religious outlook,
> these are either simply babbling or else, like mathematical formulas employed
> in a poetic text, they have vastly different functions and meanings than they
> had in their original settings.[7]

The engagement in thinking about the relationship between religions cannot for
Lindbeck simply be an engagement in identifying common cores or comparing the
veracities of truth claims. For the purposes of the present book, Lindbeck's observations apply similarly to the theological critique of religion, and it is not possible
to rank religions in terms of inferiority or superiority simply with regard to how
much of a shared concern there is for self-critique within individual traditions.[8]

Indeed, a negative assessment of religion from a Christian theological perspective
may doubly determine that this inability to find a common core or a set of proposi-
tional objectives by which to compare traditions is possible: not seeing religion as
a positive aspect of Christianity suggests that identification of this supposed commonality across traditions cannot be the basis for a positive engagement with the
other. Therefore, whether a religion is supposedly superior or inferior *qua* religion
is of no significance. In this way, a theology of religions against religion is nervous
of the sorts of taxonomy of religious traditions that one sees in Schleiermacher.[9]
Barth himself is deeply critical of this kind of approach in his own discussions of
Schleiermacher. Barth describes Schleiermacher's theology of religions thus:

> The Christian religion is 'the purest form of monotheism that has appeared in
> history,' for Judaism, as shown by its exclusiveness and its open relapses into

---

7   Lindbeck, *The Nature of Doctrine*, p. 49.

8   Cf. ibid., p. 55.

9   David Clough relates this matter well to Barth's theology in discussion of CD §17: 'Barth sought
to bring down the edifice of nineteenth- and early twentieth-century German theology that followed
Schleiermacher in charting a way to God starting with religious experience. Barth witnessed to how
this focus on the human leads to all manner of murky relationships between religion and nationhood,
culture, race, and language.' Clough, 'Karl Barth on Religious and Irreligious Idolatry', p. 216.

idolatry, is still thought to be akin to fetishism, while Mohammedanism with its passionate nature and the strong sensory content of its ideas carries reminiscences of polytheism. I need hardly refer expressly to the historical dilettantism of the expositions in this paragraph; indeed, the whole schema of development which is used here finds no support in modern religious scholarship. I will also refer only in passing to the increasing obscurity of the fundamental principle; it is only with serious unwillingness that one can follow the evolutions of the chameleon known as the sense of absolute dependence. What concerns us is the question what Schleiermacher is really after here. . . . [H]e wants to prove that in the historical world of this mysterious basic factor Christianity takes one of the highest places, indeed, the very highest place. He does this by postulating a series in which monotheism as its climax is secretly declared to be Christian monotheism . . . [10]

For Barth, however, any form of taxonomy of religions can never be the basis for either a positive or negative judgement about their relationship with Christ.[11]

The relationship between individual empirical religions, for Barth, is a deeply complex and dynamic one. He writes: 'By God's revealing of Himself the divine particular is hidden in a human universal, the divine content in a human form, and therefore that which is divinely unique in something which is humanly only singular.'[12] Barth recognizes that there is a degree to which there is continuity in terms of the human phenomenon of religion, but that revelation creates a condition in which even in human terms there is a singularity about the Christian faith, which brings about particularity and distinctiveness.[13] We might wish to push Barth further on this point, as there seems at this juncture in his work to be a willingness to affirm a universal category in relation to other empirical religious traditions. However, the crucial point to realize is that these claims come specifically *within* a theological context of reflection on religion *theologically* (as a subset of Barth's engagement with pneumatology). For Barth, the paragraph on religion is not a theology of the religions (plural), although it might have implications for

---

10   ToS, p. 226. Cf. Schleiermacher, *The Christian Faith*, §§ 8–9.

11   Cf. I/2, p. 79: 'Even to meet this doctrine of Schleiermacher's and his already clearly expressed wish to see the Old Testament removed from the Canon of the Christian Church, a sound objection can scarcely be made, so long as it is not realised that the whole concern is neither "Judaism" nor "Christianity," neither Old Testament nor New Testament piety, but Jesus Christ as the object of the Old Testament and the New Testament witness. Therefore it is not a matter of an historical relation between two religions, nor yet of one that can be described by the concepts of "kinship" or of "homogeneity," but of unity of revelation in both cases which connects the two socalled religions.'

12   CD I/2, p. 282. This is a difficult passage to translate, and in Green's most recent translation, he suggests in the place of 'humanly only singular' the phrase 'merely humanly remarkable' (Green, *Barth on Religion*, p. 35).

13   For more detailed exegesis of this passage, see Greggs, 'Bringing Barth's Critique of Religion to the Inter-Faith Table', 85–8.

one. It is, instead, a theology of religion (singular), and in this has a very specific
and particular focus – the church, as one would expect for a *church* dogmatics.
The context for Barth's reflections on religion is offered by him as follows:

> The event of God's revelation has to be understood and expounded as it is
> attested to the Church of Jesus Christ by Holy Scripture. It is within this con-
> crete relationship that theology has to work. That is why when we asked how
> God does and can come to man in His revelation, we were compelled to give
> the clear answer that both the reality and the possibility of this event are the
> being and action only of God, and especially of God the Holy Spirit. Both the
> reality and the possibility! . . . Not only the objective but also the subjective
> element in revelation, not only its actuality but also its potentiality, is the
> being and action of the self-revealing God alone. . . . But this revelation is in
> fact an event which encounters man. It is an event which has at least the form
> of human competence, experience and activity. And it is at this point that we
> come up against the problem of man's religion.[14]

Barth works from the particular context of Christian revelation to discuss the
nature of religion *for Christian theology*. His concern is not other faiths, but the
Christian faith, and all his judgements take place around that subject and within
that context.

However, this very concern with the singularity of Christianity in terms of religion is a wise place with which to begin reflection on a Christian theology of
religions. This is not because of some form of universalized religious experience,
but because the theological conceptualization offers fruit which is helpful in relation to empirical religious traditions. The singularity Barth posits recognizes the
correct level of complexity in terms of the relationship between the internal definition of religion for an individual tradition, the basis of reflection on particular
revelation (in the instance of Christianity), and the exclusive and particular claims
of distinctive traditions that cannot easily be categorized. Speaking from a singular position on the basis of exclusive claims, rather than working on the basis of
identifying common cores or corresponding elements of different faiths, or of
reading one's own traditions onto the distinctiveness of another, is the correct
basis from which to articulate something which seeks genuinely to be a theology
of religions. For Barth, the basis for making a *theological* claim stems from reflection on God's revelation in Jesus Christ. The exclusivity of the basis for theological reflection does not, however, lead to a bigoted or narrow theological reflection.
Nor does it lead to a series of comparative judgements in which Christ is seen to
be the pinnacle of God's works or of human religion (quite the opposite, Christ is
religion's *Aufhebung*). Jesus is, instead, the source from which all other works of

---

14   CD I/2, p. 281.

God are derived.[15] This determines that there can be no substantialized syncretism between Christianity and other religions, as this would be meaningless in relation to Jesus Christ who is the basis of all of God's ways with the world.

However, this lack of a capacity to engage in a syncretistic approach to other faiths does not determine that every word that flows from other faiths might need to be considered as some form of false gospel. In reflecting on Barth's engagement with what it means to speak of Jesus as the light of life,[16] there is the need to affirm that Jesus is the light of life 'in all its fulness', and therefore that there is 'no other light of life outside or alongside His, outside or along- side the light which He is.'[17] But in observing the exclusivity of this unique- ness of Jesus' being the light of life (with no possibility of comparable lights of life which may be syncretized with Him, even if of lesser status),[18] there is nevertheless the capacity to affirm that it is also the case that not every state- ment outside of the church or Christian scriptures should be understood as being untrue or of no value.[19] There can be no syncretism, but the distance between Christ and the religion that seeks to worship Him (Christianity) deter- mines that we cannot simply say that truth only exists within Christianity and that there is no truth outside of Christianity: Christianity is not in and of itself true, and the Christian religion has no higher religious status than any other empirical religion.

This concern not to articulate a substantialized syncretism is also found in Barth in his deep reticence to give concrete examples of the secular parables of the Kingdom. Paul Chung helpfully observes in relation to this:

> If Barth canonizes or gives dogmatic examples of secular parables, he would inevitably run into a relativistic syncretism that would result in an expropri- ation of God's particular covenant with Israel in a concrete, historical reality. WE (*sic*) should not totalize all different, particular religious experiences and belief systems to the Western metaphysics of sameness.[20]

The capacity for a substantialized theology of religions is significantly under- mined by Christ's unique status, but this is a status which relativizes *all* words or lights, as the revelation which stands against the Christian religion more than any (see the section 'Relativizing Theological Speech: Speaking as a Religionist'

---

15 Cf. Thompson, 'Religious Diversity, Christian Doctrine and Karl Barth', 19.

16 On this topic, see ibid., pp. 11–18; Hunsinger, *How to Read Karl Barth*, postscript; and Chapter 4 of this book.

17 CD IV/3, p. 86.

18 CD IV/3, p. 87.

19 CD IV/3, p. 97.

20 Paul S. Chung, 'On Karl Barth in Interreligious Studies and Cross-Cultural Perspective', *Studies in Interreligious Dialogue* 18, no. 2 (2008), 217.

below). Thus, in Barth's earlier reflections, even in confronting what he terms the 'Japanese Protestantism' of Genku and Shinran,

> we ought not to be startled even momentarily by the striking parallelism of it to the truth of Christianity, but that we should be grateful for the lesson which it so abundantly and evidently teaches. And the lesson is this: that in its historical form, as a mode of doctrine, life and order, the Christian religion cannot be the one to which the truth belongs *per se* – not even if that form be the Reformed.[21]

It is futile to compare these religions of 'grace' as this is in and of itself meaningless without the one decisive factor of Christianity, which is the basis of all else and without which all else (even grace) is meaningless – the name of Jesus Christ.[22] The only basis for any Christian reflection has to come from being 'enclosed in the one name of Jesus Christ, and nothing else . . . in all the formal simplicity of this name as the very heart of the divine reality of revelation'.[23] Any attempt at substantializing some version of commonality between individual empirical faiths is theologically impossible, or – perhaps better – pointless, for Barth.

This impossibility, however, simply provides the basis for theological reflection on the nature of plurality and genuine otherness. Freed from reflecting on continuities and discontinuities, a theology of religions framed by a theology against religion disallows any violence towards the otherness of the other, who can all too often be read as oneself or described in one's own terms.[24] Genuine exclusivity and particularity (as required of real pluralism)[25] is given its place. The need, thus, arises to engage in describing our relationship to another who is other *to us*. In doing this, there can be no presumption of a uniform description: the different attitudes and forms of engagement for early Christians in their dealings with Jews and pagans makes this evidently clear, and we should not simply accept the secular judgement against the plurality of individual traditions by lumping these various and distinctive others together as one universalized 'religion'.[26] A dynamic

---

21   CD I/2, p. 342.

22   Barth's point made to Berkouwer about the danger of a principle of grace abstracted from the person of Jesus Christ should be noted here; see CD IV/3, pp. 173–80.

23   CD I/2, p. 343.

24   Michael Barnes helpfully describes the way in which even the idea of theologies of religions implies some form of Christian meta-narrative. Michael Barnes, SJ, *Theology and the Dialogue of Religions* (Cambridge: CUP, 2002), p. 7.

25   See Chapter 7 of this book on pluralism.

26   As discussed in Chapter 7 of this book. A similar point is made by David Grumett regarding the engagement of Henri de Lubac with Buddhism: a singular 'one size fits all' mode of engagement with all distinctive and particular traditions was considered insufficient for de Lubac who thought that certain traditions would relate variously to Christianity; on de Lubac and theologies of the religions, see David Grumett, *De Lubac: A Guide for the Perplexed* (London: T&T Clark, 2007), chapter 7; and

and non-substantialized articulation of a theology of religions will realize the distinctive situations, dialogues and discourses in which it is necessary to engage in a contemporary pluralist society, and these are likely to be situations, dialogues and discourses that we are unlikely to be able to anticipate in advance.

RELATIVIZING THEOLOGICAL SPEECH: SPEAKING AS A RELIGIONIST

The dynamic variety of engagements in which Christian theology will have to take part in seeking to articulate a theology of religions will receive further detailed reflection in the next chapter of this book which seeks to look at inter-faith issues. However, the relativization of Christian theological speech through theological reflection on the category of religion for Christianity requires further attendance in terms of its implications for a theology of religions. For the Christian who seeks to engage in theological articulation against religion, the recognition of the religious nature of theological speech is significant in forcing an awareness of the limits of theological speech. Theological speech is never a first order enterprise, but is instead a much humbler engagement. As Lindbeck observes:

> Just as grammar by itself affirms nothing either true or false regarding the world in which language is used, but only about language, so theology and doctrine, to the extent that they are second order activities, assert nothing true or false about God and his relation to creatures, but only speak about such assertions. These assertions, in turn, cannot be made except when speaking religiously . . . [27]

For Lindbeck, the religious expression of assertions is not considered as a negative thing.[28] However, following the trajectory on which we are set, we may say that, while of course even in a desire to speak non-religiously there will be religious contexts and elements to theological self-expression, this is no good thing, and undermines our capacity genuinely to reflect upon the nature of God and His ways with the world. When it comes to theological speech, therefore, according to Barth, '[t]he issue is not an ultimate "assuring" but always a penultimate "de-assuring" of theology, or, as one might put it, a theological warning

---

David Grumett, 'De Lubac, Buddhism and Catholicism', paper given at the Department of Theology and Religious Studies, Univeristy of Bristol (Bristol, 2010).

27   Lindbeck, *The Nature of Doctrine*, p. 69.

28   However, Lindbeck does point to ways in which Christians should certainly not be proud in relation to their claims about faith: 'it is ridiculous for Christians to boast. They are like infants mouthing scraps out of Shakespeare or the *Principia Mathematica*, parrot-like, by rote' (ibid., p. 61).

against theology'.[29] Theology, too, is bound by religion, which is contradicted by God's revelation in Jesus Christ. What this means is that an attempt to engage in comparative or syncretizing reflections on the revelation of God is impossible for Christian theology (much as they will inevitably creep in): 'Above all, we should on principle spare revelation itself, i.e., Jesus Christ, all our direct or relatively indirect desire to prove its superiority over all other religions'.[30]

The effect of this heightening of the status of God's revelation in Jesus Christ,[31] over Christian theology, is a recognition of the incapacity of theology to remove itself from its religious preconditions (on which its subject might reflect).[32] This in turn makes theology unable to engage in value judgements about religions, even those which seek to make Christ superior to all other religions: such an engagement is in and of itself religious and reduces Jesus Christ, who is the *Aufhebung* of religion, to a religious object. However, even in seeking to avoid such value judgements, theology will inevitably fall back into reflection on religious categories, as a discipline which reflects formatively on the teaching of the church: most decidedly, theology is not the revelation of Jesus Christ but a reflection upon that revelation within the religious expression of revelation in the community. Even in seeking to think theologically about the category of religion in order to recognize the pitfalls of religious speech and behaviour (as has been the condition of this book), there is an inevitable doing that which we wish not to do and a failing to do that which we wish to do (a religious version of Romans chapter 7), as theology is the reflection upon God's relationship to the world, which is inevitably expressed religiously despite itself.[33] Barth writes: 'Jesus Christ cannot be absorbed and dissolved in practice into the Christian *kerygma*, Christian faith and the Christian community. He cannot be replaced by Christianity. He remains sovereign even in this respect.'[34] The community, faith and even kerygma are not Jesus Christ, and theology, as reflections on these reflections on Jesus Christ, must recognize humbly that it, too, is not Jesus Christ. It is the task of theology (even in its own failings) to articulate this to the church and the Christian people. Nicholas Lash puts this well:

> [O]ne of the principal functions of doctrine, as a regulative of Christian speech and action, would be to help protect the corrupt reference by describing our

---

29   CD I/1, pp. 164–5.

30   CD I/1, p. 168.

31   For an unpacking of the meaning of this, see Chapters 3 and 4.

32   This is even true, to a degree, in Barth's early theology of revelation with regard to the Bible and to preaching. See Hart, 'The Word, the Words and the Witness', esp. 88.

33   Even terminological difficulties present themselves in this: how to speak of empirical religions without affirming some kind of essentialized religion or religious core between the religions, and so on. In this way, the present book becomes easy prey to its own charges, but this is an inevitable feature of the turning back of the critique of religion onto oneself – even when one is seeking to critique religion.

34   CD IV/3, p. 349.

manifest propensity towards idolatry. Idolatry is a matter of getting the reference wrong: of taking that to be God which is not God, of making some fact or thing or nation or person or dream or possession or ideal for our heart's desire and the mystery 'that moves the sun and other stars'.[35]

For Lash, the doctrine which arises from religion has to turn the critique of idolatry back onto Christian faith and speech, in order to remind the church of the true referent of its speech.

What does this mean for a theology of the religions? It means decidedly that theological speech (and all Christian speech) only takes place in the context of theologians and Christians being religionists. A theology against religion still takes shape within all of the failings of religiosity. This point relativizes even this form of theological speech, which is all too aware of its religionist propensities.[36] But it is *the capacity to be aware of its religious failings that is of significant dogmatic value*. A theological de-assuring of theology is the right and appropriate form that a theology which is nervous of idolatry should take: it is not only idols made of clay and gold which need to be recognized as non-continuous with God, but idols which are ideas, constructs, rituals and communities.[37] The theological point of the commandment against making a graven image of God is not simply that this is a bad thing to do, but that God cannot be captured within the confines of an image.[38] Glimpses of God in scripture illustrate this: Moses sees only God's back; Isaiah only the hem of the robe which fills the temple. There is always more to God, and theology cannot engage in believing it articulates the ultimate word on God's nature (even in seeking to avoid religion), but must recognize that even the community of faith from which it springs cannot offer the ultimate creedal or confessional description of God adequate to the subject it seeks to describe. Innate to the nature of the Christian faith, within which even Jesus has a name which is unknown (Rev. 19.12), is the affirmation that there is always more to God beyond our imagination or comprehension, and found sometimes in the most unusual places (even in the mouth of an ass).[39] This is not, however, the claim of the nameless God of liberalism,[40] but the God who reveals Himself as supremely above our capacity to master and name Him in our religion; this is the God who despite Moses' desire to know His name points to His presence, history and activity

---

35   Lash, *The Beginning and End of 'Religon'*, p. 134.
36   Cf. Hunsinger, *How to Read Karl Barth*, p. 245.
37   Cf. Lash, *The Beginning and End of 'Religon'*, p. 50: 'We worship things as naturally as we breathe and speak. But that is the problem – untutored, we set out hearts on *things*: on forces, ideas; on people, dreams and institutions; on the world or some item of its furnishings. We are spontaneously idolatrous.'
38   'God is not an object whose nature we are capable of describing' (ibid., p. 136).
39   CD IV/3, p. 119.
40   Cf. Soulen, '"Go Tell Pharaoh" or, Why Empires Prefer a Nameless God', 12–13.

within creation, as well as His self-sufficiency in Himself.[41] But in our desire to speak about and to conceptualize this God of history, at best all that might be achieved in even the purest and most fulsome reflections on church confession can only be a reflection on the penultimate statement about the ultimate – never the ultimate thing in itself.[42]

In this way, an engagement in articulating a theology of religions for a Christian theologian, who is aware of the dangers of religion and her inevitable religionist discourse, can never take a God's-eye perspective which offers God's judgement on these other religionist traditions. She can only seek to articulate at best penultimately (and thereby one might hope more humbly) the otherness of the other *to us* (rather than to God). This religious other remains other to our own perspective on the revelation of God in our own continued religious failings. Put otherwise: it is an engagement in articulating how *I* (and my community) might see you from the perspective of my religionist theological discourse, which the God about whose revelation I speak relativizes in the majesty and breadth of His revelation, a revelation my religion contradicts and fails even to glimpse. A theology of religions can never offer a God's-eye perspective on other faiths, but only ever the view from below of those who engage in theological speech about (or against) their own religious community. The self of an individual or community's divine self-assurance is undermined by the theological de-assuring of theology. Before his turn to religionlessness, Bonhoeffer suggestively asserted: 'my suspicion and fear of "religiosity" have become greater here [in prison] than ever. That the Israelites *never* say the name of God aloud is something I often ponder, and I understand it increasingly better.'[43] Within a couple of weeks, he also writes: 'Only when one knows that the name of God may not be uttered may one sometimes speak the name of Jesus Christ.'[44] Perhaps these are places in which we might see Bonhoeffer pointing towards, or setting us on a path towards, the theological de-assurance of theology as a fruitful engagement with other faiths.

To engage in this anti-idolatrous de-assuring is not to say nothing, however: the very basis for these claims lie in the basis of reflection on revelation, and the path to atheism is not a possibility, since the charge against idolatry applies as powerfully to the great sceptics of religion as to religious protagonists.[45] The reason for this is that it is only the revelation of God in Jesus Christ that is able to characterize

---

41 On naming God, see Soskice, *The Kindness of God.*

42 See preceding discussions here on ultimates and penultimates in Bonhoeffer's thought.

43 LPP, p. 189.

44 LPP, p. 213. For further reflection on this and the preceding quotation from Bonhoeffer, see Greggs, 'Religionless Christianity in a Complexly Religious and Secular World: Thinking through and Beyond Bonhoeffer'; and Tom Greggs, 'Religionless Christianity and the Political Implications of Theological Speech: What Bonhoeffer's Theology Yields to a World of Fundamentalisms', *International Journal of Systematic Theology* 11, no. 3 (2009).

45 Clough, 'Karl Barth on Religious and Irreligious Idolatry', p. 227; cf. CD I/2, pp. 320–5.

Christian religion as unbelief, idolatry and self-righteousness, and thereby to rela-
tivize its relation to other words about God.[46] Indeed, in Barth's critique of religion,
he offers manifold biblical examples as the basis for why it is necessary to take this
stance:[47] it is his deep particularism which is the basis on which he proceeds. This
christocentric, theological de-assuring, furthermore, underscores the impossibility
of engaging in correspondences or substantialized engagements in a theology of
religions, since from a Christian theological perspective even Christian speech is
undermined by the object about which it seeks to offer articulation – the revelation
of Jesus Christ. Christian theological reflection points to this absolute which precedes all else and is sovereign to all else. Drawing lines of continuity or seeking to
point to differentiated religious particularizations of a universal essence is a futile
engagement for Christian theology since the superior reign of Christ is itself con-
tradictory of Christianity's own religion: even if this substantializing were engaged
in, it would bear no relation to God's relationship to humanity. However, while
atheism is condemned, and his critique of religion does not hold back from critiquing the atheist critiques, Barth is still able to say:

> Godlessness appears in a worse form in religion than it does in theoretical
> atheism, for here it does not make open confession as it tries to do in atheism,
> but thinks it has sought and found a positive substitute for what is lacking . . .
> In religion the world tries to domesticate the God who is known and yet also
> unknown and strange, to bring him into its own natural and intellectual sphere
> of vision and power.[48]

A comparison of various attempted domestications of God with our own (which
is worst of all in us as Christians) is of no worth and has as much to do with the
God, who reveals Himself, as Baal and the golden calf do: indeed, it is tantamount
to comparing Baal and the golden calf to each other. The reason for this worthless-
ness is not because we are right; it is because we are those who give gold to the
building of the idol while God is revealing His Word.

MULTIPLE DENSITIES OF GOD'S HOLY SPIRIT

Can Christian theology say nothing, therefore, about other traditions which are
seen as also being religious? Are there other grounds for thinking about people
who are other to us in our religious traditions? I wish to suggest here that there are
things Christians can (and perhaps should) say about other faiths in relation to
themselves. To do this, Christians will need to speak out of their own tradition.

---

46   CD I/2, p. 314.
47   CD I/2, pp. 328–31.
48   ChrL, pp. 129–30.

This is not to undermine what has been said thus far, but it is to recognize, with Lindbeck, the following point:

> To hold that a particular language is the only one that has the words and concepts that can authentically speak of the ground of being, the goal of history, and true humanity (for Christians believe they cannot genuinely speak of these apart from telling and retelling the biblical story) is not at all the same as denying that other religions have resources for speaking truths and referring to realities . . . [49]

Again, for Lindbeck, there is a positive use of the term religion in what he says. However, if we remember that the negativity of the theological concept that we have outlined has first and foremost to be applied to Christianity as a religion, watchful of and open to the fact that there is nothing essentialist in these other expressions of religion *qua* religion that makes them positive, it is still possible to affirm within Christian theological discourse that (most especially given God's revelation within Christianity despite its religion which is the worst of all forms) God may well act in the world in a way that the church does not know.[50]

If we emphasize the negativity of Christian religion and recognize God's revelation despite it, we can recognize that there is nothing innately good in the category of religion, and that it stands in radical discontinuity with God. It is only from the *presence of the Holy Spirit from without* that the words of the Christian can become true and offer a true witness to the triune God.[51] In terms of life within the world, Paul speaks of these concrete virtues of witness as fruits of the Spirit, which he contrasts to unwise life in the flesh:

> For what the flesh desires is opposed to the Spirit, and what the Spirit desires is opposed to the flesh; for these are opposed to each other, to prevent you from doing what you want. But if you are led by the Spirit, you are not subject to the law. Now the works of the flesh are obvious: fornication, impurity, licentiousness, idolatry, sorcery, enmities, strife, jealousy, anger, quarrels, dissensions, factions, envy, drunkenness, carousing, and things like these. I am warning you, as I warned you before: those who do such things will not inherit the kingdom of God. By contrast, the fruit of the Spirit is love, joy, peace, patience, kindness, generosity, faithfulness, gentleness, and self-control.[52]

The natural (or perhaps more appropriately unnatural) works of sinful humans are contrasted to the fruits that those who are led by the Spirit display. If we take

---

49   Lindbeck, *The Nature of Doctrine*, p. 61.
50   Cf. Barnes, *Theology and the Dialogue of Religions*, p. 28.
51   See the discussion in this book on the pneumatological context of Barth's reflections for the context in which to understand the following (Chapter 2).
52   Gal. 5.17–23a.

seriously the sinful nature of all humanity and the failed ability of humans to rescue themselves from sinfulness according to the Christian tradition,[53] we must recognize that sanctification always comes from without the human being, as a work of the Holy Spirit who makes others holy by virtue of His presence. Any display, therefore, of holiness as an operative work of God the *Holy* Spirit must be seen as a work of that same Holy Spirit. In and of themselves, fallen humans are incapable of love, joy, peace, patience, kindness, generosity, faithfulness, gentleness, and self-control without the Spirit's help. We may, therefore, suggest (though nothing more) that communities and individuals in which these fruits are displayed are communities and individuals in which the Holy Spirit, who dwells extensively in the world, is more fully intensely present. This may well be a shining of the lights in the outer-sphere, 'other lights which are quite clear and other revelations which are quite real.'[54] The very reality and clarity of these lights as fruits of the Spirit stems from the operative work of the Holy Spirit, as the presence of God which crosses boundaries, opening us up to other humans and to God. This is a work of the God who maintains and deepens particularity.[55] In this way, it may be possible to suggest that empirical religions, as forms which bring together the sorts of virtues that the fruits of the Spirit speak about, are places where the Spirit is variously and multiply intensely present. This has nothing to do with the religions *qua* religion, or a line of substantive continuity between the Spirit's act and the religion, but with the reality that the fruits of the Spirit can come only from outside of the individual or community – from the Spirit Himself.

This is a theme which is related to religious variance directly within the witness of scripture. When confronted with a religious other who asks questions about ritualistic propriety,[56] Jesus states:

Woman, believe me, the hour is coming when you will worship the Father neither on this mountain nor in Jerusalem. You worship what you do not know; we worship what we know, for salvation is from the Jews. But the hour is coming, and is now here, when the true worshipers will worship the Father in spirit and truth, for the Father seeks such as these to worship him. God is spirit, and those who worship him must worship in spirit and truth.[57]

Here, there is no denial of particularity: the Samaritans worship what they do not know as salvation is from the Jews. But in terms of the coming hour (from the point

---

53   See Chapter 5 on pessimism and salvation. The inability of humans to rescue themselves from sinfulness is the issue at the heart of the Pelagian controversy, with orthodoxy recognizing the heretical nature of speech which suggests the human ability to save itself.
54   CD IV/3, p. 97.
55   Gunton, *The One, the Three and the Many*, pp. 181–3.
56   On Jewish–Samaritan relations at the time of Christ, see Greggs, 'Preaching Inter-Faith: Finding Hints about the Religious Other from the Good Samaritan', 62–3.
57   Jn 4.21–4.

of view of the eschaton), true worshipers will worship the Father in spirit and truth. Religious propriety is not the issue: worship will not simply be localized to Gerezim or even to Jerusalem because worship will involve full reality ('truth') and be determined by the presence of the Spirit who blows wherever He wills (Jn 3.8). The Spirit does not make people worship on Jerusalem, even though Jerusalem is the 'correct' place to worship; the precise point is that worship of God cannot ultimately be spatio-religiously defined. In this much, while we may recognize the concern of Bonhoeffer in speaking about 'unconscious Christianity', some form of unconscious or anonymous Christianity to a degree misses the point.[58] The issue is not about being defined in relation to *Christianity*: even though salvation comes through Jesus Christ, the hour is coming when true worshippers will not worship in the church either. The issue is understanding that true worship of the Father is in Spirit and truth. Patronizingly seeing the others as some form of Christian is itself unchristian if Christianity relates to the biblical narrative in which religious self-identification and commitment is relativized in relation to the eschatological Kingdom of God, which will be inherited by those who display the fruits of the Spirit, as the Spirit gives them from without (Gal. 22–3). In thinking about these texts in this kind of a way, it might be possible to detect the beginnings of a non-religious interpretation of biblical texts which is meaningful for an age of secularism *and pluralism*, an age which is complexly secular and multi-religious.[59] The fruits of the Spirit might be understood to be an intense presence of the Spirit who is extensively and multiply intensively present in the world, and who is the operating condition for true worship of the Father, as the one who is present in all of the reality (and truth) of particular life and who offers and brings about the foretaste of the coming eschatological community.

DIFFERENTIATED EXCLUSIVISMS

In terms of the model of engagement that this chapter seeks to offer for a theology of religion, it may have been possible to detect what might be termed 'differentiated

---

58   Bonhoeffer discusses 'unconscious Christianity' on two occasions: first in relation to 'natural piety' (LPP, p. 489); and second in notes, in which he relates it to the left hand not knowing what the right hand is doing and to Mt. 25 (LPP, p. 491). A third mention in LPP comes from Bethge, who thinks the idea very important and asks for Bonhoeffer's further thoughts (LPP, p. 546). For a parallel concept to Bonhoeffer's 'unconscious Christianity', see Karl Rahner, S.J., 'Anonymous Christians', in *Theological Investigations Vol 6: Concerning Vatican Council 2* (London: Darton, Longman & Todd, 1974); for discussion of the relationship between Rahner's conceptualization and Bonhoeffer, see Geffrey B. Kelly, '"Unconscious Christianity" and the "Anonymous Christian" in the Theology of Dietrich Bonhoeffer and Karl Rahner', *Philosophy & Theology* 9, no. 2 (1995); on the problematic nature of such thinking (especially for a theology similar to that outlined herein), see Lindbeck, *The Nature of Doctrine*, pp. 61–3. While what follows is offered as a mild corrective to Bonhoeffer's language, in terms of the concepts which underscore this phrase, it is important to remember that for Bonhoeffer, to be Christian is not to be a religious person in a certain way (LPP, p. 480).
59   For further examples of this sort of reading, see the next chapter.

exclusivisms' in the description that has been offered thus far.[60] In his reflections on Karl Barth in light of a theology of religions, Gavin D'Costa recognizes something of this issue when he describes Barth as simultaneously 'exclusivist, inclusivist and universalist'.[61] Sensitive readers of Barth may be able to detect that there is complete christological exclusivism in his work; but that the situation is somewhat more complex when it comes to revelational exclusivism and also eschatological exclusivism, which denies salvation to the non-Christian.[62]

As has already been noted in this book, Barth's complete christological exclusivism is the basis for his hopeful assertion of eschatological universalism.[63] It is worth considering these concerns in a little more detail. Lindbeck's words are helpful here, and reflective of Barth's concerns as well: 'The major doctrinal concern has been to preserve the *Christus solus*, not to deny the possibility of salvation to non-Christians.'[64] Furthermore, this hope of universal salvation does not seek to suggest that salvation is even a concern for those of other faiths. Di Noia asks the question: 'Is it possible . . . to account theologically for the availability of salvation to the non-Christians without ascribing to them the pursuit of an aim of life that they either explicitly reject or could not recognize as their own?'[65] Inasmuch as these others are other *to us*, and inasmuch as salvation is a central Christian concern, the answer here has *for us* to be in the affirmative. This is not to deny the identity, concerns and preoccupations of the other, but it is also not to undermine our own identity in relating to theirs: there can be no theology of religions from nowhere, so to speak; and we must recognize that Christian concerns about the other are *Christian* concerns for Christians about the other. To move away from concerns about salvation is to deny the real nature of this concern for Christianity, and to move away from authentic expressions of the Christian faith. To ask about the salvation of others outside of the church is not simply to engage in a top-down or ultimate view of the other, but a penultimate view *within our own community* of the ultimacy of the other before God; it can never more than that.

---

60 I have discussed differentiated exclusivisms before. See Greggs, 'Bringing Barth's Critique of Religion to the Inter-Faith Table', p. 79, n. 16; and Tom Greggs, 'The Lord of All: Rediscovering the Christian Doctrine of Providence for a Pluralist Society', in *Theology, Religion and Exclusion: Towards Transformation*, ed. Hannah Bacon and Wayne Morris (London: T&T Clark, 2011). These themes are also discussed in relation to evangelical theology by Veli-Matti Kärkkäinen, 'Evangelical Theology and the Religions', in *The Cambridge Companion to Evangelical Theology*, ed. Timothy Larsen and Daniel J. Treier (Cambridge: CUP, 2007), p. 206.

61 Gavin D'Costa, 'Theology of Religions', in *The Modern Theologians: An Introduction to Christian Theology in the Twentieth Century. Second Edition*, ed. David F. Ford (Oxford: Blackwell, 1997), p. 630. For a further unpacking of what these terms mean, see Gavin D'Costa, *Theology and Religious Pluralism: The Challenge of Other Religions* (Oxford: Basil Blackwell, 1986).

62 Cf. Hunsinger, *How to Read Karl Barth*, p. 281.

63 See Chapter 5 of this book.

64 Lindbeck, *The Nature of Doctrine*, p. 56.

65 J. A. Di Noia, *The Diversity of Religions: A Christian Perspective* (Washington: Catholic University of America Press, 1992), p. 94.

With regard to revelational exclusivism, the situation is even more complex. Revelation for Barth can never be separated from the one event of Jesus Christ, which means that theological pluralism must necessarily be rejected as there can be no sources of revelation outside of Him. Therefore, an exclusivity exists in the words of scripture and (at least in the early volumes of *Church Dogmatics*) in the proclamation of the church, as they attest to the one revelation of God in Jesus Christ.[66] However, this exclusivism exists in the dialectical tension that also comes with the recognition that the one Word of Jesus Christ relativizes all human words.[67] Thus Barth offers a generous form of christological exclusivism while still retaining a proper level of internal coherence with basic expressions of belief for Christianity. It is inside the exclusivity of his christological claims that Barth can make positive statements of hope for those who do not themselves make those claims. A similar point is made by Bonhoeffer. His observations that only in faith can one know the nature of revelation as being independent of faith present comparable differentiations with regard to traditional exclusivity.[68]

One can see similar concerns to those over revelation with regard to the providential work of God in creation.[69] Barth advocates that the exclusive subject of providence is revelation,[70] but the subject of that revelation is the universal Lordship of God. At once, therefore, Barth is radically inclusive of all creation, and simultaneously exclusivist in the way in which he makes this assertion. The only way to know God's providential power in general world-occurrence is through the special history of God with His particular people. Thus Barth writes:

> That world history in its totality is the history in which God executes His will of grace must thus be taken to mean that in its totality it belongs to this special history; that its lines can have no other starting-point or goal than the one divine will of grace; that they must converge on this one thin line and finally run in its direction. This is the theme of the doctrine of providence. It has to do with the history of the covenant, with the one thin line as such. Or rather, it has to do with it only to the extent that it for its part is undoubtedly one

---

66   Cf. CD I/1, §4, on the threefold nature of the word of God.

67   Cf. CD I/1, pp. 164–9, and Barth's later work on truth *extra muros ecclesiae* (IV/4, §69).

68   A&B, p. 118.

69   This is a theme I have tackled in detail in Greggs, 'The Lord of All: Rediscovering the Christian Doctrine of Providence for a Pluralist Society'. J. A. Di Noia, *The Diversity of Religions* offers a sustained engagement with this theme of providence in relation to other religions. Despite his previous concerns expressed above, he writes: 'The acknowledgement of the providential diversity of religious aims is compatible with a strong Christian affirmation of the universality of salvation. A Christian theology of religions, shaped by this development of traditional doctrines, preserves the unique valuation of the role of the Christian community in the divine plan of humankind. Furthermore, such a theology of religions can acknowledge the distinctive identity of non-Christian religious schemes and patterns of life' (p. 72).

70   CD III/3, p. 33.

among the many other lines of general world-occurrence, and that these many other lines of general world-occurrence have their ontic and noetic basis in the fact that the God from whom they come and to whom they return pursues on this one line the special work which the creature must serve on these other lines. The doctrine of providence must not level down the special history of the covenant, grace and salvation; it must not reduce it to the common denominator of a doctrine of general world occurrence. In so doing it would lose sight of the starting-point and therefore of its concept of the subject. And then it would no longer be speaking of the world dominion of God revealed in His Word. This God is the Father of Jesus Christ, the God of Abraham, Isaac and Jacob, the God of the prophets and apostles, the God who pursues His special work on this special line of world-occurrence. The doctrine of providence presupposes that this special history is exalted above all other history.[71]

Barth cautions that we cannot draw lines of continuity between other expressions of providence and providence as expressed within Christianity (no parallelism or substantialization is possible regarding other empirical religions),[72] but this does not prevent there from being an immensely strong sense of God's guiding hand in all of history. Indeed, the breadth and depth of God's providential reach is almost beyond imagination. It is worth quoting Barth at length again to gain a sense of this:

Everything was open and present to Him: everything in its own time and within its own limits; but everything open and present to Him. Similarly, everything that is, as well as everything that was, is open and present to Him, within its own limits. And everything that will be, as well as everything that was and is, will be open and present to Him, within its own limits. And one day – to speak in temporal terms – when the totality of everything that was and is and will be will only have been, then in the totality of its temporal duration it will still be open and present to Him, and therefore preserved: eternally preserved; revealed in all its greatness and littleness; judged according to its rightness or wrongness, its value or lack of value; but revealed in its participation in the love which He Himself has directed towards it. Therefore nothing will escape Him: no aspect of the great game of creation; no moment of human life; no thinking thought; no word spoken; no secret or insignificant enterprise or deed or omission with all its interaction and effects; no suffering or joy; no sincerity or lie; no secret event in heaven or too well-known event on earth; no ray of sunlight; no note which has ever sounded; no colour which has ever been revealed, possibly in the darkness of oceanic depths where the eye of

---

71   CD III/3, pp. 36–7.
72   CD III/3, p. 27.

man has never perceived it; no wing-beat of the day-fly in far-flung epochs of geological time.[73]

Although distinctiveness and particularity is not suspended (there will still be judgement), nothing – not even a 'wing-beat of the day-fly in far-flung epochs of geological time' – will be lost to God: it is all preserved in His eternity. Given Barth's beliefs about the lesser lights (discussed above and in Chapter 4), which are not 'Nothing' but may well reveal something of the true Light in the outer sphere, it may be possible to see here the guiding hand of God upon people of other faiths and religious traditions as well – a purpose of God worked out in creation in which the multiple intensities of God's Holy Spirit are operative. To look to God's providential guiding is not to say that there is something innately good in religion (some common experiential core), but to note determined particularity and variety. Furthermore, to point to providence as a way of understanding these differentiated exclusivisms is not to say that through religion God guides peoples and is involved in every single aspect of creation, but that providence is *so* strong that *despite of religion* God is present to communities of peoples, guiding and preserving them, just as He does even in the Christian religion.

Another way of speaking about these differentiated exclusivisms might be offered in terms of the variety of covenants of God with creation to which the Bible testifies. Within the Hebrew Bible, it is possible to identify a number of particular covenants with humanity, many involving differing 'reaches' of God (and levels of exclusivity). Among a notable number of others, these are sometimes identified as the Adamic, Noahide, Abrahamic, Sinaitic, Davidic and Ezekelic covenants.[74] This is a theme which is present (in an undeveloped way) in Barth's theology. He writes: 'The one covenant achieves historical form in the making of *a series of covenants*.'[75] Barth also asserts:

Jesus Christ is already the content and theme of this prehistory, of the Old Testament covenant. As prehistory, as revelation in expectation, the Old Testament covenant is characterised by its division into several covenants side by side, equipped with the same marks, even with the marks of the same uniqueness. Before the Sinaitic covenant we admittedly find the covenant with Abraham underlying the election of Israel, and again, before the Abrahamic covenant, the covenant with Noah, in which the particular covenant with Israel, even before it became an event, is already carried beyond its particularity and raised to universality. So, although it is already a reality

---

73   CD III/3, pp. 89–90.
74   For a presentation of the range of covenants within the Bible, see Steven L. McKenzie, *Covenant* (St Louis: Chalice, 2000); and W. J. Dumbrell, *Covenant and Creation: A Theology of the Old Testament Covenants* (Carlisle: Paternoster, 1997).
75   LJCHC, p. 52, emphasis added.

from that early beginning, Israel's election is a present reality. In Deuteronomy we find that the covenant is to some extent a lasting ordinance, under which the Israel of the present stands, although it is still based upon the free love and lordship of God.[76]

It is important to recognize that for Barth Jesus Christ is the one covenant God for humanity. However, this singular covenant of God with humanity in Jesus Christ does not determine that there is no historical particularity and variance in the different historical instantiations of covenant before Jesus' historical becoming flesh, nor that His incarnation suspends these. In reflecting further upon these covenants, however, it is worth noticing the distinctive differentiations in the ways in which the covenants operate and the varying extent of their reaches. For example, the covenant with Noah seems to be universal and the Noahide laws are considered to apply to all of creation (beyond the parameters of the future people of Israel); the covenant with Abraham, however, is for his off-spring, including it seems Ishmael to whom a great nation is promised and who is brought into the sign of the covenant through circumcision;[77] the covenant at Sinai involves God's people whom He has rescued from Egypt, but laws are also laid down about the treatment of the foreigner in the land; and so on. The particular and exclusive testimony of scripture is that we cannot force a dull and monochrome meta-narrative onto the history of God's dealings with His people, expressed variously in the different covenants offered. That there are different covenants and reaches within these covenants, with different interrelations between them, determines, moreover, that there will need to be different things said in relation to those peoples who variously and distinctively stand in relation to different covenants. As an adopted people of Abraham, our dealings with the offspring of Isaac and Ishmael will be different from each other, just as they will be different to the dealings with people who stand under the Noahide covenant. Furthermore, there is clearly nothing incumbent upon other religious traditions to accept, recognize or agree with our understanding of their covenantal relationship with God; this can never be anything other than a Christian interpretation of the variety of God's engagements with different peoples. Of course, this does not reduce the importance of saying this *for Christian theology*.

---

76   CD I/2, pp. 81–2. The plurality of the covenants is not something which Barth spends a significant amount of time on, however, in his work, despite his affirmation of this. See Tom Greggs, 'Peoples of the Covenants: Evangelical Theology and the Plurality of the Covenants in Scripture', *Journal of Scriptural Reasoning* (forthcoming), in which I not only address this issue with regard to Barth's work, but also engage in discussing God's covenant in relation to Ishmael and to Muslim people in the present.

77   It is worth noting here that as well as the Judaeo-Christian tradition of Ishmael being the father or a powerful nation, in *The Tales of the Prophet*, the first part of Mohammad's biography, Ishmael is understood not only to be the father of the Arab nations but also the father of the greater *Ummah* (community) of Muslim people.

CONCLUSION: REALIZING ESCHATOLOGY IS NOT FULLY REALIZED

One further way of thinking of these differentiated covenants is in terms of the non-realized and future nature of the eschaton: they are covenants which might display the breadth of God's ways with the world that we do not yet know or recognize, grounded in God's covenantal act of creation.[78] To a Roman (and one might presume pagan) centurion, Jesus says in Matthew's Gospel: 'I tell you, many will come from east and west and will eat with Abraham and Isaac and Jacob in the kingdom of heaven, while the heirs of the kingdom will be thrown into the outer darkness, where there will be weeping and gnashing of teeth.'[79] Read as a text about our contemporary self-understanding as Christians regarding our own self-identification as 'heirs of the kingdom',[80] this is a radically de-assuring text for us. However, it is also a text which helps us to understand (anti-religiously) the breadth of God's engagement with the world including those of other faiths. It forces us to be humble and to be optimistic. The centurion is presumably understood as one of those who exists outside of what the community understands to be God's normative scope of engagement with His people – as one who does not understand himself as an heir of God's kingdom. But implicit in this verse is also that he will be one of the many from the east and the west who will feast with Abraham, Isaac and Jacob. Eschatological kingdom identity for Jesus Christ seems not to be tied to religious affiliation. Seeking to realize this eschatological reality in the present, in proclaiming oneself as an heir, seems further to lead one not to be a member of the kingdom which lies ahead of us in the future in God. This outsider status for the so-called heir comes to one who confuses this future kingdom with a religious community in the present.

Engagement with those of other faiths, therefore, always involves the humility for Christians of realizing that they (as insiders) could well find themselves as outsiders, and the outsiders could well find themselves insiders. In this way, no God's-eye perspective is allowed and no pronouncement *vox dei* is possible. The others may well be (even if they do not themselves know or even desire this) the most treasured members of the eschatological kingdom. By our desire to keep

---

78 On creation and covenant, see CD III/1, § 41.

79 Mt. 8.11–12.

80 I am, therefore, offering an hermeneutical engagement with a text which could be interpreted in worryingly anti-Jewish ways, as a text which is specifically Christian and meaningful only to the Christian tradition. For those for whom these texts are authoritative, the argument is that the danger exists for those who understand themselves as the heirs of the eschatological kingdom (Christians): the historical issue is that of being a religious insider, not the issue of being a member of any specific historical faith community. This approach could equally be applied to texts such as those about the sheep and the goats, or texts involving the Pharisees (who should be understood for the community for whom the New Testament is authoritative as typological anticipations of Christian religiosity).

the inheritance for ourselves as Christians, we may we find ourselves outside the kingdom we thought we stood to inherit. For the Christian, this may mean that the only judgement that can be offered to those of other faiths is one of positive and hospitable engagement with those many who will join the feast with the patriarchs, and whom we should welcome as table guests now, if we seek to be an proleptic anticipation of the future kingdom and desire not to find ourselves on the outside and in darkness by seeing ourselves as the only true heirs. It is to what this engagement with those of other faiths in the present might look like that this book now turns.

Chapter 9

FROM THEORY TO PRACTICE: INTER-FAITH DIALOGUE

Having outlined in the previous chapter a possible shape to a theology of religions which arises from a critical theological approach to the nature of religion, it is now necessary to move from considering how to *think* about the question of other empirical religions to the question of how to *engage* with other empirical religionists, both in terms of general themes about Christian attitudes towards members of other religions and in terms of practical examples of fruitful engagement. The purpose of this chapter is to identify potentially wise modes of engagement for Christians with members of other faiths, arising from a Christian theological appropriation of the critique of religion. Clearly, there is a degree of progression here from the last chapter. It is not difficult to imagine how, for example, recognizing that as Christians we speak as religionists rather than with *vox dei* might inform a more generous manner of behaviour towards those who are members of other religions. However, in a complexly secular and multi-religious world, it is insufficient merely to rest at the level of theory with regard to the religious other who is not simply a speculative theoretical possibility but a genuine physical neighbour. Given that there is little direct engagement in Barth and Bonhoeffer with theologies of the religions, it is hardly surprising that there is no engagement in their corpuses in discussing the potential for modes of engaging in inter-faith dialogue: this simply was not a concern for them.[1] However, this reality does not mean that fruit cannot be borne from their theologies for the area of inter-faith engagement. The benefits that can be gained from them come not least from the arena of their critical engagement with and theologizing of the category of religion. In this chapter, impetuses for engaging in inter-religious dialogue will be discussed, and there will be some suggested practical modes of engagement. The chapter will begin by outlining the need for dynamic engagement with other faiths – an engagement which will differ from faith to faith, and which will vary in terms of the reasons for entering into it. The chapter will then consider the need, arising from the critical stance that Christians must take with regard to their own religion, to engage humbly with those of other religions, with a full

---

1 Perhaps the closest we come to this is with regard to Judaism, but within the very specific setting of the issues in Nazi Germany.

recognition that Christians will not always be in the 'driving seat' in inter-faith dialogue. The chapter will go on to outline the benefits of engaging in inter-faith dialogue in terms of becoming and understanding ourselves more fully. After discussion of the need to engage in inter-faith and secular-faith discussion simultaneously, and of Jesus' own engagement with those of other faiths, the chapter will consider Scriptural Reasoning (the reading together and study of scriptures from different religious traditions) as one possible means of discovering a 'non-religious' interpretation of scripture, and as a way for Christians to engage in inter-faith dialogue arising from a theological appropriation of the critique of religion.

DYNAMIC ENGAGEMENTS

One implication of there being no substantialized theology of the religions is that there thus needs to be dynamic engagement in inter-faith dialogue.[2] By this is meant that since there can be no 'one size fits all' attitude to the theology of religions, there can equally be no 'one size fits all' approach to inter-faith dialogue or to the reasons for engaging in it. While Barth does not deal frequently with other religions, there are for him definitive differentiations that exist between the ways in which Christianity should deal with different empirical religions, which are not all treated as one, but are considered variously. About Judaism, for example, Barth writes:

> It is a good thing to seek union between Presbyterians and Episcopalians and so on, and between Eastern Orthodox and Roman Catholics, but the big thing is our fundamental unity with the synagogue, because we all came from Israel. Christ was a Jew and so long as we understand Judaism only as another kind of religion, there will be at the root of the ecumenical movement something lacking.[3]

For all that Barth talks about 'religion' as a category, he nevertheless deals variously with different empirical religions: his approach demonstrates that there is no singular, 'one size fits all' approach to other faiths. For example, although Barth is hardly enlightened in his discussions of Islam, he nevertheless discusses this religion in relation to monotheism (distinguishing Christian monotheism from it),[4] and in relation to the Old and New Testaments, to which he believes Islam stands in historical relation.[5] In comparison to his engagement with Islam, his discussions of Buddhism (especially Genku and Shinran) revolve around discussions

---

2 See the section 'Against a Substantialized Theology of Religions' in Chapter 8 of this book.

3 Karl Barth, *Gespräche 1959–1962* (Zürich: Theologische Verlag, 1995), pp. 450–1.

4 See, for example, CD I/1, p. 353 and II/1, pp. 448–9; and GD, p. 430; these are hardly positive endorsements of Islam, however.

5 CD I/2, p. 828.

of grace.[6] While his engagements with empirical religions are normally to differentiate Christian theology from them, the points at which dialogue and discussion take place are various for Barth. The reason for this varied and plural engagement with other empirical religions is because – perhaps surprisingly – there is genuine place for dialogue in Barth's theology. However, this needs to be described carefully.

Rather than dialogue being overcome by a desire to find shared ground or a fear of saying something which is different to that believed by the other, for Barth, dialogue has to be genuinely dialogical: it has to take place on the basis of difference. Dialogues take place in recognition that there may be shared issues and concerns, but that these issues and concerns, while they may be shared and overlapping, are not the same. To a degree dialogue is based, therefore, upon some level of disagreement. Inter-faith dialogue is in some ways the form of dialogue in which this disagreement is most strong, difficult and meaningful for those who partake in it, since it revolves around what should be the most deeply held beliefs that people have. If we fail to recognize the very real differences between faith communities and belief systems, dialogue will not only fail but we will do violence towards the other whom we will see simply as a repetition of ourselves. For inter-faith dialogue to be genuinely inter-*faith*, there will inevitably be places of difference, disagreement and deep felt pain; the seats at the table of inter-faith are never going to be terribly comfortable, but nor indeed should they ever seek to be. In this much, the hyphenated nature of this term is key: when the dynamic engagement between religions is replaced by a substantialized 'thing' called 'interfaith', the nature and purpose of inter-faith engagements are destroyed. If the very enterprise of inter-faith dialogue replaces or overwhelms the distinctive faith communities, or becomes the primary identifier (over their own individual tradition) for those who engage in it, then inter-faith activity ceases to be the very means for genuine dialogue that it was designed to be. Barth's at times brutal (and for the contemporary world, we might say, unwise) disagreements with the beliefs of other faiths are going to exist (even if they could be expressed more wisely) for those who proclaim 'Jesus Christ is Lord!': no one can serve two masters. Christians are and should be Christian, just as Sikhs are and should be Sikh, Jews Jewish and so on. However, there are two further significant features of Barth's engagement with other faiths. First, even to enter into some dialogue with the others presupposes some degree of 'attraction' (for want of a better term) between Christianity and other faiths: to engage with other faiths is an expression of what Barth terms the singularity of Christianity (as opposed to its uniqueness or to the universality of religion),[7] and we might think of this as some shared – if very distinctive – concerns. Secondly, the pluriformity of engagement in which Barth

---

6   CD I/2, pp. 340–2.
7   CD I/2, p. 282; cf. the section 'Against a Substantialized Theology of Religions' in Chapter 8 of this book for further discussion of this term.

discusses other empirical religions is crucial. The plurality and differences of the faiths will determine that engagements and dialogues with different religious groups are going to be distinctive and different. There is always a need to recognize this.

When engaging in inter-faith comes not to be about identifying a common core, establishing lines of continuity, and trying to cover over differences that can never be reduced or simply hidden, there is the possibility of dynamic and real human engagement with peoples of difference. As Lindbeck puts it:

> This lack of a common foundation is a weakness, but is also a strength. It means, on the one hand, that the partners in dialogue do not start with the conviction that they really basically agree, but it also means that they are not forced into the dilemma of thinking of themselves as representing a superior (or an inferior) articulation of a common experience of which other religions are inferior (or superior) expressions.[8]

Not engaging in inter-faith on the basis of a positive belief in a shared essence determines, furthermore, that there is the appropriate recognition of the plurality of reasons and theological bases for engaging in inter-faith dialogue. Not presupposing a positive common core shared by all religions means that there is a need to examine the various foundations for engagement with other faiths, which require engagement internal to the Christian tradition and theology, rather than accepting some foundational external norm of a perceived and positive common religious core.[9] For a Christian theology which does not see religion as a positive thing, there can nevertheless be various theological reasons for engaging with other empirical religions in the world. These will be on the basis of Christian theology and will be unlikely to be affirmed by those of the other religion, but arising from the Christian tradition there can nevertheless be a reaching out dialogically to those others within the world who do not share the Christian belief system. Not having a common core which one wishes to affirm determines, however, that these engagements will be dynamic and plural.

In some ways, the need for a dynamic engagement is hardly surprising. Inter-faith dialogue, after all, concerns real life human beings in real life situations and contexts. Thus, as Barnes puts it, a 'certain pluralism of response to other faiths is inevitable'.[10] Bonhoeffer recognizes in his *Ethics* that the basis of responsible action is grounded in reality rather than ideology for the Christian because God became a real human being. He writes: 'Responsible action is nourished not by an ideology but by reality, which is why one can only act within the boundaries of

---

8   Lindbeck, *The Nature of Doctrine*, p. 55.
9   Cf. Ibid., pp. 53–4 in his critique of the experiential-expressivist.
10 Cf. Barnes, *Theology and the Dialogue of Religions*, p. 245.

that reality.'[11] For the Christian living in the twenty-first century, part of the reality of contemporary life is an existence in a situation of pluralism: this is a situation that cannot be avoided theologically or ethically. Seeking to live lives in correspondence to Christ (whom we might once again affirm as the *Aufhebung* of religion) requires that we seek to live a life for God and for other human beings – not idealized human beings, but real human beings of difference and varied otherness. In the contemporary setting, for Christians, this involves somehow living wisely for members of other faiths as well.[12] Once again to quote Bonhoeffer:

> Only because God became human is it possible to know and not despise real human beings. Real human beings may live before God, and we may let these real people live beside us and before God without either despising or idolizing them. This is not because of the real human being's inherent value, but because God has loved and taken on the real human being. The reason for God's love for human beings does not reside in them, but only in God. Our living as real human beings, and loving the real people next to us is, again, grounded only in God's becoming human, in the unfathomable love of God for us human beings.[13]

Grounded in the christological claims of our faith, Bonhoeffer points to the possibility of loving *real* other humans, who we are able to know through Jesus Christ. We know these others not as those we idolize or as those we hate, but as those who are beloved of God, and as real neighbours that we are called to love. This is a love which passes beyond difference and otherness to real human situations and contexts.

Moreover, it is perhaps unsurprising that the need to engage in inter-faith should be thoughts of as dynamic when we consider the nature of the God who is the Lord of all creation, and not just of the Lord of the church. Barth certainly recognizes the wide diversity of God's engagement with creation. As Geoff Thompson puts it: 'God's freedom is such that the divine presence to creation can never be considered static or uniform'.[14] Barth makes this case emphatically:

> Although in His eternal being and action towards the world God is undivided and indivisibly One and the Same, although He is always wholly the One He is, the mode of His action varies. It is one thing in the incarnation of the Word, in the once-for-all and unique assumption of human nature into unity with His eternal Son, into communion with His divine being. It is another thing in the wider kingdom of His grace – in the life of the Church and the children of

---

11   Ethics, p. 225.
12   On wisdom and inter-faith dialogue, see Ford, *Christian Wisdom: Desiring God and Learning in Love*, chapter 8.
13   Ethics, p. 87.
14   Thompson, 'Religious Diversity, Christian Doctrine and Karl Barth', 18.

God, in the power of preaching and the sacraments, in the power of the new conception and birth of man to faith by the Holy Spirit. It is another thing again in the creation, preservation and government of the existence and nature of the world and man, in virtue of which they are always neutral reality. It is another thing again in the future consummation, in the return of Christ, in the resurrection of the dead, in the last judgment and the end when He will be all in all. He acts and speaks variously in the prophets and apostles, in preaching and sacrament, in Holy Scripture, in the writings of the fathers and the creeds of the Church, differently yesterday, and differently to-day, and differently to-morrow. . . . He is always infinitely diverse in His communion with each individual angel, thing, man, or believer, as compared with all the rest.[15]

Furthermore, and crucially for any engagement in inter-faith which does not proceed on the basis of some positive shared common core or on the basis of a taxonomy of religions, there is no hierarchy involved with this variety of God's engagement with the world: the unity of the works of God is not found on the basis of some form of gradation of acts. Again, Thompson summarizes this well: 'Jesus Christ is less the pinnacle of God's works, and more the all-encompassing source from which the others are derived *and* the horizon before which they are ordered.'[16] We cannot see Christianity as somehow the pinnacle of God's engagement with the world, ordering the other empirical religions in relation to the Christian one. After all, Christianity *qua* religion is contradicted by Jesus Christ, and thus we should not think that God's operations with the world take place on some form of graded religious scale. God operates diversely, variously and fully within the world in His actions *ad extra*. That God engages in a plurality of ways with creation should determine that we do not seek to enforce a flat monotony onto our engagements with other religions in the world.[17]

HUMILITY IN APPROACHING THE OTHER

While it is the case that there should be no singular engagement with other faiths, but different theological reasons for, and modes of engagement with, those of different religions, there may nevertheless be wise impetuses that we can identify within a theology against religion that can help to bring about the conditions for dialogue. Significant among these impetuses should be that of humility. Realizing that the condemnation of religion is a condemnation of *Christian* religion guards the Christian against ever thinking that she is in a position of superiority from

---

15 CD II/1, pp. 315–16.

16 Thompson, 'Religious Diversity, Christian Doctrine and Karl Barth', 19.

17 I have made this point about plurality with regard to Origen's theology; see Tom Greggs, 'The Many Names of Christ in Wisdom: Reading Scripture with Origen for a Diverse World', *Journal of Scriptural Reasoning* (2008).

which to judge the other. For the Christian to recognize in relation to other religions that she does not take the position of God, but of the worst of all idolators, and that she speaks not with God's voice but only ever as a religionist, helps her to adopt a more humble attitude towards members of other faiths. To engage thus is to re-orientate ourselves towards an outlook that can 'be developed in such a way as to oppose the boasting and sense of superiority that destroys the possibility of open and mutually enriching dialogue.'[18] Engaging in inter-faith dialogue from the perspective of a critical theological engagement with the concept of religion might not only allow for the capacity to engage in genuine dialogue, rather than a desire to engage in identifying some common essence to various religious traditions, but it might also provide the wise operative condition for engaging in dialogue with members of other faiths – humility.

Barth addresses the issue of humility with regard to the other (religious or not) variously in his writings. He describes the attitude of humility well in his discussion of the parable of the Pharisee and the publican:

> The parable of the Pharisee and the Publican (Lk. 189f.) speaks of two men who are both equally shamed before God but who are completely different because of their knowledge or ignorance of the fact. On the one hand we have here in the temple, proudly displayed before the face of God, the man who is ignorant and therefore quite unashamed. He thanks God so beautifully that he is as he is and therefore not as other men, extortioners, unjust, adulterers, or even as this publican. He can claim that he is free from carnal appetites: 'I fast twice in the week'; and he can also claim that he is free from the rule of Mammon: 'I give tithes of all that I possess.' On the other hand, also in the temple and before the face of God, we have the man who knows and is therefore ashamed. He can only stand afar off, and dare not lift up so much as his eyes unto heaven, but can only smite on his breast, his confession of faith being simply this: 'God be merciful to me a sinner.' . . . The one can only humble himself whereas the other sees many things which encourage him to exalt himself.[19]

The point in relating this parable to the issue of inter-faith dialogue is not that the other is likely to be pharisaical (far from it), but that we run the risk of and are likely to adopt the attitude of this Pharisee in our engagement with those of other faiths, rejoicing that we are religiously punctilious and correct. However, in light of our own religiosity (and our propensity in that to idolatry), it is incumbent upon the Christian at the inter-faith table to take the position of the publican, recognizing her own sin, and being led to ask for the mercy of God.

---

18 Cf. Lindbeck, *The Nature of Doctrine*, p. 59.
19 CD IV/3, p. 385.

Christians, after all, are not types of human beings, but are just human beings in the first instance.[20] Even in affirming the distinctiveness of the Christian from other human beings, Barth is able to state about Christians:

[They] too are his creatures, people like all the rest. They too exist in the depths of all creaturely human being. Not on the heights with God, but out of these clearly recognizable depths they call upon him, upon him who is who he is in heaven, in the heights of his own unapproachable place, in the distance which he alone can overcome from his side. They are in the world. Yet they are not so in vain. They are significant and important for the world as world. As they thank and praise God and pray to him, in contrast to all religious hubris and moral heaven-storming; in contrast also to all wild dissipation and indolent negligence, they realize the only legitimate possibility in relation to the world; in contrast to all optimistic and pessimistic illusions they fulfill the truth of being of the world and man in relation to him who is God as Creator and Lord of the world and man.[21]

Realizing that God is the Creator of all the world and all humans, moreover, brings with it the realization that scripture attests to revelations of God outside of the bounds of the church.[22] We know this only from scripture and God's revelation, thus we cannot deny God's revealing presence outside of the bounds of the church.

That there are other words outside of the revelation known by Christians should guard the Christian from arrogantly jumping to condemn the lights of the outer-sphere as false.[23] Chung's words regarding this seem correct: 'Barth is not convinced of the absoluteness of Christianity over other religions but is concerned rather to lead the Christian church to self-criticism with a humble attitude and radical openness toward religious outsiders.'[24] The correct mode of Christian engagement with non-Christian religions is, therefore, humility.

Furthermore, this humility does not only arise because of the failings of the Christian in her religion. The humility is grounded in the absolute superiority of Christ to Christianity and to the church. Barth writes powerfully:

There can be no question of Jesus Christ being even temporarily directed in His absence to let Himself be represented by an honoured Christianity and the holy Church, or of non-Christians having to wait to be impressed by the

---

20   LPP, p. 480.
21   ChL, pp. 98–9.
22   CD IV/3, p. 97.
23   For more on the lights and the Light and the words and the Word, see Chapter 4 of this book.
24   Chung, 'On Karl Barth in Interreligious Studies and Cross-Cultural Perspective', 222; cf. 217 and 220.

clarity, cogency and credibility of the witness of Christians. Jesus Christ . . . cannot be replaced by Christianity. He remains sovereign even in this respect.[25]

The very sovereignty of Jesus Christ is such that the Christian as a member of her faith at the inter-faith table can be nothing other than humble in attitude towards the other; for she knows the chasm that exists between Jesus Christ as the object of Christian worship and the church and religion that seeks to worship Him.

Not only is humility appropriate in light of Christ's sovereignty as Lord, it is also fitting as an attitude for one who seeks to behave responsibly as a creature in the world. In his *Ethics*, Bonhoeffer sets the limits of responsible human action in terms of the surrender to God's grace and responsibility for the neighbour, who is known as encountered in Jesus Christ. He writes: 'Responsible action . . . gains its unity, and ultimately also its certainty, from this very limitation by God and neighbor. It is not its own lord and master, nor is it unbounded or frivolous. Instead, it is creaturely and humble.'[26] That responsible action is bounded not only by God but by the concrete neighbour is significant for inter-faith engagement in the twenty-first century. The question exists of how to live responsibly before God and before these others, who might be very different from us. In recognizing the way in which these two realities (God and the neighbour) place limitations on our responsible action, the Christian also recognizes that responsible action is both creaturely and humble in light of these two realities. This point is significant not only in situations in which Christians might take the lead or act as the catalyst or initiator of inter-faith engagement, but also in situations in which Christians do not find themselves in the driving seat with regard to members of other faiths. One sees such an example in Jesus' famous parable of the Good Samaritan (Lk. 10.25–37). In this story, it is the presumed religious insider who is in need, and the member of another religious tradition (the Samaritan) who is the hero, and in the position of strength to offer help to the religious insider. The story could easily have been told to similar effect with the Samaritan as the needy one, but by making the Samaritan the hero the point is made clearly that it is not simply the case in relations with members of other religions of our assisting and aiding the religious other who needs us; it can also be a case of our needing to be assisted and aided by the religious other (as in the case of the victim here).[27] And this is a point which challenges our presupposed idea of who our neighbour is (the very question which introduces the parable). Assuming that we will have the dominant position in inter-faith dialogue, or that we will be paragons of virtues which need to be displayed to others is hardly a humble attitude, but is instead one born of religious

---

25   CD IV/3 p. 349.

26   *Ethics*, p. 269.

27   For further on this theme, see Greggs, 'Preaching Inter-Faith: Finding Hints About the Religious Other from the Good Samaritan'.

superiority and arrogance: we ourselves may need at times to be helped by the religious other, and we may find that it is we who are to emulate that gracious service directed towards us. We see a contemporary example of this in the gift of Muslim scholars, intellectuals and clerics to the Christian church, *A Common Word Between Us and You.* This letter is the first coming together of significant numbers of Muslim leaders (at present 307 from every school of thought in Islam) since the time of Mohammad, and they have come together to affirm the traditional and mainstream Islamic teaching of respecting the Christian scripture and calling Christians to be more faithful to it.[28] This gift to the Christian church was and is one to be gratefully received in humility for what it is, and the leaders of the major Christian denominations (including the Pope and the Archbishop of Canterbury) that thanked the signatories for their gracious gift to the church at a time of strained relationships between Christians and Muslims should be congratulated for their actions. The wise and humble response to the generosity of this gift is to receive it in the spirit in which it was given, not to point out the places in which Christians continue to disagree or feel religiously superior.

Understanding Oneself Better

Through approaching the member of another religious faith in real humility, the possibility may arise of understanding ourselves better than we might otherwise have done. As Geoff Thompson reminds us, Barth's discussion of salvation outside the walls of the church is not simply an end in itself. It is also a significant place for the church itself to gain knowledge of God.[29] He writes regarding Barth on extra ecclesial words: 'these words are not anticipatory expressions of the one Word which are superseded by the church's own knowledge of God. They themselves contribute to the church's own hearing of the Word. Moreover, they do so with a certain "shock" value.'[30] Just as we might not always be in the position of the initiator or of the strongest voice in an inter-faith setting, so too, we should not presume we are there only to teach and instruct. We should also realize the need to listen and learn.

Furthermore, beyond the simply theoretical way in which these words aid the Christian in knowing more of God, the reality of pluralism confronts the church with the fundamental issue of otherness, and the need to respond to others in love. Mathewes identifies this issue well when he states:

> The challenge of otherness is very profound, for it reveals that in religious pluralism theology confronts a primordial theological problem: the problem

---

28   See http://www.acommonword.com/ (accessed on 25 March 2010).
29   Thompson, 'Religious Diversity, Christian Doctrine and Karl Barth', 13; cf. CD IV/3, p. 688.
30   Thompson, 'Religious Diversity, Christian Doctrine and Karl Barth', 13–14.

of otherness. What the contemporary world calls pluralism we should see, in theological terms, as the fundamental challenge of otherness . . . [31]

However, in confronting this ostensible problem, the church may actually learn to become more truly the church that it is called to be. As Bonhoeffer points out, the person who truly loves God 'must, by God's will, really love the neighbour.'[32] Neighbours are not just repetitions of ourselves, but are people of difference. In the contemporary world, this involves members of other world religions and none. Love of them is at the heart of the call to be the church, and is deeply connected with love of God. This should, moreover, be a love of the other for their own sake (a genuine love) as a child of God, and not because of any tribal affiliation or personal benefit. Furthermore, this orientation on the other is the way in which we might become truly human. Barth describes emphatically how to be human, we must be involved in 'fellow-humanity':

Between humanity and inhumanity, divided by the criterion of fellow-humanity, there is no middle term; just as there is no middle term between wisdom and folly, between the knowledge of God and ignorance of God. 'Inhuman' means to be without one's fellow-men. We can either be with them, i.e., orientated on them, and therefore human, thinking and willing and speaking and acting as men; or we can be without them, and therefore not human, but inhuman, in all our acts and attitudes.[33]

This does not mean, however, simple tolerant co-existence with other human beings. Merely to tolerate would be to seek in reality to live without those we are tolerating. It also does not mean that we can simply keep a distance from our neighbours; we are, instead, called to be with them and for them. Barth continues:

If we are without them we are against them. And as the stupidity of man does not have its origin in the theoretical denial of God, but is merely practised in a particular and not indispensable way in this denial, so inhumanity does not have its basis in individual actions and attitudes towards our neighbours, but either in these or without them in the fact that we think we can and should be without our neighbours and therefore alone – a distorted attitude which will necessarily find powerful expression in corresponding actions or omissions.[34]

To think that as human beings we can live without or at a distance from our neighbours, whoever they should be, is to fail to be genuinely human as God willed and

---

31   Mathewes, *A Theology of Public Life*, p. 108.
32   SC, p. 169.
33   CD IV/2, p. 434.
34   CD IV/2, p. 434.

determined us. Keeping distance from those around us, rather than being for them, will lead to actions and omissions which do not correspond to God's will.[35] There are real life implications for this issue, moreover. As Hauerwas reminds us: 'if we understand theology wrong, we get the world wrong.'[36] Recognizing theologically the need to be for our neighbours (including those of other religions) will determine the need to think differently about the world, and to behave differently within the world. But there is also reciprocity here: confronted with the other whom we are to love and to be for, we are enabled to be more genuinely and fully participants in God's will for creation, as those who are truly human.

REMEMBERING SECULAR ISSUES

Focusing on the neighbour within the world determines that there is a need to hold secular-faith and inter-faith issues together. This is not only in terms of a politics in which notions of the secular state have often controlled or interfered in inter-faith engagements,[37] but also in terms of the need to engage with the this-worldly needs of those of other faiths. Rather than simply a discussion of various of the theological and philosophical differences between the belief systems of the different world religions, inter-faith dialogue should arise for Christians out of a sense of being genuinely for the other. Thus, it should be an activity in which real friendship can be built up, and which can bring real difference to the world in this age (the *saeculum*, we might say). This is not to sidestep the questions of God's nature and of exclusivity, but it is to seek to perform inter-faith activities genuinely before God and for His sake: since from a Christian perspective, an aspect of love of God is love of neighbour.

For Barth, a significant negative aspect of religion is its propensity to turn inwards towards the self.[38] Thus, seeking to engage in inter-faith dialogue from the perspective of a theology which is against religion determines that in that very dialogue the heart cannot be turned towards the self, but must be turned out towards the other. This means that dialogue cannot only take place for our own benefit, but should also take place for the sake of the other, and – ultimately – for the sake of God. In seeking to be for the other, it is necessary to ask the questions: How are my actions loving towards them? How am I being *for* them?[39]

---

35   Cf. Lindbeck, *The Nature of Doctrine*, p. 54, in which he suggests that true Christian mission might even be to make members of other faiths more genuinely members of those faiths.

36   Hauerwas, *With the Grain of the Universe*, p. 183.

37   See Chapter 7 of this volume. See also Barth's discussion in CD §17 of the relationship between politics and pluralism: CD I/2, pp. 333–7.

38   CD I/2, p. 315.

39   'Being *against* others in trying to demonstrate the superiority of God's omnipotence would be the denial of the God who wants to be there *for* others in the transforming suffering on the cross.'

Talk must turn into action; and action must lead to further talk. In contrast to Schleiermacher's description of the community of the church as a religious grouping,[40] Barth reminds the church that it is formed in the image of Christ. In acknowledging this, Barth reminds us of Christ: 'He Himself, God's grace to the world in person, is the first and supreme Guest and Stranger who found no room in the inn and still cannot find any.'[41] By seeking to be a community founded on Jesus, the church must also seek to offer hospitality towards the other, and be prepared to receive it as well – in real concrete situations (pregnant mothers requiring inns), rather than simply in metaphysical speculations. The Jesus who taught and healed, and talked and ate with others is the Jesus on whom the church must be focused by the power and activity of the Spirit.

Looking at Jesus' engagement with members of other religious communities, it is deeply striking that the attendance to real human needs stands centrally within the narrative. Whether it is the desire for Jesus to heal someone beloved (as in the case of the Roman centurion and of the Syro-Phoenician woman), or a story in which a member of another religious community needs desperate help and receives it from the most unexpected corner (as in the story of the Good Samaritan), or an outcast coming to be an insider through healing (as with the Samaritan leper), Jesus does not in his engagements with members of other religious communities attend primarily to high-level theological discourse, but to real and urgent human need.[42] Even in the one place in which there is prolonged discourse relating to other religious communities (the Samaritan woman at the well in John 4), the context for this conversation is Jesus' asking for some water – a basic human provision that it seems should be denied because of religious difference. Interestingly, here, it is Jesus' physical need (and not that of the woman) which is the basis for the engagement between them. Jesus attends to (and is attended to in terms of) physical, human needs in his engagements with members of other religions; in this way, He is genuinely for these people, and being genuinely for these others is thereby truly human. If Jesus is truly the *Aufhebung* of religion, then attending to his engagements with members of other empirical religious communities is surely wise. Bonhoeffer describes the nature of responsible action as modelled by Jesus' engagement with reality in a way which is helpful to the current discussion:

> Again and again Jesus . . . . becomes the one who breaks through the law for the sake of the 'law' or, more clearly put, for the sake of the freedom of God's

---

Schwöbel, ' "Religion" and "Religionlessness" in *Letters and Papers from Prison*: A Perspective for Religious Pluralism?', p. 182.

40   For example, Schleiermacher, *The Christian Faith*, §7.

41   CD IV/3, p. 743.

42   This is even true of the Syro-Phoenician woman pericope: the context of Jesus' discourse is the desire for a miracle.

love. Love accepts what is real [das Wirkliche] just as it is, as proper to love. Love does not despise what is real for the sake of an idea, but accepts it as a given and as loved by God. Love does not derive its way of dealing with what is real independently from the real, but from the reality of the real, from its being-loved-by-God. The nature of all concrete responsible action is to grasp in what is real the love of God with which the real, the world, was loved.[43]

In a world situation in which we are confronted with the reality of neighbours of other faiths or none, loving concretely the real life neighbours we have is the challenge and responsibility of Christian living. We must ask the question of how it is that we may break through 'laws' in order to fulfil the law of love in the societies in which we now live, and of how we can see the reality of otherness around us as beloved of God.

SCRIPTURAL REASONING AS ONE POSSIBLE NON-RELIGIOUS INTERPRETATION

One possible practice of engagement in inter-faith dialogue, which has the potential to fulfil the described modes of engagement between the church and other empirical religions (as discussed above), is that of Scriptural Reasoning.[44] Scriptural Reasoning is a method of inter-faith dialogue which originated with Peter Ochs, David Ford, Daniel Hardy and Basit Koshul. Drawing on the model of engagement between Jewish philosophers (called 'Textual Reasoning'), Scriptural Reasoning offers a mode of inter-faith dialogue for members of different religious communities (dominantly Abrahamic communities in practice) with each other. Crucially, the manner of this engagement does not involve the rejection of deeply held faith commitments in order to enter some 'shared' (liberal) secular space that relativizes truth claims, undermines faith commitment and underplays differences.[45] Scriptural Reasoning takes place, rather, in the shared reading and discussion of the sacred texts of the faiths – the very particular and exclusive basis for the faiths. The practice, therefore, revolves around a shared sense of mutual hospitality in order to facilitate the dialogue. In Christian terms, we might express this as the fundamental need to be for the other. In this mutual hospitality, there is a simultaneous engagement in being the host (with one's own text) and the guest (at someone else's sacred text). This is a helpful image for

---

43 Ethics, p. 233.
44 The following section is an adaptation of a section of an essay I have previously published as Tom Greggs, 'Inter-Faith Pedagogy for Muslims and Christians: Scriptural Reasoning and Christian and Muslim Youth Work', *Discourse* 9, no. 2 (2010).
45 Cf. Chapter 7 of this volume on secular space.

those who follow Jesus, who was Himself both a guest and a host in His engagements with others.

Steven Kepnes has summarized the practice as follows:[46]

> SR [Scriptural Reasoning] is a practice of group reading of the scriptures of Judaism, Christianity, and Islam that builds sociality among its practitioners and releases sources of reason, compassion, and divine spirit for healing our separate communities and for repair of the world. Thus, SR theory aims at a scripturally reasoned triadic response to the problems of the world that is motivated and sustained by the healing and divine spirit of scripture.[47]

This mode of inter-faith dialogue has spread tremendously throughout the world, re-creating itself in various forms to fit the needs of the communities engaging in the practice:[48] it marks (in the terms of this book) a dynamic rather than a static approach to inter-faith, therefore (see above). What is continuous in all of the versions of the practice is a commitment to the reading of the scriptures of others before God for the sake of the world. Texts are not simply read in a modernist, historico-critical manner (as in the manner of singularly outsider study), nor are they read individualistically and piously as if they were religiously authoritative for all at the table (as in the manner of singularly insider study),[49] but are read as living texts which provide (variously and differently) the theological basis for the speech of each of the traditions of the book present at the table. The dominant concern is, therefore, primarily hermeneutical, and this hermeneutics is neither one of modern liberalism nor one of religious piety particular to one tradition.

In order to explain the practice, Scriptural Reasoning is sometimes spoken of figuratively in terms of the biblical image (present in all three Abrahamic traditions) of the tent of meeting. This is an image drawn from the provisional tent which features throughout the Torah. The image of the tent is used in a non-competitive way with the image of a house. The term 'house' is used figuratively in this inter-faith practice as a term for the institutional places of worship of the participants in Scriptural Reasoning

---

46   There is no master-descriptor of Scriptural Reasoning, and Kepnes' description should not be treated as such. Rather, it is offered as one particular kind of Jewish description which is put forward as an 'hypothesis' to participants from other traditions (and other members of his own tradition). For other summaries of scriptural reasoning, see Ford, *Christian Wisdom: Desiring God and Learning in Love*, pp. 273–303; David F. Ford and C. C. Pecknold, eds, *The Promise of Scriptural Reasoning* (Oxford: Blackwell, 2006); and Ford, 'God and Our Public Life: A Scriptural Wisdom', pp. 71–3.

47   Steven Kepnes, 'A Handbook for Scriptural Reasoning', *Modern Theology* 22, no. 3 (2006), 367. Much of the thinking that follows owes a good deal to Kepnes' article. On Scriptural Reasoning and triadic logic, see Ochs, *Peirce, Pragmatism and the Logic of Scripture*.

48   There is, for example, a medieval research group that meets in Princeton, and a civic focused group that meets in London. See here David F. Ford, 'An Interfaith Wisdom: Scriptural Reasoning between Jews, Christians and Muslims', *Modern Theology* 22, no. 3 (2006), 364–5, n. 9.

49   In this way, translated into Bonhoefferian terms, one might say that Scriptural Reasoning involves a mode of reading scripture which is neither liberal nor positivist; cf. LPP, pp. 372–3.

(the synagogue, church and mosque). That the tent exists in a non-competitive relationship to the houses is important in two ways. First, Scriptural Reasoning does not seek to supplant or to remove individual faith commitment, exclusivity or particularity, but seeks rather to enable genuine dialogue as dialogue between people who share similarities but also differences. There is no requirement to give up any deeply held faith commitments; indeed, such faith commitment is affirmed. This determines that, secondly, as opposed to the modernist assumption that religion should either be a homogeneous glue that binds people together, or that – if heterogeneous – it should be replaced by a non-religious secular space, Scriptural Reasoning seeks to allow for a space in which particularity is needed and welcomed: difference does not stand in aggressive opposition to dialogue and conversation, but is required for dialogue and conversation.[50] In this way, Scriptural Reasoning is a genuine engagement in and with pluralism, rather than an attempt to displace it.[51] As Taylor puts it: 'Rather than turning aside from our differences in an attempt to preserve some putative peace (not really peace at all), it is precisely through exploring these differences together that we learn the meaning of our profound interdependence.'[52] Kevin Hughes discusses these issues in his *The Premises of Scriptural Reasoning*.[53] Outlining the problems that are often assumed to exist as the result of religious difference, Hughes offers the following diagnosis:

> Too often it is assumed, both by experts in conflict resolution and diplomats alike, that religion is always the problem and never part of the solution to the inter-ethnic and inter-religious conflicts raging in the world today. This assumption is strengthened by the observation that usually it is the most fervent adherents of a religious tradition who initiate or at the very least exacerbate these conflicts.[54]

However, he goes on to offer a different set of hypotheses, of which the fourth to eighth are:

> 4. That, after centuries of terrible conflict, political and religious, this civilization introduced a competing model: an effort to achieve religious peace by

---

50   I have spoken elsewhere of the danger of engaging in 'in a dishonest dialogue dishonestly'. See Greggs, 'Bringing Barth's Critique of Religion to the Inter-Faith Table', 81.
51   Cf. Chapter 7 of this book.
52   William Taylor, *How to Pitch a Tent: A Beginners Guide to Scriptural Reasoning* (London: St Ethelburga's Centre for Reconciliation and Peace, 2008), p. 5.
53   The following quotations are taken from Kevin Hughes, 'The Premises of "Scriptural Reasoning"', *Journal of Scriptural Reasoning Forum* (http://etext.lib.virginia.edu/journals/jsrforum/writings/HugPrem.html).
54   Cf. Ben Quash, 'Deep Calls to Deep: Reading Scripture in a Multi-Faith Society', in *Remembering Our Future: Explorations in Deep Church* ed. L. Bretherton and A. Walker (Milton Keynes: Paternoster, 2007), p. 114: 'religions might in the end be better at healing their own conflicts . . . than any secular alternative based on "neutral criteria"'.

eliminating religious difference, either through secularization of religious
elites or through assimilation of any two of the Abrahamic religions to the
cultural and political of the other one;

5. That, while the modern model has made some lasting contributions to inter-
religious peace, it has also given rise to the most destructive inter-ethnic and
inter-religious conflicts the world has ever known;

6. That there is strong evidence that the modern model cannot simply correct
its own errors;

7. That the modern model must therefore be repaired and supplemented by
additional models;

8. That scriptural reasoning offers one such model.

Scriptural reasoning seeks, therefore, to offer one possibility of dialogue based on
the affirmation of each individual participant's faith commitment through the
mutual hospitality offered to each other. This involves a commitment to both
reaching out to members of other faiths and to dialoguing with them, simultaneous to a commitment to one's own particularity and faith for that reaching out and
dialogue to be remotely meaningful.

In practice, this activity of scriptural reasoning normally arises in the form of
small groups (ideally 6–8 people), with roughly equal numbers of each faith
present. The group is convened by a person who facilitates the discussion and
often – though not necessarily – chooses the texts (normally reasonably short
ones) in consultation with members of the various faith traditions. The sensitive
issues that are inevitably present in such discussions determine that the convenor
is crucial to the successful engagement in the practice, especially for those new to
it. It is impossible to describe any group and its individual dynamics, and each
will vary considerably from group to group: *this is a dynamic rather than a static
mode of engagement*. As Kepnes puts it:

> SR is a practice before it is a theory. It properly can only be known in its per-
> formance. The performative dimension gives SR a time-bound and context-
> specific characteristic. This means that every SR event is dependent upon the
> specific time and place and the particular group of individuals that assemble
> to practice SR.[55]

However, it is hoped that a by-product of Scriptural Reasoning is the building of
sociality between members, with friendships and relationships arising from the
shared study and dialogue. The never-ending nature of scriptural study for people of the Book determines that dialogue is able to be maintained, deepening
friendships, based not on shared social (or liberal) values, but on the very basis

---

55   Kepnes, 'A Handbook for Scriptural Reasoning', p. 370

of difference. In this way, attending to the world and others arises from attending to faithful love of God.

Scriptural Reasoning certainly seeks to have an applicative nature and purpose in reply to the questions which have prompted engagement in inter-faith dialogue in the first instance. However, Scriptural Reasoning is also an academic practice which is suited to the university.[56] The aspect of 'reasoning' determines that there is a need for due attention to be paid to the manner in which these dialogues take place. Peter Ochs describes this aspect of scriptural reasoning well:

1. Study is a group as well as individual activity. Good scholars display social as well as strictly intellectual virtues. These include extending hospitality to fellow learners, listening, and speaking to the heart as well as mind.
2. The primary intellectual virtue is reading well. Group study should focus, first, on a religion's primary scriptural sources, as they appear to have been received by their early reception communities and as they are scrutinized by text-historical scholars. Group study should focus, secondly, on the ways these sources are received by contemporary communities of practitioners.
3. Group study should address at least two different scriptural sources and scriptural traditions. After introductory instruction by specialists and representatives of each tradition, all scholars/students should contribute equally to the work of discussing and interpreting all of the sources. This work should move gradually through all appropriate levels of study: from philological, semantic and rhetorical studies to intra-scriptural readings to comparative interpretations of the source texts' societal, ethical, and theological implications.
4. Comparative interpretations should be stimulated by a range of interests: from formal studies of hermeneutical and narrative patterns, to ethical and theological dialogue among the traditions studied, to the implications of such studies for addressing contemporary intellectual and societal debates.[57]

The practice is largely undertaken by people of faith from the perspective of faith, and it seeks to offer participants the possibility of thinking rationally from within their tradition, and of recognizing that modes of reasoning arise from

---

56   The practice of Scriptural Reasoning hopes to allow for what Nick Adams has termed 'reparative reasoning'. See Nicholas Adams, 'Reparative Reasoning', *Modern Theology* 24, no. 3 (2008), 447–57; and Nicholas Adams, 'Making Deep Reasonings Public', *Modern Theology* 22, no. 3 (2006), 385–401. This is a philosophical term, which Adams explains in detail, but which might be summarized as 'a system of repair of systems of repair' (Adams, 'Reparative Reasoning', 453). In other (and applicative) terms, one might say that there are second order ethical implications to engaging in the practice of Scriptural Reasoning: it not only facilitates dialogue, but repairs modes of dialogue to allow for the promotion of peace in the hope of healing the world.
57   Peter Ochs, 'SR as an Academic Practice', *Journal of Scriptural Reasoning Forum* (http://etext. lib.virginia.edu/journals/jsrforum/writings/OchFeat.html). Cf. Peter Ochs, 'Scripture', in *Fields of Faith: Theology and Religious Studies for the Twenty-First Century*, ed. D. F. Ford, B. Quash, and J. M. Soskice (Cambridge: CUP, 2005), pp. 104–18.

within different traditional discourses. Furthermore, the practice recognizes that others (from different faiths) may be simultaneously pursuing such concerns variously also. Engaging, therefore, in theological study of foundational texts does not undermine the process of reasoning and dialogue, and may indeed help to underscore the need to recognize the danger of the modernist meta-narrative. This does not mean that the ability to reason across traditions breaks down. Instead, the use of scriptural texts as a means of facilitating dialogue arises precisely out of such a possibility of hearing and sharing traditions. This is particularly true for Abrahamic peoples. Kepnes justifies the use of scripture as the primary text of study and interfaith dialogue as follows: 'We do this, most simply, because Jews, Christians and Muslims share common narratives and they share a common respect for scripture as fundamental documents of revelation and religious foundation.'[58]

In his *Letters and Papers from Prison*, Bonhoeffer suggests the potential for a 'non-religious' interpretation of scripture.[59] Although he never offers a fulsome description of what such an interpretation might look like (suggesting it is '*too hot*'),[60] he does describe what form he believes a religious interpretation takes: 'It means, in my opinion, to speak metaphysically, on the one hand, and on the other hand, individualistically.'[61] To read the Bible with members of other faiths is neither to engage in a form of interpretation which is metaphysical (the plain sense is what is sought), nor is it to engage in reading the text individually (pious and ecclesial readings are not the focus of the discussion). Reading in this way, with members of other religions, is curiously a non-religious way of reading (as defined in this book's theological interpretation of religion), allowing the text to speak rather than seeing it simply as concerning the pious self or the religious group to which we belong. This is a way of reading which is done for God and for the world, and before both. Furthermore, engaging in readings with others can accentuate the dangers of tying God too closely to religion. Reading and interpreting the story of Ishmael and Hagar with Jews and Muslims, for example, brings out real and concrete depths of meaning, not easily accessible to a Christian only reading: what does it mean for God to still be the God of Ishmael and there to be enmity between the brothers? How is a Christian before Jewish and Muslim readers to place herself in the text? And so on.[62] As Ben Quash puts it:

> The introduction of an 'other' (or more than one 'other') to the activity of studying Scripture within a particular tradition can have radical and helpful

---

58   Kepnes, 'A Handbook for Scriptural Reasoning', 370.

59   LPP, pp. 372–3 and 455–7.

60   LPP, p. 457.

61   LPP, p. 372.

62   For further discussion of this text in relation to Scriptural Reasoning, see Steven Kepnes, 'Hagar and Esau: From Others to Sisters and Brothers', in *Crisis, Call, and Leadership in the Abrahamic Traditions*, ed. Peter Ochs and William Stacy Johnson (New York: Palgrave Macmillan, 2009); and Greggs, 'Peoples of the Covenants: Evangelical Theology and the Plurality of the Covenants in Scripture'.

effects, many of which are precisely a deepening of the relation of a particular tradition's Scripture readers to their own Scriptures.[63]

Reading scripture in this way not only moves Christians beyond their religious presuppositions with regard to their own texts; it may also facilitate a critical engagement with the propensity to offer religious interpretations of texts, as the plain sense of the text is read with members of other religious communities, who more easily recognize a movement away from the text into metaphysics, individual piety or religion. Moreover, while the practice of Scriptural Reasoning is not an engagement in proselytizing (though the fact that we might wish the others to come to know the reality of our own faith is not to be put aside), Scriptural Reasoning surely is an engagement in witness for Christians.[64] It is a place in which Jesus Christ is discussed, and we do well to remember the words of Bonhoeffer in *Ethics* here:

> Wherever the name of Jesus is still mentioned – even if in ignorance, even if only in recognizing its objective power without following it with personal obedience, even if with stammering and embarrassment – there this name creates a space for itself to which the slandering of Jesus has no access; there the power of Christ still has a sphere of influence; there one ought not interfere, but allow the name of Jesus Christ to do its work.[65]

Scriptural Reasoning is one example of such an enterprise for Christians who desire to allow the power of Christ to work within His sphere of influence by the operation of the Holy Spirit. Scriptural Reasoning can, after all, be a place in which the fruits of the Spirit of Christ can be seen – a place in which there can be love, joy, peace, patience, kindness, generosity, faithfulness, gentleness and self-control, and a place in which the Spirit of God may be understood to dwell in multiply intense ways.[66] It may be a place in which we can display these gifts and realize them more fully in light of the other, but also a place in which we may be challenged by the others' displaying of them also.

CONCLUSION: THE QUEST FOR PEACE

The engagement in inter-faith dialogue is an exercise in seeking peace. In this way it is an incumbent calling upon the Christian church which seeks to live a life modelled by that of Christ. Bonhoeffer points to the biblical reality that 'Christ

---

63 Quash, 'Deep Calls to Deep: Reading Scripture in a Multi-Faith Society', pp. 111–12.

64 See Chapter 6 of this book on the church's calling to witness.

65 *Ethics*, p. 342.

66 Cf. the section 'Multiple Densities of God's Holy Spirit' in Chapter 8 of this book.

helps us not by virtue of his omnipotence but rather by virtue of his weakness and suffering'.[67] The church must place itself in positions in which it does not seek to be the dominant and powerful voice, but in which it may be weak (and may even feel it is suffering). These may be places in which the church is as reliant on the hospitality of others as the others are on the hospitality of the church. Rather than seeking the re-establishment of a Constantinian religious monopoly, which is based on power and strength, or engaging in some latter-day crusade, the church in an age of pluralism must confront the theological issue of otherness, and see it not as an obstacle *to* Christ-like living, but as an opportunity *for* Christ-like living. Painful and difficult as the engagement in inter-faith dialogue may be, it may nevertheless confront the Christian with her wrongful religiosity, and help her to engage in a life lived for God and for the other. In seeking to live such a life, the Christian seeks to fulfil the commandment of love, a commandment which has powerful potential in bringing peace. Furthermore, this peace will be a genuine peace: not a violent peace that exists by suppression of the other, nor an easy peace through suppression of self, it will be a peace in which the relationship between the self and the other is not one of animosity and hatred, but one of mutual hospitality, love and respect. For Christians, this will be a peace that arises out of being genuinely for the concrete other in all of her otherness. And this peace may well be a proleptic anticipation of the kingdom in which the lion will lie down with the lamb – a kingdom in which difference does not lead to violence, but in which the co-existence of even the most profoundly different is a co-existence of genuine peace in otherness. In an age of conflict brought about by religion, it is this peace that the church must seek.

---

67   LPP, p. 479; cf. Mt. 8.17.

Chapter 10

CONCLUSION: A CODA ON MYSTERY AND HOPE

SUMMARY

This book has sought to articulate a theology arising from the critique of religion, and has sought to do so in constructive dialogue with Bonhoeffer and Barth. As well as addressing the historical theological relationship between Bonhoeffer and Barth regarding their approaches to 'religion', this book has sought to offer some constructive (or, better, formative) reflection on their work for a different theological era. To do this, certain provisional motifs were elicited from Barth and Bonhoeffer's work in order to think constructively about salvation, the church, the public square, other religions and inter-faith dialogue from the perspective of a theology which is critical of religion. The topics addressed in the constructive sections of this book are hardly considered exhaustive, and the topics that have been addressed have been done so in a far from exhaustive manner. The theology herein is a theology which is *in via*, but that very process of being 'on the way' is to a degree innate to the task of theologizing with the critique of religion: the critique must itself be a theological de-assuring of theology, even of this kind of theology itself. Nevertheless, with this proviso, it is hoped that the motifs identified might help as guidelines for future theological enterprises, beyond the specific topics addressed by this book, which seek to be against religion by virtue of:

- being *radically christocentric*;
- being *christocentrically world affirming*;
- emphasizing the *promeity and reconciliatory work and nature of God*;
- identifying a *pneumatological realness*, which emphasizes the work of God the Spirit in relating the ways and works of God to creation, human communities and individuals;
- seeking to preserve *created, human and historical particularity*;
- affirming *mystery*;

- seeking to be fiercely *anidolatrous* in an articulation of the doctrine of God;
- being resolutely *unwilling to engage in articulating binaries*;
- not *differentiating between secular and sacred spaces*;
- and, seeking to meet people in the fullness of their lives, and to deal with the *whole person*.

These motifs have been variously considered in the preceding chapters.

In many ways, what has preceded in this book has sought to be a theological exposition of Jesus' teaching on the greatest commandments. The theological critique of religion has been aimed at ensuring that it is *God* (and not an idol) who is loved with all of our hearts, souls and minds. Realizing that it is God and not religion which is our focus opens up the possibility of loving our neighbours, who are other than us, as ourselves (Mt. 22.37–40). For that reason, as well as focusing throughout on the doctrine of God, there has been an examination of salvation and ecclesiology, as doctrines in which it is easy to engage in articulating a separation of those outside from those inside the Christian faith. The co-connected themes of loving God and neighbour were then articulated in relation to the public square and to people of other faiths: without the secular–religious or inter-religious divide, the freedom to be *for* the world and members of other faiths opens up: realizing the theological critique of religion moves theology away from creating dividing binary lines, and away from locating God in certain areas or spheres and not others.

APPROPRIATE MYSTERY

This theological focus expresses itself in terms of recognizing the appropriate form of mystery for Christian theology. A theology which takes a critical stance regarding religion should express Jesus' commandment to love God with all our hearts, souls and minds in relation to the first and second commandments of the Decalogue: the prohibition against worshiping any 'god' before God and the prohibition against idolatry. This theological emphasis seeks to offer a reminder of the Godness of God. It seeks to guard against any suggestion that human beings may have been able fully to locate, describe or define God, and advocates that the religious attempt to do so is fraught with danger and deceit. This criticism of religion, however, arises neither from atheism nor mysticism, which are both subject to critique in their own religiosity, but from an appropriate understanding and emphasis on mystery.

All too often, the mystery of God can become the last bastion of apologetics. It can become a mystery which arises from ignorance, and the boundaries of human knowledge which remain unanswered. Such was Bonhoeffer's condemnation of a form of mystery in which '[r]eligious people speak of God where human knowledge is at an end (or sometimes when they're too lazy to think further), or when human strength fails'.[1] In this kind of mystery that Bonhoeffer espouses, the God of the Bible is replaced by the human creation of an increasingly superfluous *deus ex machina*.[2] Human progress in knowledge determines that the space in which so-called 'God' is allowed is rapidly reduced: answering questions of which we are ignorant of the answer, even seemingly ultimate ones, by pointing to a 'God' who fills gaps in our knowledge is no longer possible.[3] However, this makes way for true God, in His true divinity and true humanity. Although not directly related to discussions on religionless Christianity, in contrast to this mystery born of ignorance, Bonhoeffer points to the unutterability of God's name within his prison writings.[4] In this discussion, we may find an appropriate form of mystery befitting the very Godness of God. To reclaim this otherness of the God is to begin to move away from a sense that God can ever be captured within the confines of a religion. A theology against religion needs, therefore, to reclaim a true and appropriate doctrine of the mystery of God. Is articulating an appropriate form of mystery the means by which we may discover the ' "arcane discipline" . . . through which the mysteries of the Christian faith are sheltered against profanation'?[5]

Despite Bonhoeffer's linking of this theme to 'positivism',[6] it does seem that in articulating an appropriate form of mystery, befitting a theology which takes the first two commandments seriously, Barth's work offers much. Given that Barth wrote so much, and often did so in such a forthright tone,[7] it might seem surprising that the theme of mystery is pervasive throughout his work.[8] However, Barth constantly affirms the mystery of God throughout *Church Dogmatics*. For him, crucially, mystery is not an attempt at filling holes that exist in human knowledge; mystery, instead, arises from faith and revelation, rather than from unbelief and ignorance. Simply defining a mystery as something unknowable except through revelation is inadequate for Barth. For him, mystery does not precede revelation; it follows from it. It is the very nature of God to be inscrutable to humanity: 'the *Deus revelatus* is also the *Deus absconditus* and the *Deus absconditus* the *Deus revelatus*'.[9] Therefore, for Barth, it is necessary to affirm: 'In faith itself we are forced to say that our knowledge of God begins in all seriousness

---

1 LPP, p. 366.

2 LPP, p. 366.

3 LPP, pp. 425–8.

4 LPP, p. 213; cf. p. 189.

5 LPP, p. 373; cf. pp. 365 and 390.

6 LPP, p. 373; cf. section 'Positivism on Revelation' in Chapter 3 of this book.

7 One might think famously here of his '*Nein!*' to Brunner. As has been discussed, in terms of what David Ford has termed the 'moods' of theology, Barth generally writes in the indicative; see Ford, *Christian Wisdom*, pp. 45–6.

8 Mystery is not, however, to be confused with mysticism, about which Barth was deeply critical: e.g. CD I/2, pp. 318–20.

9 CD I/1, p. 330.

with the knowledge of the hiddenness of God.'[10] It is faith which enables humans to have the *knowledge* of God's mystery.[11]

Indeed, for Barth, the whole of scripture points to this theme of God's hiddenness, witnessing to the revelation in which God remains hidden, and in which God declares Godself to be the hidden God by revelation:[12] the Word of God is primarily what God speaks by and to Godself in God's eternal concealment. Furthermore, this hiddenness of God is not brought to an end in the coming of Jesus Christ, but carries on beyond the closure of the canon.[13] Even in pointing to Jesus, the prophets point to the hidden God: they point to His revelation as such. Thus, mystery in the Old Testament and the New Testament is no different: neither concerns an abstract hiddenness of God; both concern a hiddenness which points towards Christ (in the manger and on the cross).[14] Indeed, for Barth, the cross is the final culmination of this hiddenness of God: 'In the cross of Christ God is really and finally to become hidden from the world'.[15] In this way, Barth rules out God's hiddenness as a general theory of knowledge and in relation to some form of supreme being formed by religion. Instead, God encounters humanity as the hidden one; and humanity knows His hiddenness by revelation. Hiddenness becomes, therefore, a statement of faith, as it is truly a quality of God.[16]

Furthermore, for Barth this theme is directly related to worldliness and secularity. Mystery is crucial to Barth's discussion of indirect revelation because of human secularity. In this, he argues that speech about God is and remains a mystery supremely in its secularity: there is, thus, a similarity between Christianity and other empirical religions, and between theology and philosophy, as humanity has to deal with the Word of God in the mystery of its secularity (the indirect self-presentation of God to humans – dimly through a mirror). The revelation of God comes despite of, rather than because of, the cosmos; and because of this, it has to be indirect. There is in this indirect nature of revelation, therefore, a loving, merciful and gracious act in God's concealment.[17] The same is true of the derivative form of revelation in Holy Scripture. Scripture reveals God indirectly as testimony, and as a sign of human existence with God Himself (which comes only from the act of God).[18] Even the prophets hear God only indirectly through the 'the historical events, forms and relationships which are His work' and which confront them.[19] In the revelation of Jesus Christ, the hidden God has made Himself apprehensible not

---

10   CD II/1, p. 183.

11   Soskice helpfully points to this aspect of Barth's theology, and especially his christology: Soskice, *The Kindness of God*, p. 61.

12   For example, CD I/2, p. 84.

13   Barth suggests that one can see this point in the way in which Israel has reacted to Christ: CD I/2, p. 89.

14   CD I/2, p. 90.

15   CD I/2, p. 86.

16   CD II/1, pp. 183–4.

17   CD I/1, pp. 165–73.

18   CD I/2, p. 500.

19   CD II/1, p. 19.

directly but indirectly, in faith and in sign – 'Not, then, by the dissolution of His hiddenness – but apprehensibly.'[20]

Mystery provides a theological reminder that theology should be de-assured, a theological warning against theology.[21] The hiddenness and veiled nature of the object that theology studies determines that theology has continual need of correcting, and can never be perfect. It must be self-critical of what can only ever be its mere 'approximations'.[22] There is, therefore, a need for humility in theology and in Christian speech. This provides an openness to other voices and discourses, confident that the God of all creation is able to move in ways unimaginable to even the greatest of theological minds. God's own hiddenness means that all our ideas, however pious and religious, are unsuitable and inadequate for comprehension of Him,[23] and that there is always infinitely more to God. This is not to say, however, that theology should say nothing. Theology is not to be apophatic but engaged in the dynamic tension between the kataphatic and the apophatic:[24] 'We are allowed to view and conceive the inconceivable God in obedience, to proclaim the Ineffable in obedience. . . . And woe betide us if we rely upon our impotence and omit to praise Him!'[25] However, the very worshipful nature of God, determines that there is ever more to the God who is eternally deserving of ever greater praise,[26] and so Barth describes the task of theology as follows: 'We are drawing upon the ocean. We are therefore faced by a task to which there is no end.'[27] This inexhaustible ocean is not religion, but the God who will be the all in all, and can never be captured within the confines of human religiosity. St Augustine puts this positively when he speaks of the God not in terms of the darkness of unknowing, but in terms of the one who is so gloriously mysterious that His 'ineffable light beat back our gaze'.[28] The blindingly bright revelation of God is the revelation of the God who makes Himself known as the one who is beyond all human comprehension.

APPROPRIATE HOPING

In light of this God who will be all in all, it is necessary to capture something of the significance of the right kind of hope for a theology against religion. It is here

---

20   CD II/1, p. 199.

21   CD I/1, p. 165. See further Chapter 8 of this book.

22   CD II/1, p. 202.

23   CD II/1, p. 335.

24   For further on the tension between the apophatic and the kataphatic, see Tom Greggs, 'The Eschatological Tension of Theological Method: Some Reflections after Reading Daniel W. Hardy's "Creation and Eschatology"', *Theology* CXIII, no. 875 (2010).

25   CD II/1, p. 204.

26   Cf. CD II/1 §31.3 on the glory of God.

27   CD II/1, p. 406.

28   *De Trinitate*, 15.10.

where love of neighbour may come into focus. This form of hope is not the hope of a utopian, overly realized eschatology, but neither is it a form of hope which is so futurist orientated as to divert attention away from this world too hastily. The hope for which a theology against religion should strive is one which is a presentist trusting in God as creator and redeemer of the world. Emphasizing that God is the creator of the world allows theology to move beyond finding God simply in locatable and identifiable so-called sacred settings: God is the creator of all, and we should not concern ourselves simply with trying to increase that which we see as the ostensively pious. Neither should we confuse the world as it is created with the world as it will be redeemed. Creation and redemption belong in consideration together, but they should not be subsumed into each other. As Pannenberg puts it: 'Creation and eschatology belong together because it is only in the eschatological consummation that the destiny of the creature, especially the human creature, will come to fulfilment. Yet creation and eschatology are not directly identical.'[29] In Bonhoeffer's terms, there needs to be a recognition of the symbiotic but differentiated relationship between the ultimate and the penultimate, realizing that 'the penultimate must be preserved for the sake of the ultimate.'[30] Or, as he puts it in his *Letters and Papers from Prison*:

> The Christian hope of resurrection is different from the mythological way in that it refers people to their life on earth in a wholly new way, and more sharply than the OT. Unlike believers in the redemption myths, Christians do not have an ultimate escape route out of their earthly tasks and difficulties into eternity.... This-worldliness must not be abolished ahead of its time; on this, NT and OT are united.[31]

The hope of the Christian faith is a hope which leads humans back to the world, rather than focusing them on some angelic heavenly kingdom in the future.[32] In the words of Philip Ziegler: 'The eschatological qualification of all things by the redeeming lordship of Christ – the rendering of all things properly *penultimate* in relation to him – is the first and final secularising of the world.'[33] Or again: 'Neither present preoccupation, nor utopian longing, but rather only a pledge from

---

29   Wolfhart Pannenberg, *Systematic Theology*, vol. 2, trans. Geoffrey W. Bromiley (Edinburgh: T&T Clark, 1994), p. 139.

30   Ethics, p. 160.

31   LPP, pp. 447–8.

32   As Moltmann puts it: 'What business do we have in heaven among the angels? Human beings are not candidates for angelic status. They are the image of God on earth. Consequently we cannot talk about the new creation of human beings without talking about the new creation of the earth.' Jürgen Moltmann, *In the end – the Beginning: The Life of Hope*, trans. Margaret Kohl (London: SCM, 2004), p. 151.

33   Philip Ziegler, 'Eschatology and Secularity in the Late Writings of Dietrich Bonhoeffer', in *Dietrich Bonhoeffers Theologie Heute Ein Weg Zwischen Fundamentalismus Und Säkularismus?*, ed. John De Gruchy, Stephen Plant and Christiane Tietz (Guetersloh: Guetersloher Verlagshaus, 2009), p. 134.

God is able to obviate the disconsolate grind of the present. Only the latter makes the present penultimate by lending it an ultimate horizon and thus investing it with promise.'[34] In trusting creation to God's redemptive purposes, the Christian engages neither in a compromising confusion of the kingdom with creation, which denies God's redemptive works, nor in the religious denial of the breadth of God's creation, which fails to see God as creator of all.

In emphasizing hope, the Christian should demonstrate patience with creation, and seek to emphasize the character of God's patience to the world which stands as God's creation awaiting redemption. Christians should not be too swift to move their thoughts to the beyond, and certainly should be slow ever to offer any condemnation of the creation over which God is sovereignly Lord. We should, instead, see the time between Christ's ascension and His return as a function of God's loving patience. And Christians should orientate their lives in correspondence to that loving patience on the neighbours that God has given them. Barth discusses God's patience as a perfection of His love in *Church Dogmatics* II/1,[35] and points to the manner in which God makes space and time for the other (even in creation's fallenness) to allow the time for response and for faith. All of this is because of Jesus Christ: God is patient because Christ stands in the place of all of creation and for all of creation. Thus, Barth writes: 'For the sake of this One, God has patience with the many.'[36] In realizing that God has time for creation in His inexhaustible mercy, Christians must also attend with patience to the world in all is variety and difference, even as they are desirous for Christ's return.

It is notable, furthermore, how many passages in scripture which point to the eschaton present the outcome of eschatological judgement as arising from the basis of attendance to the realities of this world, and to other human beings. In his eschatological discourse which includes discussion of the judgement of the sheep and the goats, Jesus points to the basis of judgement as being the engagement with others in the world:

> I was hungry and you gave me food, I was thirsty and you gave me something to drink, I was a stranger and you welcomed me, I was naked and you gave me clothing, I was sick and you took care of me, I was in prison and you visited me. (Mt. 25.35–6)

This theme is also reflected in the parable of Lazarus (Lk. 16.19–31). Attendance to the other in the world in the present is the basis for genuine eschatological hope. In focusing our consideration onto the present and the neighbours around

---

34 Philip Ziegler, ' "Voices in the Night": Human Solidarity and Eschatological Hope', in *Who Am I? Bonhoeffer's Theology through His Poetry*, ed. Bernd Wannenswetsch (London: T&T Clark, 2009), p. 139.
35 §3.3.
36 CD II/1, p. 418.

us, we are freed to live in an expectant hope of the Kingdom of God which we foretaste in proleptic anticipate in genuine community and love of the other for their own sake. Since the image of heaven in scripture is of a heavenly city in which there is no temple as the Lord Himself is the temple (Rev. 21.22), this political dimension of hope is surely not surprising, and it should not be surprising if the Kingdom of God, which encroaches on the world, is one in which there is an awakening of human beings to be for the other. This awakening will not take place out of any tribal or religious links, but simply for the sake of the other, as one created and loved of God. After all, Jesus taught: 'If you love only those who love you, what good is that . . . ?' The hope of the Kingdom of God is not brought about by religiously focusing on some heavenly realm, but is instead brought about by focusing on the present world and the needs of other humans.

An appropriate sense of mystery and an appropriate form of hope is perhaps in the end what a theology which focuses upon the 'God who is beyond in the midst of our lives' will always concern. It is hoped that a theology which is against religion, aware of its own need for constant revisioning, reforming and reshaping in light of even its own religious propensities, will ever and again seek to speak of this God, and not of an idol of religious fashioning. In speaking of this God, we may be led to the others around us in the world that God has created, providentially guided, and will redeem.

BIBLIOGRAPHY OF
SECONDARY SOURCES

Adams, Nicholas. 'Making Deep Reasonings Public'. *Modern Theology* 22, no. 3 (2006): 385–401.

——. 'Reparative Reasoning'. *Modern Theology* 24, no. 3 (2008): 447–57.

Albertz, R. *A History of Israelite Religion in the Old Testament Period, Vol. 1.* London: SCM, 1994.

Alt, Albrecht. *Essays in Old Testament History and Religion.* Sheffield: JSOT, 1989.

Asad, Talal. *Formations of the Secular: Christianity, Islam, Modernity.* Stanford: Stanford University Press, 2003.

Barnes, Michael, SJ. *Theology and the Dialogue of Religions.* Cambridge: CUP, 2002.

Barr, James. *Fundamentalism.* London: SCM, 1977.

Bauckham, Richard. 'Universalism: A Historic Survey'. *Themelios* 4, no. 2 (1978): 47–54.

Berger, Peter L. 'The Desecularization of the World: A Global Overview'. In *The Desecularization of the West*, edited by Peter L. Berger. Grand Rapids: Wm. B. Eerdmans, 1999.

Berkouwer, G. C. *The Triumph of Grace in the Theology of Karl Barth.* Translated by Harry R. Boer. London: Paternoster, 1956.

Bethge, Eberhard. *Dietrich Bonhoeffer.* Translated by Eric Mosbacher, Peter Ross, Betty Ross, Frank Clarke and William Glen-Doepel. Edited by Edwin Robertson. London: Collins, 1970.

Bettis, Joseph D. 'Is Karl Barth a Universalist?' *Scottish Journal of Theology* 20, no. 4 (1967): 423–36.

Boring, M. Eugene. 'The Language of Universal Salvation in Paul'. *Journal of Biblical Literature* 105, no. 2 (1986): 269–92.

Boulton, Matthew Myer. *God against Religion: Rethinking Christian Theology through Worship.* Grand Rapids: Wm. B. Eerdmans, 2008.

Buckley, James J. 'A Field of Living Fire: Karl Barth on the Spirit and the Church'. *Modern Theology* 10, no. 1 (1994): 81–102.

Bultmann, Rudolf. *New Testament and Mythology and Other Basic Writings.* Translated and edited by Schubert M. Ogden. London: SCM, 1985.

Busch, Eberhard. 'Indissoluble Unity: Barth's Position on the Jews During the Hitler Era'. In *For the Sake of the World. Karl Barth and the Future of Ecclesial Theology*, edited by George Hunsinger, 53–79. Cambridge and Grand Rapids: Wm. B. Eerdmans, 2004.

Chesnutt, Glenn. 'The Secular Parables of the Kingdom'. Paper presented at the Society for the Study of Theology, Leeds, 2006.

—. 'The Theological and Political Ramifications of a Theology of Israel'. In *New Perspectives for Evangelical Theology: Engaging with God, Scripture and the World*, edited by Tom Greggs, 200–15. Abingdon: Routledge, 2010.

Chia, Clement. 'Is Barth a Supercessionist? Reconsidering the Case in the Historical Context of the Nazi Jewish Question'. Paper presented at the Society for the Study of Theology, Leeds, 2006.

Choueiri, Youssef. 'The Political Discourse of Contemporary Islamicist Movements'. In *Islamic Fundamentalism*, edited by Abdel Salam Sidahmed and Anoushiravan Ehteshami. Boulder: Westview, 1996.

Choueiri, Youssef M. *Islamic Fundamentalism. Revised Edition*. London: Cassell, 1997.

Chung, Paul S. 'On Karl Barth in Interreligious Studies and Cross-Cultural Perspective'. *Studies in Interreligious Dialogue* 18, no. 2 (2008): 212–27.

Clough, David. 'Karl Barth on Religious and Irreligious Idolatry'. In *Idolatry: False Worship in the Bible, Early Judaism and Christianity*, edited by Stephen C. Barton, 213–27. London: T&T Clark, 2007.

—. *On Animals: Systematic Theology*. London: Continuum, forthcoming.

Colwell, John. 'The Contemporaneity of Divine Decision: Reflections on Barth's Denial of Universalism'. In *Universalism and the Doctrine of Hell. Papers Presented at the Fourth Edinburgh Conference on Christian Dogmatics 1991*, edited by Nigel M. de S. Cameron, 139–60. Carlisle: Paternoster, 1992.

Cortez, Marc. 'What Does It Mean to Call Karl Barth a "Christocentric" Theologian?' *Scottish Journal of Theology* 60, no. 2 (2007): 127–43.

—. 'Body, Soul, and (Holy) Spirit: Karl Barth's Theololgical Framework for Understanding Human Ontology'. *International Journal of Systematic Theology* 10, no. 3 (2008): 328–45.

Cray, Graham, ed. *Mission-Shaped Church: Church Planting and Fresh Expressions of Church in a Changing Context*. London: Church House, 2004.

Crisp, Oliver. 'On Barth's Denial of Universalism'. *Themelios* 29 (2003): 18–29.

—. 'On the Letter and Spirit of Karl Barth's Doctrine of Election: A Reply to O'Neil'. *Evangelical Quarterly* 79, no. 1 (2003): 53–67.

—. 'I Do Teach It, but I Also Do Not Teach It: The Universalism of Karl Barth (1886–1968)'. In *"All Shall Be Well": Explorations in Universal Salvation and Christian Theology, from Origen to Moltmann*, edited by Gregory MacDonald, 299–318. Eugene: Wipf and Stock, 2010.

D'Costa, Gavin. *Theology and Religious Pluralism: The Challenge of Other Religions*. Oxford: Basil Blackwell, 1986.

—. 'Theology of Religions'. In *The Modern Theologians: An Introduction to Christian Theology in the Twentieth Century*. Second Edition, edited by David F. Ford, 626–44. Oxford: Blackwell, 1997.

Davie, Grace. *Religion in Britain since 1945*. Oxford: Blackwell, 1994.

—. *Europe: The Exceptional Case. Parameters of Faith and the Modern World.* London: Darton, Longmann & Todd, 2000.

Dawkins, Richard. *The God Delusion.* London: Black Swan, 2007.

Day, John. *Yahweh and the Gods and Goddesses of Canaan.* Sheffield: Sheffield Academic Press, 2000.

de Gruchy, John W. 'With Bonhoeffer, Beyond Bonhoeffer: Transmitting Bonhoeffer's Legacy'. In *Dietrich Bonheoffer's Theology Today: A Way between Fundamentalism and Secularism?*, edited by John W. de Gruchy, Stephen Plant and Christiane Tietz, 55–72. Gütersloh: Gütersloh Verlaghaus, 2009.

DeHart, Paul J. *The Trial of the Witnesses: The Rise and Decline of Postliberal Theology.* Oxford: Blackwells, 2006.

de S. Cameron, Nigel M. 'Universalism and the Logic of Revelation'. In *The Best in Theology Vol. 3*, edited by J. I. Packer, 153–68. Carol Stream: Christianity Today, Inc., 1989.

Di Noia, J. A. *The Diversity of Religions: A Christian Perspective.* Washington, DC: Catholic University of America Press, 1992.

—. 'Religion and the Religions'. In *The Cambridge Companion to Karl Barth*, edited by John Webster, 243–57. Cambridge: CUP, 2000.

Dramm, Sabine. *Dietrich Bonhoeffer: An Introduction to His Thought.* Translated by Thomas Rice. Peabody: Hendrickson, 2007.

Drane, John. *The Mcdonaldization of the Church: Spirituality, Creativity, and the Future of the Church.* London: Darton, Longman & Todd, 2000.

—. *After Mcdonaldization: Mission, Ministry and Christian Discipleship in an Age of Uncertainty.* London: Darton, Longman & Todd, 2008.

Driel, Edward Chr. van. 'Karl Barth on the Eternal Existence of Jesus Christ'. *Scottish Journal of Theology* 60, no. 1 (2007): 45–61.

Dulles, Avery, SJ. *Models of the Church.* New York: Doubleday, 1987.

Dumas, André. *Dietrich Bonhoeffer: Theologian of Reality.* Translated by Robert McAffee Brown. London: SCM, 1971.

Dumbrell, W. J. *Covenant and Creation: A Theology of the Old Testament Covenants.* Carlisle: Paternoster, 1997.

Fergusson, David. *Community, Liberalism & Christian Ethics.* Cambridge: CUP, 1998.

—. *Rudolf Bultmann*, Outstanding Christian Thinkers. London: Continuum, 2000.

—. *State, Church and Civil Society.* Cambridge: CUP, 2004.

—. *Faith and Its Critics: A Conversation.* Oxford: OUP, 2009.

Feuerbach, Ludwig. *The Essence of Christianity.* Translated by George Eliot. New York: Harper & Row, 1957.

Ford, David F. 'Barth's Interpretation of the Bible'. In *Karl Barth: Studies of His Theological Method*, edited by S. W. Sykes, 55–87. Oxford: Clarendon Press, 1979.

—. *Self and Salvation: Being Transformed.* Cambridge: CUP, 1999.

—. 'An Interfaith Wisdom: Scriptural Reasoning between Jews, Christians and Muslims'. *Modern Theology* 22, no. 3 (2006): 345–66.

—. *Christian Wisdom: Desiring God and Learning in Love*. Cambrigde: CUP, 2007.

—. 'God and Our Public Life: A Scriptural Wisdom'. *International Journal of Public Theology* 1 (2007): 65–84.

Ford, David F., and Pecknold, C. C., eds. *The Promise of Scriptural Reasoning*. Oxford: Blackwell, 2006.

Frick, Peter. 'Friedrich Nietzsche's Aphorisms and Dietrich Bonhoeffer's Theology'. In *Bonhoeffer's Intellectual Formation*, edited by Peter Frick, 175–200. Tübingen: Mohr Siebeck, 2008.

Frick, Peter, ed. *Bonhoeffer's Intellectual Formation*. Tübingen: Mohr Siebeck, 2008.

Gibbs, Eddie and Bolger, Ryan K., *Emerging Churches: Creating Christian Community in Postmodern Cultures*. Grand Rapids: Baker Academic, 2005.

Glasse, John. 'Barth on Feuerbach'. *The Harvard Theological Review* 57, no. 2 (1964): 69–96.

Gockel, Matthias. *Barth and Schleiermacher on the Doctrine of Election: A Systematic-Theological Comparison*. New York: OUP, 2006.

Graham, Jeannine Michele. *Representation and Substitution in the Atonement Theologies of Dorothee Sölle, John Macquarrie and Karl Barth*. New York: Peter Lang, 2005.

Green, Clifford. 'Trinity and Christology in Bonhoeffer and Barth'. *Union Seminary Quarterly Review* 60, no. 1 (2006): 1–22.

Green, Clifford J. *Bonhoeffer: A Theology of Sociality. Revised Edition*. Grand Rapids: Wm. B. Eerdmans, 1999.

Green, Garrett. 'Challenging the Religious Studies Canon: Karl Barth's Theory of Religion'. *Journal of Religion* 75 (1995): 473–86.

—. *Barth on Religion: The Revelation of God as the Sublimation of Religion*. London: T&T Clark, 2007.

—. 'Imaginary Gods and the Anonymous Christ: Thinking About the Religions with Karl Barth'. Paper presented at the Karl Barth on Religion and the Religions Conference, Princeton Theological Seminary (Princeton, 2009).

Greggs, Tom. 'Irenaeus and Augustine on the Problem of Evil Reconsidered'. *New Theologian* 14, no. 2 (2004).

—. 'Exclusivist or Universalist? Origen "the Wise Steward of the Word" (Commrom V.1.7) and the Issue of Genre'. *International Journal of Systematic Theology* 9, no. 3 (2007).

—. '"Jesus Is Victor": Passing the Impasse of Barth on Universalism'. *Scottish Journal of Theology* 60, no. 2 (2007).

—. 'Bringing Barth's Critique of Religion to the Inter-Faith Table'. *Journal of Religion* 88, no. 1 (2008): 75–94.

—. 'The Many Names of Christ in Wisdom: Reading Scripture with Origen for a Diverse World'. *Journal of Scriptural Reasoning* (2008).

—. 'Religionless Christianity in a Complexly Religious and Secular World: Thinking through and Beyond Bonhoeffer'. In *Religion, Religionlessness and Contemporary Western Culture*, edited by Stephen Plant and Ralf K. Wüstenberg, 111–25. Frankfurt am Main: Peter Lang, 2008.

—. *Barth, Origen, and Universal Salvation: Restoring Particularity*. Oxford: OUP, 2009.

—. 'Preaching Inter-Faith: Finding Hints About the Religious Other from the Good Samaritan'. *Epworth Review* 36, no. 3 (2009): 60–70.

—. 'Religionless Christianity and the Political Implications of Theological Speech: What Bonhoeffer's Theology Yields to a World of Fundamentalisms'. *International Journal of Systematic Theology* 11, no. 3 (2009): 293–308.

—. 'Beyond the Binary: Forming Evangelical Eschatology'. In *New Perspectives for Evangelical Theology: Engaging with God, Scripture and the World*, edited by Tom Greggs, 153–67. Abingdon: Routledge, 2010.

—. 'The Eschatological Tension of Theological Method: Some Reflections after Reading Daniel W. Hardy's "Creation and Eschatology" '. *Theology* CXIII, no. 875 (2010): 339–47.

—. 'Inter-Faith Pedagogy for Muslims and Christians'. *Discourse* 9, no. 2 (2010): 201–26.

—. 'Legitimizing and Necessitating Inter-Faith Dialogue: The Dynamics of Inter-Faith for Individual Faith Communities'. *International Journal of Public Theology* 4, no. 2 (2010): 194–211.

—. 'Pessimistic Universalism: Rethinking the Wider Hope with Bonhoeffer and Barth'. *Modern Theology* 26, no. 4 (2010): 495–510.

—. 'The Lord of All: Rediscovering the Christian Doctrine of Providence for a Pluralist Society'. In *Theology, Religion and Exclusion: Towards Transformation*, edited by Hannah Bacon and Wayne Morris. London: T&T Clark, 2011.

—. 'Peoples of the Covenants: Evangelical Theology and the Plurality of the Covenants in Scripture'. *Journal of Scriptural Reasoning* (forthcoming).

Grumett, David. *De Lubac: A Guide for the Perplexed*. London: T&T Clark, 2007.

—. 'De Lubac, Buddhism and Catholicism'. Paper presented at the Department of Theology and Religious Studies Seminar, University of Bristol (Bristol, 2010).

Gunton, Colin. 'Karl Barth's Doctrine of Election as Part of His Doctrine of God'. *Journal of Theological Studies* 25, no. 2 (1974): 381–92.

Gunton, Colin E. 'The Church on Earth: The Roots of Community'. In *On Being the Church: Essays on the Christian Community*, edited by Colin E. Gunton, 48–80. Edinburgh: T&T Clark, 1989.

—. 'The Triune God and the Freedom of the Creature'. In *Karl Barth: Centenary Essays*, edited by S. W. Sykes. Cambridge: CUP, 1989.

—. *The One, the Three and the Many: God, Creation and the Culture of Modernity. The 1992 Bampton Lectures.* Cambridge: CUP, 1993.

Haag, Herbert. *Clergy and Laity: Did Jesus Want a Two-Tier Church?* London: Burns and Oates, 1998.

Hardy, Daniel W. *Finding the Church.* London: SCM, 2001.

Hart, Trevor. 'Universalism: Two Distinct Types'. In *Universalism and the Doctrine of Hell. Papers Presented at the Fourth Edinburgh Conference on Christian Dogmatics 1991*, edited by Nigel M. de S. Cameron, 1–34. Carlisle: Paternoster, 1992.

—. 'The Word, the Words and the Witness: Proclamation as Divine and Human Reality in the Theology of Karl Barth'. *Tyndale Bulletin* 46, no. 1 (1995): 81–102.

—. *Regarding Barth: Essays toward a Reading of His Theology.* Carlisle: Paternoster, 1999.

Hauerwas, Stanley. *With the Grain of the Universe: The Church's Witness and Natural Theology.* London: SCM, 2002.

—. *Hannah's Child: A Theologian's Memoir.* London: SCM, 2010.

Hays, Richard B. 'Postscript: Seeking a Centred, Generous Orthodoxy'. In *New Perspectives for Evangelical Theology: Enagaging with God, Scripture and the World*, edited by Tom Greggs, 216–18. Abingdon: Routledge, 2010.

Healy, Nicholas M. *Church, World and the Christian Life: Practical-Prophetic Ecclesiology.* Cambridge: CUP, 2000.

Hector, Kevin W. 'God's Triunity and Self-Determination: A Conversation with Karl Barth, Bruce McCormack and Paul Molnar'. *International Journal of Systematic Theology* 7, no. 3 (2005): 246–61.

Hick, John. *Evil and the God of Love.* London: Macmillan, 1966.

—. *God and the Universe of Faiths : Essays in the Philosophy of Religion.* London: Macmillan, 1973.

—. *God Has Many Names: Britain's New Religious Pluralism.* London: Macmillan, 1980.

—. *Problems of Religious Pluralism.* London: Macmillan, 1985.

—. *An Interpretation of Religion: Human Responses to the Transcendent.* London: Macmillan, 1989.

Hodge, A. A. *Evangelical Theology: A Course of Popular Lectures.* London: Banner of Truth, 1976.

Hughes, Kevin. 'The Premises of "Scriptural Reasoning"'. Journal of Scriptural Reasoning Forum, http://etext.lib.virginia.edu/journals/jsrforum/writings/HugPrem.html (accessed 22 September 2010).

Hunsinger, George. *How to Read Karl Barth. The Shape of His Theology.* New York and Oxford: OUP, 1991.

—. 'Review of Charles Marsh, *Reclaiming Dietrich Bonhoeffer: The Promise of His Theology*'. *Modern Theology* 12, no. 1 (1996): 121–3.

—. *Disruptive Grace. Studies in the Theology of Karl Barth.* Grand Rapids and Cambridge: Eerdmanns, 2000.

—. 'The Mediator of Communion: Karl Barth's Doctrine of the Holy Spirit'. In *The Cambridge Companion to Karl Barth*, edited by John Webster, 177–94. Cambridge: CUP, 2000.

—. 'A Tale of Two Simultaneities: Justification and Sanctification in Calvin and Barth'. In *Conversing with Barth*, edited by John C. McDowell and Mike Higton, 68–89. Aldershot: Ashgate, 2004.

—. 'Election and the Trinity: Twenty-Five Theses on the Theology of Karl Barth'. *Modern Theology* 24, no. 2 (2008): 179–98.

Jearnold, Werner G. 'Karl Barth's Hermeneutics'. In *Reckoning with Barth: Essays in Commemoration of the Centenary of Karl Barth's Birth*, edited by Nigel Biggar, 80–97. Oxford and London: Mowbray, 1988.

Jenkins, Philip. *God's Continent: Christianity, Islam, and Europe's Religious Crisis.* New York: OUP, 2007.

Jenkins, Timothy. *Religion in English Everyday Life: An Ethnographic Approach.* New York and Oxford: Berghahn Books, 1999.

Jenkins, Timothy, and Quash, Ben. 'The Cambridge Inter-Faith Programme: Academic Profile'. Cambride Inter-faith Programme Website, http://www.interfaith. cam.ac.uk/en/resources/papers/cip-academic-profile (accessed 3 March 2010).

Jinkins, Michael. *The Church Faces Death: Ecclesiology in a Post-Modern Context.* New York and Oxford: OUP, 1999.

Jones, Paul Dafydd. 'Karl Barth on Gethsemane'. *International Journal of Systematic Theology* 9, no. 2 (2007): 148–71.

—. *The Humanity of Christ: Christology in Karl Barth's Church Dogmatics.* London: T&T Clark, 2008.

Jüngel, Eberhard. *God as the Mystery of the World: On the Foundation of the Theology of the Crucified One in the Dispute between Theism and Atheism.* Translated by Darrell L. Guder. Edinburgh: T&T Clark, 1983.

—. *Karl Barth: A Theological Legacy.* Translated by Garrett E. Paul. Philadelphia: Westminster, 1986.

—. *God's Being Is in Becoming. The Trinitarian Being of God in the Theology of Karl Barth. A Paraphrase.* Translated by John Webster. Edinburgh: T&T Clark, 2001.

Kärkkäinen, Veli-Matti. 'Evangelical Theology and the Religions'. In *The Cambridge Companion to Evangelical Theology*, edited by Timothy Larsen and Daniel J. Treier, 199–212. Cambridge: CUP, 2007.

Kelly, Geffrey B. 'Bonhoeffer and Barth: A Study of the Interaction with Karl Barth in Bonhoeffer's Theology of Revelation'. Dissertation presented to the Université de Louvain, 1970.

—. ' "Unconscious Christianity" and the "Anonymous Christian" in the Theology of Dietrich Bonhoeffer and Karl Rahner'. *Philosophy & Theology* 9, no. 2 (1995): 117–49.

—. 'Bonhoeffer's Christ-Centred, Religionless Christianity and His Critique of Religio-Political Fundamentalism'. Paper presented at the Tenth International Bonhoeffer Congress (Prague, 2008).

Kent, Elizabeth. 'Embodied Evangelicalism: The Body of Christ and the Christian Body'. In *New Perspectives for Evangelical Theology: Engaging with God, Scripture and the World*, edited by Tom Greggs, 108–22. Abingdon: Routledge, 2010.

Kepnes, Steven. 'A Handbook for Scriptural Reasoning'. *Modern Theology* 22, no. 3 (2006): 368–83.

—. 'Hagar and Esau: From Others to Sisters and Brothers'. In *Crisis, Call, and Leadership in the Abrahamic Traditions*, edited by Peter Ochs and William Stacy Johnson, 31–46. New York: Palgrave Macmillan, 2009.

Krause, Gerhard. 'Dietrich Bonhoeffer and Rudolf Bultmann'. In *The Future of Our Religious Past: Essays in Honour of Rudolf Bultmann*, edited by James M. Robinson, 279–305. London: SCM, 1971.

Krötke, Wolf. 'A New Impetus to the Theology of Religions from Karl Barth's Thought'. Paper presented at the Karl Barth Society of North America (Washington, DC, 2006).

Lash, Nicholas. *The Beginning and End of 'Religon'*. Cambridge: CUP, 1996.

Leahy, Brendan. ' "Christ Existing as Community": Dietrich Bonhoeffer's Notion of Church'. *Irish Theological Quarterly* 73, no. 1 (2008): 32–59.

Lewis, C. S. *The Screwtape Letters: Letter from a Senior to a Junior Devil*. London: Collins, 1942.

Lindbeck, George A. *The Nature of Doctrine: Religion and Theology in a Postliberal Age*. Philadelphia: Westminster, 1984.

Lindsay, Mark. 'Dialectics of Communion: Dialectical Method and Barth's Defense of Israel'. In *Karl Barth: A Future for Post Modern Theology?*, edited by Geoff Thompson and Christiaan Mostert, 122–43. Adelaide: Openbook, 2000.

Ludlow, Morwenna. *Universal Salvation: Eschatology in the Thought of Gregory of Nyssa and Karl Rahner*. Oxford: OUP, 2000.

—. 'Universalism in the History of Christianity'. In *Universal Salvation? The Current Debate*, edited by Robin A. Parry and Christopher H. Partridge, 191–218. Carlisle: Paternoster, 2003.

MacDonald, Gregory. *The Evangelical Universalist: The Biblical Hope That God's Love Will Save Us All*. London: SPCK, 2008.

MacIntyre, Alasdair. *Whose Justice? Which Rationality?* London: Duckworth, 1988.

Marquardt, Friedrich-Wilhelm. *Theologie Und Sozialismus. Das Beispiel Karl Barths*. 3rd enlarged edn. Munich: Chr. Kaiser Verlag, 1985.

Marsh, Charles. *Reclaiming Dietrich Bonhoeffer: The Promise of His Theology*. Oxford: OUP, 1994.

Marshall, B. D. 'Review of Richard Roberts, *A Theology on Its Way? Essays on Karl Barth*'. *Journal of Theological Studies* 44 (1993): 453–8.

Martin, David. *The Religious and the Secular: Studies in Secularization*. London: Routledge & Kegan Paul, 1969.

—. *Reflections on Sociology and Theology*. Oxford: Clarendon Press, 1997.

Mathewes, Charles. *A Theology of Public Life*. Cambridge: CUP, 2007.

McCormack, Bruce. 'Grace and Being: The Role of God's Gracious Election in Karl Barth's Theological Ontology'. In *Cambridge Companion to Karl Barth*, edited by John Webster, 92–110. Cambridge: CUP, 2000.

—. 'Participation in God, Yes, Deification, No: Two Modern Protestant Responses to an Ancient Question'. In *Denkwürdiges Geheimnis: Beiträge Zur Gotteslehre. Festschrift Für Eberhard Jüngel Zum 70. Geburtstag*, edited by Ingolf U. Dalfferth, Johannes Fischer and Hans-Peter Grosshans, 347–74. Tübingen: Mohr Siebeck, 2004.

—. 'Seek God Where He May Be Found: A Response to Edwin Chr. Van Driel'. *Scottish Journal of Theology* 60, no. 1 (2007): 62–79.

—. 'Election and the Trinity: Theses in Response to George Hunsinger'. *Scottish Journal of Theology* 63, no. 2 (2010): 203–24.

McCormack, Bruce L. *Karl Barth's Critically Realistic Dialectical Theology*. Oxford: Clarendon Press, 1995.

—. *Orthodox and Modern: Studies in the Theology of Karl Barth*. Grand Rapids: Baker Academic, 2008.

McDowell, J. C. 'Learning Where to Place One's Hope: The Eschatological Significance of Election in Barth'. *Scottish Journal of Theology* 53, no. 3 (2000): 326–38.

—. *Hope in Barth's Eschatology: Interrogations and Transformations Beyond Tragedy*. Aldershot: Ashgate, 2001.

McIntyre, John. *The Shape of Pneumatology: Studies in the Doctrine of the Holy Spirit*. Edinburgh: T&T Clark, 1997.

McKenzie, Steven L. *Covenant*. St Louis: Chalice, 2000.

McLean, Stuart. *Humanity in the Thought of Karl Barth*. Edinburgh: T&T Clark, 1981.

McNeill, John T., ed. *Calvin Institutes of the Christian Religion*. Louisville: Westminster John Knox, 2006.

Meyendorff, John. *Byzantine Theology: Historical Trends and Doctrinal Themes*. New York: Fordham University Press, 1987.

Moberly, R. W. L. *The Old Testament of the Old Testament: Patriarchal Narratives and Mosaic Yahwism*. Minneapolis: Fortress, 1992.

Molnar, Paul D. *Divine Freedom and the Doctrine of the Immanent Trinity: In Dialogue with Karl Barth and Contemporary Theology*. Edinburgh: T&T Clark, 2002.

Moltmann, Jürgen. *In the end – the Beginning: The Life of Hope*. Translated by Margaret Kohl. London: SCM, 2004.

Neder, Adam. *Participation in Christ: An Entry into Karl Barth's Church Dogmatics*. Louisville: Westminster John Knox, 2009.

Nimmo, Paul T. *Being in Action: The Theological Shape of Barth's Ethical Vision.* London: T&T Clark, 2007.

—. 'Barth and the Christian as Ethical Agent: An Ontological Study of the Shape of Christian Ethics'. In *Commanding Grace: Studies in Karl Barth's Ethics*, edited by Daniel L. Migliore, 216–38. Grand Rapids: Wm. B. Eerdmans, 2010.

—. 'Election and Evangelical Thinking: Challenging Our Way of Conceiving the Doctrine of God'. In *New Perspectives for Evangelical Theology: Engaging with God, Scripture and the World*, edited by Tom Greggs, 29–43. Abingdon: Routledge, 2010.

Northcott, Michael. '"Who Am I?": Human Identity and the Spiritual Disciplines in the Witness of Dietrich Bonhoeffer'. In *Who Am I? Bonhoeffer's Theology through His Poetry*, edited by Bernd Wannenswetsch, 11–30. London: T&T Clark, 2009.

O'Collins, Gerald. *Salvation for All: God's Other Peoples.* Oxford: OUP, 2008.

O'Grady, Colm. *The Church in the Theology of Karl Barth.* Washington: Corpus Books, 1969.

Ochs, Peter. *Peirce, Pragmatism and the Logic of Scripture.* Cambridge: CUP, 2004.

—. 'Scripture'. In *Fields of Faith: Theology and Religious Studies for the Twenty-First Century*, edited by D. F. Ford, B. Quash and J. M. Soskice. Cambridge: CUP, 2005.

—. 'SR as an Academic Practice'. Journal of Scriptural Reasoning Forum http://etext.lib.virginia.edu/journals/jsrforum/writings/OchFeat.html (accessed 4 April 2010).

Osborn, Robert T. 'Positivism and Promise in the Theology of Karl Barth'. *Interpretation* 25, no. 3 (1971): 283–302.

Ott, Heinrich. *Reality and Faith: The Theological Legacy of Dietrich Bonhoeffer.* Translated by Alex A. Morrison. London: Lutterworth Press, 1971.

Pangritz, Andreas. *Karl Barth in the Theology of Dietrich Bonhoeffer.* Translated by Barbara Rumscheidt and Martin Rumscheidt. Grand Rapids: Wm. B. Eerdmans, 2000.

Pannenberg, Wolfhart. *Christianity in a Secularized World.* London: SCM, 1988.

—. *Systematic Theology Vol 2.* Translated by Geoffrey W. Bromiley. Edinburgh: T&T Clark, 1994.

—. *Basic Questions in Theology: Collected Essays Volume 2.* Minneapolis: Fortress, 2007.

Percy, Martyn. *Words, Wonders and Power: Understanding Contemporary Fundamentalism and Revivalism.* London: SPCK, 1996.

Plant, Raymond. *Politics, Theology and History.* Cambridge: CUP, 2001.

Plant, Stephen. *Bonhoeffer.* London: Continuum, 2004.

Prenter, Regin. 'Dietrich Bonhoeffer Und Karl Barths Offenbarungpositivismus'. In *Mündige Welt*, edited by E. Bethge. Munich: Chr. Kaiser Verlag, 1960.

Pugh, Jeffrey. *Religionless Christianity: Dietrich Bonhoeffer in Troubled Times.* London: T&T Clark, 2008.

Quash, Ben. *Theology and the Drama of History.* Cambridge: CUP, 2005.

—. 'Deep Calls to Deep: Reading Scripture in a Multi-Faith Society'. In *Remembering Our Future: Explorations in Deep Church*, edited by L. Bretherton and A. Walker, 108–30. Milton Keynes: Paternoster, 2007.

—. 'Revelation'. In *The Oxford Handbook of Systematic Theology*, edited by John Webster, Kathryn Tanner and Iain Torrance, 325–44. Oxford: OUP, 2007.

Rahner, Karl, S.J. 'Anonymous Christians'. In *Theological Investigations Vol 6: Concerning Vatican Council 2*, 390–8. London: Darton, Longman & Todd, 1974.

Roberts, Richard H. 'Spirit, Structure and Truth'. *Modern Theology* 3, no. 1 (1986): 77–106.

—. *A Theology on Its Way? Essays on Karl Barth.* Edinburgh: T&T Clark, 1991.

Rogers Jr., Eugene F. 'Supplementing Barth on Jews and Gender: Identifying God by Analogy and Spirit'. *Modern Theology* 14, no. 1 (1998): 43–82.

—. 'The Eclipse of the Spirit in Karl Barth'. In *Conversing with Barth*, edited by John C. McDowell and Mike Higton, 173–90. Aldershot: Ashgate, 2004.

Rosato, Philip J. *The Spirit as Lord. The Pneumatology of Karl Barth.* Edinburgh: T&T Clark, 1981.

Rowland, Christopher. 'The Lamb and the Beast, the Sheep and the Goats: "The Mystery of Salvation" in Revelation'. In *A Vision for the Church: Studies in Early Christian Ecclesiology in Honour of J. P. M. Sweet*, edited by Markus Bockmuehl and Michael B. Thompson, 181–91. Edinburgh: T&T Clark, 1997.

Rowley, H. H. *Worship in Ancient Israel: Its Forms and Meaning.* London: SPCK, 1967.

Russell, Norman. *The Doctrine of Deification in the Greek Patristic Tradition.* Oxford: OUP, 2006.

Sauter, Gerhart. 'Why Is Karl Barth's Church Dogmatics Not a "Theology of Hope"? Some Observations on Barth's Understanding of Eschatology'. *Scottish Journal of Theology* 52, no. 4 (1999): 407–29.

Schleiermacher, Freidrich. *The Christian Faith.* Translated by H. R. Mackintosh and J. S. Stewart. Edited by H. R. Mackintosh and J. S. Stewart. English translation of the 2nd German edn. Edinburgh: T&T Clark, 1968.

Schwöbel, Christoph. 'Theology'. In *The Cambridge Companion to Karl Barth*, edited by John Webster, 17–36. Cambridge: CUP, 2000.

—. ' "Religion" and "Religionlessness" in *Letters and Papers from Prison*: A Perspective for Religious Pluralism?' In *Mysteries in the Theology of Dietrich Bonhoeffer: A Copenhagen Bonhoeffer Symposium*, edited by Kirsten Busch Nielsen, Ulrik Nissen and Christiane Tietz. Göttingen: Vandenhoeck & Ruprecht, 2007.

Selby, Peter. 'Christianity in a World Come of Age'. In *The Cambridge Companion to Dietrich Bonhoeffer*, edited by John W. de Gruchy, 226–45. Cambridge: CUP, 1999.

Smith, R. Gregor, ed. *World Come of Age: A Symposium on Dietrich Bonhoeffer*. London: Collins, 1967.

Sonderegger, Katherine. *That Jesus Was Born a Jew: Karl Barth's 'Doctrine of Israel'*. Pennsylvania: Pennsylvania State University Press, 1992.

Soskice, Janet Martin. *The Kindness of God: Metaphor, Gender, and Religious Language*. Oxford: OUP, 2007.

Soulen, R. Kendall. ' "Go Tell Pharaoh" or, Why Empires Prefer a Nameless God'. *Cultural Encounters* Sample Issue (2005): 5–15.

Stenger, Mary Ann. 'Faith (and Religion)'. In *The Cambridge Companion to Paul Tillich*, edited by Russell Re Manning, 91–104. Cambridge: CUP, 2009.

Storrar, William F. and Morton, Andrew R. 'Introduction'. In *Public Theology for the 21st Century: Essays in Honour of Duncan B. Forrester*, edited by William F. Storrar and Andrew R. Morton. London: T&T Clark, 2004.

Stout, Jeffrey. *Democracy and Tradition*. Princeton: Princeton University Press, 2004.

Taylor, William. *How to Pitch a Tent: A Beginners Guide to Scriptural Reasoning*. London: St Ethelburga's Centre for Reconciliation and Peace, 2008.

Thiselton, Anthony C. *The Hermeneutics of Doctrine*. Grand Rapids: William B. Eerdmans, 2007.

Thompson, Geoff. 'Religious Diversity, Christian Doctrine and Karl Barth'. *International Journal of Systematic Theology* 8, no. 1 (2006): 3–24.

Thompson, John. 'The Humanity of God in the Theology of Karl Barth'. *Scottish Journal of Theology* 29, no. 3 (1976): 249–69.

Tietz, Christiane. 'Friedrich Schleiermacher and Dietrich Bonhoeffer'. In *Bonhoeffer's Intellectual Formation: Theology and Philosophy in His Thought*, edited by Peter Frick, 121–43. Tübingen: Mohr Siebeck, 2008.

Tillich, Paul. *Systematic Theology: Combined Volume*. Welwyn: James Nisbet & Co., 1968.

Veitch, J. A. 'Revelation and Religion in the Theology of Karl Barth'. *Scottish Journal of Theology* 24, no. 1 (1971): 1–22.

Volf, Miroslav, *Exclusion and Embrace: A Theological Exploration of Identity, Otherness, and Reconciliation*. Nashville: Abingdon, 1996.

von Weizäcker, Carl Friedrich. 'Gedanken Eines Nichttheologen Zur Theologischen Entwicklung Dietrich Bonhoeffer'. In *Der Garten Des Menschlichen: Beiträge Zur Geschichlichen Anthropologie*. Munich: C. Hanser, 1977.

Wannenwetsch, Bernd. ' "Christians and Pagans": Towards a Trans-Religious Second Naivité or How to Be a Christological Creature'. In *Who Am I? Bonhoeffer's Theology through His Poetry*, edited by Bernd Wannenwetsch, 175–96. London: T&T Clark, 2009.

Webster, John. *Barth's Moral Theology: Human Action in Barth's Thought*. Edinburgh: T&T Clark, 1998.

—. 'Trinity and Creation'. *International Journal of Systematic Theology* 12, no. 1 (2010): 4–19.

Wenham, John W. 'The Case for Conditional Immortality'. In *Universalism and the Doctrine of Hell. Papers Presented at the Fourth Edinburgh Conference on Christian Dogmatics 1991*, edited by Nigel M. de S. Cameron, 161–91. Carlisle: Paternoster, 1992.

Williams, Rowan. 'The Suspicion of Suspicion: Wittgenstein and Bonhoeffer'. In *The Grammar of the Heart: New Essays in Moral Philosophy and Theology*, edited by Richard H. Bell, 36–53. San Fransisco: Harper & Row, 1988.

Wüstenberg, Ralf K. *A Theology of Life: Dietrich Bonhoeffer's Religionless Christianity*. Translated by Doug Stott. Grand Rapids: Wm. B. Eerdmanns Publishing Co., 1998.

—. *Bonhoeffer and Beyond: Promoting a Dialogue between Religion and Politics*, International Bonhoeffer Interpretations. Frankfurt am Main: Peter Lang, 2008.

Ziegler, Philip. 'Eschatology and Secularity in the Late Writings of Dietrich Bonhoeffer'. In *Dietrich Bonhoeffers Theologie Heute Ein Weg Zwischen Fundamentalismus Und Säkularismus?*, edited by John De Gruchy, Stephen Plant and Christiane Tietz, 122–36. Guetersloh: Guetersloher Verlaghaus, 2009.

—. '"Voices in the Night": Human Solidarity and Eschatological Hope'. In *Who Am I? Bonhoeffer's Theology through His Poetry*, edited by Bernd Wannenswetsch, 115–46. London: T&T Clark, 2009.

—. 'Promeity in the Christologies of Bonhoeffer and Kierkegaard'. Paper presented at the American Academy of Religion (Atlanta, 2010).

Zimmermann, W.-D., ed., *Begegnung mit Dietrich Bonhoeffer. Ein Almanach*. Munich: Kaiser, 1965.

INDEX